CARE PROCEEDINGS WITH AN INTERNATIONAL ELEMENT

Presenting the findings of a study of 100 care cases, this book provides rigorous analysis of how jurisdictional issues are determined and how information sharing of child protection operates across borders.

It draws on the first empirical study of the operation of private international law instruments (Brussels IIa and the 1996 Hague Convention) in care proceedings in England. It also illustrates how prospective carers are assessed and the routes which are used to secure legal permanence for children living overseas. In so doing, it identifies all the ways in which children's welfare interests are compromised in the cross-border context. But it does suggest solutions: identifying how private international law instruments, their interpretation and application, should be improved to promote the best interests of children.

This is an impressive work, which will be invaluable to both scholars and practitioners.

Volume 40 in the series Studies in Private International Law

Studies in Private International Law

Recent titles in the series

Place of Performance: A Comparative Analysis
Chukwuma Okoli

Private International Law in Nigeria
Chukwuma Okoli and Richard Oppong

Planning the Future of Cross Border Families: A Path Through Coordination
Edited by Ilaria Viarengo and Francesca Villata

The Private International Law of Authentic Instruments
Jonathan Fitchen

The Hague Judgments Convention and Commonwealth Model Law: A Pragmatic Perspective
Abubakri Yekini

A Guide to Global Private International Law
Edited by Paul Beaumont and Jayne Holliday

Parental Child Abduction to Islamic Law Countries
Nazia Yaqub

The Application of Foreign Law in the British and German Courts
Alex Critchley

The HCCH 2019 Judgments Convention: Cornerstones, Prospects, Outlook
Edited by Matthias Weller, João Ribeiro-Bidaoui, Moritz Brinkmann and Nina Dethloff

Jurisdiction Over Non-EU Defendants: Should the Brussels Ia Regulation be Extended?
Edited by Tobias Lutzi, Ennio Piovesani and Dora Zgrabljic Rotar

Private International Law and Competition Litigation in a Global Context
Mihail Danov

Private International Law in Russia
Edited by Anton Asoskov, Daria Levina, and Milana Karayanidi

Private International Law in BRICS: Convergence, Divergence and Reciprocal Lessons
Edited by Stellina Jolly and Saloni Khanderia

Care Proceedings with an International Element: An Empirical Study
Maria Sofia Wright

Care Proceedings with an International Element

An Empirical Study

Maria Sofia Wright

•HART•
OXFORD • LONDON • NEW YORK • NEW DELHI • SYDNEY

HART PUBLISHING
Bloomsbury Publishing Plc
Kemp House, Chawley Park, Cumnor Hill, Oxford, OX2 9PH, UK
1385 Broadway, New York, NY 10018, USA
Bloomsbury Publishing Ireland Limited, 29 Earlsfort Terrace, Dublin 2, D02 AY28, Ireland

HART PUBLISHING, the Hart/Stag logo, BLOOMSBURY and the Diana logo are trademarks of Bloomsbury Publishing Plc

First published in Great Britain 2025

A catalogue record for this book is available from the British Library.

A catalogue record for this book is available from the Library of Congress.

Library of Congress Control Number: 2025941450

ISBN: HB: 978-1-50997-730-7
ePDF: 978-1-50997-732-1
ePub: 978-1-50997-731-4

Typeset by Compuscript Ltd, Shannon

FOREWORD

In this unique study of the operation of child protection cases with an international element in England, Dr Wright combines thorough review of the relevant international instruments with a detailed analysis of a sample of 100 cases, drawn from the Cafcass e-casefile system. This analysis highlights the range of circumstances where children must be protected – those at significant risk in England whose parents have overseas connections such as recent immigrants and refugees, and those whose families are fleeing child protection authorities to or from England. Such cases pose difficulties for local authorities and courts beyond questions of jurisdiction and the enforcement of orders. Achieving good outcomes for children in a timely way in these cases is particularly challenging. Good outcomes are not simply a matter of proportionate orders but must include lasting placements which can support recovery after neglect or abuse and provide the foundation for a positive childhood. Despite the legalistic approach in the legal instruments, the focus should be on function rather than form.

At the time of the study, the UK was a member of the European Union; *Council Regulation (EC) No 2201/2003 of 27 November 2003 concerning jurisdiction and the recognition and enforcement of judgments in matrimonial matters and the matters of parental responsibility, repealing Regulation (EC) No 1347/2000* (Blla) applied to cases where the child had links to an EU state; Convention of 19 October 1996 on Jurisdiction, Applicable Law, Recognition, Enforcement and Co-operation in respect of Parental Responsibility and Measures for the Protection of Children (HC96) HC96 applied where the child's links were to a Convention Country that was not an EU Member State; and national law to all other countries. Brexit has removed BIIa from the equation, so practitioners now must work with either HC96 or national law. However, the differences between these regimes and their operation explored in the study sample highlights the advantages and shortcoming of each system particularly in facilitating the co-operation between states which is essential for achieving timely decisions in the best interests of the children concerned.

Courts make decisions in individual cases; reported cases usually raise points of difficulty which may or may not be encountered in others but never identify the complete range of issues that can exist in these complex cases. Judicial guidance, whether given in judgments or elsewhere, is largely developed in response to small numbers of cases, sometimes only one. Such guidance is limited and one dimensional – drawn from the legal perspective. Although this may provide useful pointers, it can also highlight legal issues which are uncommon in practice and omit or obscure matters important for children who are the subjects of proceedings and for good practice. In contrast to this individual approach, the empirical analysis of cases in the family courts shines a light onto proceedings and the lives affected by them which even the greater transparency now allowed in family proceedings cannot match. Such analysis can reveal patterns in the facts, issues and court practice. It can identify recurring issues which need attention and practices which can avoid or resolve difficulties. Interviews of local authority lawyers and social workers reveal the challenges in working with the guidance and applying the law, not apparently considered by those who intended to facilitate cross border child protection decisions.

Although the HC96 was prepared in the 'wake' of the U.N Convention on the Rights of the Child and although the Preamble to the Hague Convention confirms 'that the best interests of children are to be a primary consideration', the Convention's focus on jurisdiction, applicable law, recognition and enforcement, combined with weak mechanisms for co-operation, creates the risk that decisions may pay insufficient attention to their effects on children's lives.

As with other socio-legal studies, a discussion of the legal provisions in the context of the analysis of a sample of cases where they were applied and the experiences of practitioners brings to life the operation of the law and the practical effects of applying it. The cases provide examples of how lawyers and social workers can work with the law to improve outcomes for children and the different approach demanded for care cases with an international element. The book therefore provides valuable insights to all those who practice in in this area of work: judges, local authority lawyers and those in private practice, social workers and cafcass guardians.

Judith Masson PhD, K.C (hon)
Professor Emeritus, University of Bristol, School of Law

SERIES EDITOR'S PREFACE

This is an excellent book based on the writer's PhD from the University of Bristol. It combines very thorough empirical research into 100 English cases concerning public law care proceedings with a potential cross-border element, with careful analytical research on the Brussels IIa Regulation (with developments in Brussels IIb – or IIter – as it is referred to in this book being flagged where appropriate) and on the Hague Child Protection Convention of 1996 (HC96). Given that post-Brexit it is the latter which applies in the UK the writer correctly focuses her very well thought through recommendations on how to best utilise HC96. The recommendations set out in the final chapter are wisely divided between those that can be applied in all HC96 Contracting States and those that can be applied to the practice in these cases in England and Wales. It is to be hoped that the Hague Conference on Private International Law (HCCH) will take account of Dr Wright's recommendations as it develops good practice in relation to HC96. It is also desirable that the relevant authorities in England and Wales consider her recommendations for practice in that jurisdiction as they are based on lessons learned from practice and from careful consideration of the interaction of law and social work expertise.

Dr Wright's second chapter is an excellent historical account of the development of international instruments on custody and access issues explaining how private international law had to embrace public law care proceedings in cross-border cases as being included within its scope. In HC96 the material scope is not just in relation to parental responsibility (broadly defined in Article 1(2) to include "parental authority, or any analogous relationship of authority determining the rights, powers and responsibilities of parents, guardians or other legal representatives in relation to the person or the property of the child.") but also all "measures of protection" of "the person or property of the child" (Article 1(1)(a)). Article 3 clarifies that the measures in Article 1 extend to:

c) guardianship, curatorship and analogous institutions;
d) the designation and functions of any person or body having charge of the child's person or property, representing or assisting the child;
e) the placement of the child in a foster family or in institutional care, or the provision of care by *kafala* or an analogous institution;
f) the supervision by a public authority of the care of a child by any person having charge of the child

Dr Wright's study is invaluable in developing private international lawyers' understanding of HC96 by coming to the Convention through the lens of public law proceedings and yet seeing how those public law proceedings can be turned into private law outcomes where a child is well cared for by a relative in another jurisdiction. After setting out the legal framework created by HC96 (and Brussels IIa) in chapter three she carefully analyses the lessons that can be learned from her empirical study in four specific areas discussed in four chapters: jurisdiction and transfer of jurisdiction; requesting and exchanging information across borders in child protection cases; overseas assessments in care proceedings; and overseas kinship placements. Her final chapter sets out the conclusions and recommendations drawn from her study. There is a wealth of interesting data and analysis in the book (including in the appendix which sets out in more detail the empirical findings) that I commend to readers. The rest of this short preface will pick out a few issues concerning the application of HC96 starting with transfer of jurisdiction.

I wrote about the transfer of jurisdiction system in HC96 (comparing it to the system in Brussels IIa) in "Private international law concerning children in the UK after Brexit: comparing Hague Treaty law with EU Regulations" (2017) *Child and Family Law Quarterly* 213. I was considering primarily private law cases concerning parental responsibility when I said that:

> transfer of the jurisdiction to decide the issue in hand does not require the child to move to the place where the case will be decided, if the child is not already present there, pending the decision on the merits ... Under Hague 1996 the court considering offering a transfer or considering making a transfer request has to compare which of the possible courts to hear the case is best placed to hear it from the perspective of *determining* the child's best interests. Therefore, no consideration should be given to substantive law (as the CJEU rightly stated in relation to Article 15 of Brussels IIa) but the examination of the relative merits of the two courts should focus on the ease with which those courts can determine the best interests of the child. Thus the most important factors seem to be the location of the child, the people contesting parental responsibility and any witnesses from whom oral testimony would be desirable. Other relevant factors may include the likely length of time of the respective proceedings, whether the parties (and possibly the child depending on the circumstances) can be legally represented and, where appropriate, the availability and cost-effectiveness of experts (for example child psychologists and social workers) to assist in the determination of the child's best interests.

I also noted one of the key origins of the transfer system in HC96 is the plea of *forum non conveniens* in Scotland, as observed by Professor Paul Lagarde in the explanatory report to HC96, and suggested a rewording of what he said in that report on the transfer provisions as follows:

> These Articles introduce into the Convention a ... mechanism for *forum non conveniens* and *forum conveniens*, where it appears that authorities other than those of the State of the habitual residence are better placed to determine what measures of protection are needed in the child's best interests.

In this book Maria is concerned about when to use the HC96 transfer system in public law cases where child protection considerations come very clearly into view. Her study is on cases where an English local authority was sufficiently concerned about the suitability of the person that was caring for the child in England (usually one of the parents) to exercise parental responsibility for the child to want to take the child into care. The study has a particular focus on cases where it is appropriate to consider a permanent placement of the child with an adult relative (a kinship placement) in another HC96 Contracting State. From the empirical study and her doctrinal analysis, she recommends the following as good practice under HC96:

> 8. In cases where there is a plan to place a child with a parent or kinship carer in a different Contracting State, it may be appropriate for jurisdiction to be transferred to that Contracting State using the provisions in Articles 8 or 9 of the HC96 so that the legal and practical framework for that placement can be resolved by the authorities in the country where the child will be living. This may be appropriate in cases where there is certainty about a child's placement with a parent or kinship carer, but the legal framework, or arrangements for post-placement support by local state-based services, needs to be resolved by the authorities in the requested Contracting State. This may not be appropriate where there is a risk of further litigation in the requested Contracting State which may undermine the plan formulated and judged to be in the child's best interests by the competent authorities of the requesting Contracting States.
>
> 9. It should also be recalled that transfer of jurisdiction under Art 8 or Art 9 does not necessarily need to coincide with a child's physical move to the requested Contracting State. In cases where a child has been placed in interim foster care, for example, it may be appropriate for the authorities of the requesting Contracting State to continue to exercise jurisdiction on the basis of a child's presence under Articles 11 and 12 of the HC96, until there is certainty as to the child's placement in the requested state, its legal framework and arrangements for post-placement support. At this point arrangements can be made for the child's transition into their final placement in the requested Contracting State.

What Maria is envisaging here is that the HC96 Contracting State which is taking care proceedings, because of child protection concerns about the way the parent or parents were caring for the child, might begin to exercise its jurisdiction to take child protection measures in relation to that child (usually on the basis of the child's habitual residence there). In doing so it should make appropriate use of the cooperation mechanisms available through HC96 to see if a kinship placement order in another HC96 Contracting State might be in the best interests of the child (eg getting an assessment of the adult relative done by a qualified person in that country). Apart from the specific provisions imposing duties of cooperation on the Central Authorities of Contracting States referred to by Dr Wright (eg Articles 33 and 36) much useful practical cooperation can be achieved by diligent Central and Competent Authorities through the general obligation under Article 30(1). Indeed, the following was stated in para 80 of the Conclusions and Recommendations of the HCCH Special Commission reviewing the operation of HC96 and the Hague Child Abduction Convention 1980 in October 2023:

> The Special Commission noted that in addition to cooperating in relation to matters provided for under Articles 31 to 36, Central Authorities are also strongly encouraged

> to cooperate regarding other matters, under Article 30, to achieve the purposes of the 1996 Child Protection Convention.

Article 30(1) of HC96 says:

> Central Authorities shall co-operate with each other and promote co-operation amongst the competent authorities in their States to achieve the purposes of the Convention.

The purposes of the Convention, as set out in its preamble just below, include international cooperation in improving protection of children where the best interests of the child is a primary consideration:

> Considering the need to improve the protection of children in international situations,
>
> Wishing to avoid conflicts between their legal systems in respect of jurisdiction, applicable law, recognition and enforcement of measures for the protection of children,
>
> Recalling the importance of international co-operation for the protection of children,
>
> Confirming that the best interests of the child are to be a primary consideration

Dr Wright encourages the idea that it is only once the competent authorities are satisfied that a kinship placement in the other HC96 Contracting State is likely to be in the best interests of the child may they then seek to transfer the jurisdiction over the case to the HC Contracting State where the adult relative is habitually resident. The competent authorities in the HC96 Contracting State where the adult relative lives would then be able to make the appropriate type of order under that legal system to give "permanence" to the adult relative's legal right to exercise parental responsibility in relation to that child. The general obligation of cooperation between the competent authorities under Article 30(1) HC96 could be used to enable communication between those authorities in these delicate cases. The exact timing of the move of the child from the State exercising initial jurisdiction over the case to the State exercising final jurisdiction will depend on what is in the best interests of the child. It may be appropriate for the child to move to live with the adult relative in the new State once the competent authority there has at least given an interim order of parental responsibility to their adult relative there. This has the advantage of the authorities in that State being able to monitor how that interim order is working before making it permanent.

So the important lesson to be learned is that, at least in public law proceedings where a kinship placement in another Contracting State is being envisaged, it may be wise to delay the transfer of the proceedings until quite a lot of work has already been done by the competent authorities in the habitual residence of the child rather than at a very early stage in the proceedings. It is also good that this empirical study confirms that the transfer of jurisdiction from one HC96 Contracting State to another should not always coincide with the child being moved from the one State to the other.

Of course, Maria also rightly recommends the best use of HC96 in cases where the competent authorities in the State where the care proceedings are initially brought do not transfer the case to another HC96 Contracting State. This may well involve the competent authorities largely applying their own law as envisaged by HC96 (Article 15(1)) but supplementing that with the use of the law of the State where the adult relative lives that the competent authority is thinking about giving parental responsibility to (Article 15(2)). The advantage of using the foreign law as a supplement could be that the parental responsibility order can be framed in a way that fits the types of order used in the State where the child is going to live with the adult relative and therefore is more likely to be recognised and operate well there. This solution can be used in relation to States that are not Contracting States to HC96 due to the universal application of the applicable law rules under HC96.

Another important route recommended by Dr Wright is the use of Article 24 of HC96 to seek advanced recognition of a kinship placement order made in one HC96 Contracting State in the HC96 Contracting State where the adult relative lives before the child leaves the Contracting State where the kinship placement order has been made. This has the advantage that if the Contracting State where the adult relative lives refuses to recognise that person's parental responsibility then alternative arrangements can be made for the child by the competent authorities of the Contracting State that made the order before the child has experienced any disruption from the care arrangements in that country (often foster care).

I unconditionally recommend this book to anyone interested in HC96 (or Brussels IIb) as it fills a significant gap in the literature on cases that start as care proceedings but end up with a cross-border private law resolution, both from an analytical perspective and by insights and recommendations drawn from a significant sample of cross-border cases. HC96 currently has 57 Contracting States and it is to be hoped that many more States will join in so that children moving across borders can benefit from having their best interests protected by appropriate measures of protection which are recognised in all the States to which they are connected.

Professor Paul Beaumont FRSE
Professor of Private International Law
University of Stirling

ACKNOWLEDGEMENTS

This book is derived from the author's thesis 'Care Proceedings with an International Element: An Empirical Study' from a PhD awarded by the University of Bristol School of Law on 5 December 2023, funded by a studentship from the Economic and Social Research Council.

In addition, this book is derived in part from the following articles.

- M Wright, 'Special Guardianship Orders and Overseas Placements' (2019) *Family Law Week*
- M Wright, '"Working" the international child protection case: a snapshot of local authorities' experiences within an evolving legal context' (2019) 41 *Journal of Social Welfare and Family Law* 15
- M Wright, 'Care Proceedings and International Kinship Care' (2022) 6 *Child and Family Law Quarterly* 381

TABLE OF CONTENTS

LIST OF ABBREVIATIONS

1902 Guardianship Convention	Convention du 12 Juin 1902 Pour Régler la Tutelle des Mineurs
1961 Convention	Convention Concerning the Powers of Authorities and the Law Applicable in Respect of the Protection of Infants
1965 Adoption Convention	Convention of 15 November 1965 on Jurisdiction, Applicable Law and Recognition of Decrees Relating to Adoptions
HC96	Convention of 19 October 1996 on Jurisdiction, Applicable Law, Recognition, Enforcement and Co-operation in Respect of Parental Responsibility and Measures for the Protection of Children
1980 Hague Convention	Convention of 25 October 1980 on the Civil Aspects of International Child Abduction
ACA 2002	Adoption and Children Act 2002
ADCS	Association of Directors of Children's Services
BIIa	Council Regulation (EC) No 2201/2003 of 27 November 2003 concerning jurisdiction and the recognition and enforcement of judgments in matrimonial matters and the matters of parental responsibility, repealing Regulation (EC) No 1347/2000 [2003] OJ L338/1
BII ter	Council Regulation (EU) 2019/1111 of 25 June 2019 on jurisdiction, the recognition and enforcement of decisions in matrimonial matters and the matters of parental responsibility, and on international child abduction [2019] OJ L178/1
CA89	Children Act 1989
CAO	Child Arrangements Order
Cafcass	Children and Family Court Advisory and Support Service
CFAB	Children and Families Across Borders

CMH	Case Management Hearing
CJEU	Court of Justice for the European Union
FPR	Family Procedure Rules 2010
HCA 1993	Convention of 29 May 1993 on Protection of Children and Co-operation in Respect of Intercountry Adoption
HCCH	Hague Conference on Private International Law (Conférence de La Haye de Droit International Privé)
ICACU	International Child Abduction and Contact Unit (the Central Authority for England and Wales for the purposes of BIIa and England for the HC96)
ICJ	International Court of Justice
IRH	Issues Resolution Hearing
ISS	International Social Services
ISW	Independent Social Worker
PD	Practice Direction
PIL	Private International Law
PLO	Public Law Outline (FPR 2010, Practice Direction 12A)
SGO	Special Guardianship Order
SWET	Social Work Evidence Template
UNCRC	UN Convention on the Rights of the Child 1989

LIST OF FIGURES AND TABLES

Figures

Tables

TABLE OF CASES

Cases: England and Wales

Cases: Court of Justice of the European Union

Cases: European Court of Human Rights

TABLE OF LEGISLATION

Statutes: International

European Agreements/Resolutions/Other International Materials

Domestic Statutes

Statutory Instruments

1

Introduction

Where a local authority in England considers that a child is at risk of harm, they may issue care proceedings under Children Act 1989 (CA 89). A local authority may apply for a care order – giving a local authority parental responsibility for the child – or a supervision order – permitting the local authority to monitor the child for a designated period.[1] In practice, care proceedings operate as a vehicle through which a court can decide whether or not the child has suffered the harm alleged and the welfare outcome which will meet the child's best interests.[2] A court will consider a range of legal and placement options for a child during care proceedings, including the child remaining with their parents, being placed with extended family or in foster care, or being placed for adoption.

Where a child who is the subject of care proceedings has an international connection, the proceedings may engage internationally and regionally agreed private international law (PIL) instruments. However, the approach to care proceedings in England has, historically, failed to consider the application and impact of these instruments. Instead, practice in this area has been shaped by the convergence of several factors, which have required courts to address how care proceedings should operate for children with connections outside of the UK.

First, the 2004 expansion of the European Union brought with it a change to the demographic make-up of local authorities in England associated with EU Freedom of Movement. Ten new countries became EU Member States in 2004 with Romania and Bulgaria joining in 2007.[3] This expansion led to a rise in net migration from the EU; the 2004 expansion led to the first major peak in EU migration experienced in the UK, and as a consequence an increase in children whose parents had migrated to the UK, primarily to work.[4] As Munby P observed in the 2014 case of *Re E (A Child) (Care Proceedings: European Dimension)*, courts

[1] CA 89 s 31.

[2] CA 89 s 1 (1).

[3] N Broberg and L Ludolph, 'Migration and Redistributive Spending: Evidence from Local Authorities in England' (2 December 2021) Robert Schuman Centre for Advanced Studies Working Paper RSC Working Paper 2021/86 https://papers.ssrn.com/sol3/papers.cfm?abstract_id=3972303. See also R Lamont, 'The Development of Child Protection Across International Borders for Children at Risk of Harm' in G Douglas, M Murch and V Stephens (eds), *International and National Perspectives on Child and Family Law* (Cambridge University Press, 2018) 235.

[4] M Sumption and PW Walsh, 'EU Migration to and from the UK' (Migration Observatory briefing, COMPAS, University of Oxford 2022). Transitional controls on the rights of Romanians and Bulgarians to live and work in the UK were not lifted until 2014.

and local authorities were increasingly encountering children with connections to other EU Member States in the context of care proceedings.[5] These connections may have arisen by way of a child's nationality, through parental, sibling or kinship links to other EU Member States or through the child having previously lived in another country. In some cases, children had been brought to the UK by their parents to avoid scrutiny or intervention by child protection authorities in their home country, creating an additional layer of complexity to the care proceedings coming before courts in England following the EU's expansion.[6]

The second significant contextual issue concerned the domestic approach to care proceedings practice in England from 2007 onwards. Courts had experienced a steady, year on year rise in the number of care proceedings applications since 2007.[7] The increase in care cases heard by the family court was also reflected in a rise in the number of children looked after by local authorities in England and Wales, placing a significant strain on public resources.[8] In response to the rising demand in care proceedings, a series of reforms were introduced which sought to minimise delay and alleviate the pressure they were placing on the family justice system. In 2008, a 'pre-proceedings' process was introduced, through statutory guidance, to operate in care proceedings.[9] This sought to divert cases from courts through pre-proceedings work with families, by way of formal meetings where local authorities would outline their concerns about children to their parents or carers (who could be legally represented at the meetings), and agree a way forward for parents or carers to make the necessary changes to avoid care proceedings.[10] Nonetheless, the 2011 Family Justice Review chaired by David Norgrove found that care proceedings were still placing a significant strain on the family justice system, and were taking too long (an average of 56 weeks).[11] Following the Family Justice Review, an extensive package of legislative and procedural reforms were introduced. The Children and Families Act 2014 introduced a 26-week time limit for care proceedings, which could only be extended where this was necessary to

[5] Re E (A Child) (Care Proceedings: European Dimension) [2014] EWHC 6 (Fam); [2014] 1 WLR 2670 [14]; R Lamont, 'Care Proceedings with a European Dimension under Brussels IIa: Jurisdiction, Mutual Trust and the Best Interests of the Child' (2016) 28 *Child and Family Law Quarterly* 67.

[6] See the discussion of the impact of EU Freedom of Movement on the family situations local authorities may encounter in a child protection context by R Lamont and C Fenton-Glynn, 'Cross-Border Public Care and Adoption Proceedings in the European Union' (2016) 38 *Journal of Social Welfare and Family Law* 94, 95–96. See also the discussion of 'known flight' cases in Chapter 6.

[7] J Munby, 'View from the President's Chambers: Care Cases – The Looming Crisis' (2016).

[8] R Preston, 'English councils need £2.7bn more for children's social care by 2025, LGA warns government' (Community Care, 25 October 2021).

[9] Department for Children, Schools and Families, The Children Act 1989 Guidance and Regulations Volume 1, Court Orders (2008, TSO).

[10] See J Masson et al, 'Partnership by Law: The Pre-Proceedings Process for Families on the Edge of Care Proceedings.' (School of Law, University of Bristol and the Centre for Research on Children and Families, University of East Anglia 2013).

[11] Family Justice Review Panel, 'Family Justice Review: Final Report' (Ministry of Justice and Welsh Government, 2011).

resolve proceedings justly.[12] The Act also amended rules surrounding the use of experts in children's proceedings, requiring there to be a focus on the necessity of expert evidence.[13] Finally, the Public Law Outline (PLO 2014) provided an array of procedural reforms which sought to 'front load' care proceedings by placing extensive evidential requirements on local authorities at the outset of proceedings.[14]

Against this background, by 2013 local authorities were feeling the effects of two significant court judgments, *Re B (A Child)*[15] and *Re B-S (Children)*.[16] These judgments emphasised that courts should only place children for adoption where 'nothing else will do'.[17] *Re B-S* in particular highlighted the importance of rigorous social work evidence in assisting the court in undertaking a 'global, holistic evaluation' of all the realistic placement options for a child's long-term future.[18] These judgments did not change the law but were interpreted by many local authorities as meaning that children should be placed for adoption less frequently, and as requiring a change in the way that children's social work is practised in care cases.[19] The combined impact of these judgments, coupled with care proceedings reforms which sought to minimise delay and complexity, meant that local authorities were required to navigate the 'irresolvable tensions between speed, justice and thoroughness.'[20]

These developments did not necessarily take into account the change in the demographic make-up of local authorities associated with the EU's expansion and the way that a child's international connections may present distinct challenges. The domestic approach to care proceedings practice also failed to fully appreciate legal changes at an international level. Council Regulation (EC) No 2201/2003 of 27 November 2003 concerning jurisdiction and the recognition and enforcement of judgments in matrimonial matters and the matters of parental responsibility, repealing Regulation (EC) No 1347/2000 (BIIa), applied in the UK from 1 March 2005.[21] BIIa provided a regionally agreed framework of PIL between EU Member States (except Denmark), with rules as to jurisdictional competence, the mutual recognition and enforcement of judgments across borders, and,

[12] Children and Families Act 2014 s 14.

[13] Children and Families Act 2014 s 13.

[14] Family Procedure Rules (FPR) 2010, Practice Direction (PD) 12A. See J Masson et al, *Child Protection in Court: Outcomes for Children* (School of Law, University of Bristol and the Centre for Research on Children and Families, University of East Anglia, 2019).

[15] [2013] UKSC 33; [2013] 1 WLR 1911.

[16] [2013] EWCA Civ 1146; [2014] 1 WLR 563.

[17] *Re B (A Child)* [2013] UKSC 33; [2013] 1 WLR 1911 [145] Lady Hale.

[18] *Re B-S (Children)* [2013] EWCA Civ 1146; [2014] 1 WLR 563 [44] (Munby P), quoting *Re G (A Child)* [2013] EWCA Civ 965, [49-50] (McFarlane LJ).

[19] J Masson et al, See J Masson et al, *Child Protection in Court: Outcomes for Children* (School of Law, University of Bristol and the Centre for Research on Children and Families, University of East Anglia, 2019) 140; J Harwin et al, 'A National Study of the Usage of Supervision Orders and Special Guardianship over Time (2007-2016)' (Nuffield Foundation, 2015) 4.

[20] J Dickens, C Beckett and S Bailey, 'Justice, Speed and Thoroughness in Child Protection Court Proceedings: Messages from England' (2014) 46 *Children and Youth Services Review* 103, 109.

[21] [2003] OJ L 338/1 Art 72.

importantly, a system for cross-border co-operation and communication between Central Authorities in relation to civil proceedings concerning children.[22] BIIa was widely considered and applied in the context of private law proceedings concerning children such as custody/ residence and contact when it entered into force.[23] However, it is clear from reported cases from 2012 onwards that courts and local authorities had been slow to appreciate the significance and application of BIIa in public law care proceedings.[24]

The convergence of these three factors – the increase in care proceedings concerning children with European connections, domestic reforms to care proceedings which did not take account of this changing demography, and the entry into force of BIIa (an instrument which did not penetrate care proceedings practice) – led to cases where there were plans to place EU national children for adoption in England. These cases began to attract political attention, and the actions of courts and local authorities became the subject of significant scrutiny at an international level. The external political attention these cases received highlighted differences in state child protection systems across the EU, in particular that in England and Wales, children may be placed for adoption at the conclusion of care proceedings – a practice which was believed to occur less frequently in other countries.[25]

[22] The term 'BIIa Member States' is used in this book to acknowledge that Denmark opted out of BIIa.

[23] For example, the Child Abduction and Custody Act 1985 and Family Law Act 1986 were amended by Statutory Instrument (The European Communities (Jurisdiction and Judgments in Matrimonial and Parental Responsibility Matters) Regulations 2005 SI 2005/265 Reg 6, 8) to reflect the application of BIIa from 1 March 2005 in international child abduction proceedings, and proceedings which fell within the scope of the FLA 1986 (including private law proceedings under the CA 89) (see also *Re J (A Child) (Custody Rights: Jurisdiction)* [2005] UKHL 40; [2006] 1 AC 80 [19]). No equivalent amendments were made in a public law children's context.

[24] See N Lowe and H Setright, 'Transferring the Problem – How Art 15 of the Revised Brussels II Regulation Operates in the Public Law Context' (2017) *International Family Law* 13. For a marked example of a lack of awareness about the relevance of BIIa in care proceedings, see the discussion of *Re S (A Child) (Care Proceedings: Jurisdiction)* [2008] EWHC 3013 (Fam); [2009] PTSR CS17 in R Lamont, 'The Development of Child Protection Across International Borders for Children at Risk of Harm' in G Douglas, M Murch and V Stephens (eds), *International and National Perspectives on Child and Family Law* (Cambridge University Press, 2018).

[25] In early discussions about the law surrounding non-consensual adoption in the UK as compared to other EU Member States, there was an assumption that the United Kingdom was unusual in having a legal framework which permitted non-consensual adoption (see *Down Lisburn Health and Social Services Trust v H* [2006] UKHL 36; [2007] 1 FLR 121 [34] (Lady Hale); *Re B-S (Children) (Adoption Order: Leave to Oppose*) [2013] EWCA Civ 1146; [2014] 1 WLR 563 [19] (Munby P); *Re D (A Child)* [2014] EWHC 3388 (Fam); [2015] 2 FLR 47 [35]). However, subsequent research has found that a number of other EU Member States have a legal mechanism for non-consensual adoption albeit that it would appear to be less widely used than in England and Wales. See also C Fenton-Glynn, 'Adoption without Consent' (Policy Department for Citizens' Rights and Constitutional Affairs, European Parliament 2015); C Fenton-Glynn, 'Adoption without Consent: Update 2016' (Policy Department for Citizens' Rights and Constitutional Affairs, European Parliament 2016); R Lamont and C Fenton-Glynn, 'Cross-Border Public Care and Adoption Proceedings in the European Union' (2016) 38 *Journal of Social Welfare and Family Law* 94; R Lamont, 'Care Proceedings with a European Dimension under Brussels IIa: Jurisdiction, Mutual Trust and the Best Interests of the Child' (2016) 28 *Child and Family Law Quarterly* 67; R Lamont, 'The Development of Child Protection Across International Borders for Children at Risk of Harm' in G Douglas, M Murch and V Stephens (eds), *International and National Perspectives on Child and Family Law* (Cambridge University Press, 2018) 238.

The Adoption and Children Act 2002 s 52 permits a court to place a child for adoption and dispense with the consent of their parents to their adoption where this is required for the child's welfare. This practice of non-consensual adoption – or 'forced adoption' – had already been the subject of criticism by campaign groups in the UK.[26] The cases of *Re B* and *Re B-S* referred to above had, to an extent, buttressed these criticisms by suggesting that courts and local authorities had taken a cavalier approach to adoption without exploring and analysing alternative placements for children with sufficient rigour.[27] Objections by overseas state authorities to the adoption of their nationals – and the suggestion that the practice of non-consensual adoption was 'out of step' with the other EU Member States – provided a further dimension to the debate around non-consensual adoption, and triggered a need to evaluate practice in care proceedings with an international element.[28] For example, the Latvian Parliament submitted a formal complaint to the House of Commons in relation to one case where a child had been placed in care in England following neglect by her mother, and had subsequently been placed for adoption.[29] The letter cited 'insufficient cross-border cooperation on the part of UK authorities in relation to the UK's national procedure of placing Latvian citizens up for adoption without parental consent.'[30]

Overseas state bodies, in the form of consulates or Central Authorities, began to attend hearings in care proceedings in England concerning their nationals, sometimes formally intervening in those proceedings and providing submissions to the court as to the appropriate welfare outcome for the child.[31] The criticisms levelled at courts and local authorities by these state bodies concerned a failure to use BIIa in care proceedings.[32] This was linked to a complaint that courts of

[26] See, for example I Josephs, 'Forced Adoption: Punishment Without Crime' (Forced Adoption) https://forced-adoption.com.

[27] The term 'forced adoption' is often used by campaign groups to describe the provision in Adoption and Children Act s 52 which permits a court to place a child for adoption and dispense with the consent of their parents to their adoption where the child's welfare requires that such consent be dispensed with. The phrase 'non-consensual adoption' to describe this provision was used by Munby P in *Re N (Children) (Adoption: Jurisdiction)* [2015] EWCA Civ 1112; [2016] 2 WLR 713 [7] and will be used throughout this book.

[28] The issue of the removal of children from the care of their parents within the EU and other European States was also explored by the Council of Europe – see O Borzova, 'Social services in Europe: Legislation and Practice of the Removal of Children from Their Families in Council of Europe Member States' (Council of Europe, 2015).

[29] O Bowcott, 'Latvia Complains to UK Parliament over Forced Adoptions' (the Guardian, 9 March 2015) https://www.theguardian.com/uk-news/2015/mar/09/latvia-complains-to-uk-parliament-over-forced-adoptions.

[30] *Merton London Borough Council v B (Central Authority of the Republic of Latvia intervening)* [2015] EWCA Civ 888; [2016] Fam 123 [90].

[31] See (but not limited to), *Re T (A Child) (Care Proceedings: Request to Assume Jurisdiction)* [2013] EWHC 521 (Fam) [2013] 2 WLR 1263; *Re T (A Child) (Care Proceedings: Request to Assume Jurisdiction)* [2013] EWCA Civ 895; [2014] 2 WLR 1204; *Merton London Borough Council v B (Central Authority of the Republic of Latvia intervening)* [2015] EWCA Civ 888; [2016] Fam 123; *Medway Council v JB* [2015] EWHC 3064 (Fam); [2016] 2 FLR 1360.

[32] See *Re E (A Child) (Care Proceedings: European Dimension)* [2014] EWHC 6 (Fam); [2014] 1 WLR 2670 [13].

England and Wales were 'exorbitant in the exercise of the care jurisdiction over children from other European countries'.[33] There were two core dimensions to this critique. First, that there was insufficient consideration of the jurisdictional provisions of BIIa in care proceedings concerning EU national children. Secondly, there was insufficient cross-border co-operation with competent authorities in other EU countries to explore family placements in those countries, as an alternative to children being placed for adoption in the UK. It was also suggested that courts and local authorities were acting unlawfully – or at least improperly – by failing to notify the relevant embassy where care proceedings were issued concerning a child with foreign nationality. This was said to be in breach of Articles 36 and 37 of the Vienna Convention on Consular Relations 1967.

In response, from 2014 onwards, there followed a proliferation of domestic guidance, in the form of reported court judgments, practice directions, amendments to procedural rules, non-statutory governmental guidance for local authorities and many other formats, which sought to assist with the practical implementation of relevant international legal instruments and the practice of care proceedings with an international dimension.[34] The decision of Munby P in *Re E (A Child) (Care Proceedings: European Dimension)* constituted the core 'guidance judgment' in this context.[35] The judgment said it was good practice for courts to consider, and record, the jurisdictional basis for care proceedings under BIIa, and to consider, in all cases with a European element, whether to seek a transfer of jurisdiction to another Member State under BIIa Article 15. In response to complaints about 'non-compliance' with the Vienna Convention on Consular Relations 1967, the judgment also said that it was good practice for the relevant embassy to be notified if a foreign national child was taken into care.[36] The Public Law Outline was amended to incorporate the President's guidance from *Re E* and

[33] Ibid. See also *Re N (Children) (Adoption: Jurisdiction)* [2015] EWCA Civ 1112; [2016] 2 WLR 713.

[34] E.g., Department for Education, 'Cross-Border Child Protection Cases: The 1996 Hague Convention. Departmental Advice for Local Authorities, Social Workers, Service Managers and Children's Services Lawyers, October 2012' (DfE, 2012); Department for Education, 'Advice on Placement of Looked After Children across Member States of the European Union. For Local Authority Children's Services, July 2013' (DfE, 2013); Department for Education, 'Working with Foreign Authorities: Child Protection Cases and Care Orders. Departmental Advice for Local Authorities, Social Workers, Service Managers and Children's Services Lawyers, July 2014' (DfE, 2014); J Munby, 'President's Guidance of 10 November 2014: The International Child Abduction and Contact Unit' (2014).

[35] *Re E (A Child) (Care Proceedings: European Dimension)* [2014] EWHC 6 (Fam); [2014] 1 WLR 2670. 'Guidance judgments' are considered in *Re B (A Child)* [2017] EWCA Civ 1579; [2017] 4 WLR 202 and include judgments handed down by the President of the Family Division which make practice points with a wider application beyond the facts of the case being considered.

[36] Munby P expressly reserved his view as to whether Articles 36 and 37 of the Vienna Convention were a part of UK law and stated that he did not intend to provide guidance to local authorities through the judgment, his comments being directed towards other judges. However, subsequently in *Merton London Borough Council v B* [2015] EWCA Civ 888; [2016] Fam 123 [79] Munby P stated it would be good practice for local authorities to be 'pro-active in bringing to the attention of the relevant consular authorities at the earliest possible opportunity the fact that care proceedings involving foreign nationals are on foot or in contemplation.'

subsequent judgments insofar as it required courts to consider jurisdiction at the outset of proceedings, as well as liaison with the Central Authority or relevant Embassy.[37] Reported cases began to evidence disputes as to jurisdiction, and applications to transfer jurisdiction to other Member States using BIIa.[38] BIIa was used to place children in foster care overseas,[39] or to safeguard kinship placements through the mutual recognition and enforcement provisions.[40] Local authorities were encouraged to use the Central Authorities designated by BIIa to communicate with counterparts overseas, to gather information for the proceedings and assess potential kinship carers.[41] Care proceedings with an international element were considered to be sufficiently complex to warrant allocation to a High Court judge, as opposed to Circuit or District judges.[42]

This national guidance has sought to clarify the relevant law in care proceedings with an international dimension, explaining how internationally and regionally agreed PIL frameworks are meant to operate when deciding cases. But the guidance has also suggested that local authorities need to work in a particular way when they have a case with an international element. This apparent 'gap' between law and practice, and the attempts to close it, raises questions about how child protection practice is modified or altered when a child has international connections, and the reach and role of law in this context.

This evolving practice environment for care proceedings with an international dimension also engages with many of the imperatives of care proceedings reform. Care proceedings with an international dimension have the potential to be slower than domestic proceedings, particularly where there is the need for an assessment of a potential carer resident overseas.[43] It may be more difficult to divert out of proceedings through pre-proceedings work with a family, for example, if a family

[37] FPR 2010 Practice Direction 12A.

[38] E.g. *Bridgend County Borough Council v G M & Anor* [2012] EWHC 3118 (Fam); *Re O-C (A Child) (Abduction: European Convention)* [2013] EWCA Civ 162; *Re T (A Child) (Care Proceedings: Request to Assume Jurisdiction)*[2013] EWHC 521 (Fam) [2013] 2 WLR 1263; Re T *(A Child) (Care Proceedings: Request to Assume Jurisdiction)* [2013] EWCA Civ 895; [2014] 2 WLR 1204; *Re M (A Child) (Foreign Care Proceedings: Transfer)* [2013] EWHC 646 (Fam); [2013] Fam. 308. See Nigel Lowe and Henry Setright, 'Transferring the Problem – How Art 15 of the Revised Brussels II Regulation Operates in the Public Law Context' (2017) *International Family Law* 13.

[39] BIIa Article 56; *HSE Ireland v SF (A Minor)* [2012] EWHC 1640 (Fam); *Re D (A Child)* [2013] EWHC 4078 (Fam).

[40] BIIa Articles 21-36. E.g., *Norfolk County Council v VE and others* [2015] EWFC 30 (Fam).

[41] *Leicester City Council v S* [2014] EWHC 1575 (Fam); [2015] 1 FLR 1182.

[42] But see *Re J (A Child) (Brussels II Revised: Article 15: Practice and Procedure)* [2014] EWFC 41; [2015] Fam Law 129.

[43] In *Re S (A Child)* [2014] EWCC B44 (Fam) [33] Munby P considered that it may be 'necessary' to extend the 26-week time limit for determination of a child protection case pursuant to Children and Families Act 2014 s 14 in cases 'with an international element where investigations or assessments have to be carried out abroad'. More recently, guidance from the Family Justice Council has confirmed that an extension to the 26-week time limit may be necessary where there are unavoidable delays associated with assessing family overseas (Family Justice Council Public Law Working Group, 'Recommendations to Achieve Best Practice in the Child Protection and Family Justice Systems: Special Guardianship Orders' (FJC, 2020) 64.

is dispersed transnationally, if the child has only recently arrived in this country or if the cross-border issues are themselves a 'trigger' for the issuing of proceedings on an emergency basis.[44] However, effective cross-border practice in care proceedings also has the potential to ease care demand: for example, through the placement of children overseas with kinship carers who have been properly assessed as being able to provide permanent homes, rather than remaining in foster care in England. The exploration of options for overseas kinship care is also consistent with the 'global holistic evaluation' of realistic placements for a child who cannot return to live with their parent/s, envisaged by *Re B-S (Children)*.[45] The extent to which internationally and regionally agreed PIL instruments facilitate care proceedings with an international dimension is therefore relevant to the overall picture of care demand, practice in child protection proceedings in England and appropriate care for children who cannot return to their parents.

Whilst the empirical study which forms the basis of this book was prompted by issues surrounding the operation of BIIa in care proceedings, it spans a period where there has been a significant change to the relevant PIL frameworks in force in the UK due to Brexit.

As set out above, BIIa applied in the UK from 1 March 2005. A second PIL instrument – the 1996 Hague Convention (hereafter 'HC96') – entered into force in the UK on 1 November 2012.[46] All EU Member States are also Contracting States to the HC96 – there are also several non-EU Contracting States including Russia, Australia and Morocco.[47] However, its provisions may have been less widely used prior to Brexit, as BIIa took priority over the HC96 in relation to matters governed by that regulation for children who had their habitual residence on the territory of a BIIa Member State.[48]

On 31 January 2020, the UK formally left the EU. During the implementation period that followed, BIIa continued to apply to care proceedings with a European

[44] For example, if the child is present in England as an unaccompanied minor, as a suspected victim of trafficking or child sexual exploitation, or where there is a risk that the child may be moved out of the jurisdiction to evade local authority intervention, or to suffer a specific form of harm such as forced marriage or female genital mutilation. Further, in *Leicester City Council v S* [2014] EWHC 1575 (Fam); [2015] 1 FLR 1182, Moylan J said that in cases where there is a potential jurisdictional issue, proceedings should be issued promptly so that there is a forum available to determine it.

[45] [2013] EWCA Civ 1146; [2014] 1 WLR 563 [44] Munby P.

[46] Convention of 19 October 1996 on Jurisdiction, Applicable Law, Recognition, Enforcement and Co-operation in Respect of Parental Responsibility and Measures for the Protection of Children. See also The Parental Responsibility and Measures for the Protection of Children (International Obligations) (England and Wales and Northern Ireland) Regulations 2010, SI 2010/1898 which supported the entry into force of the HC96.

[47] For a discussion of the interplay between the HC96 and BIIa see Chapter 2.

[48] BIIa Art 61 (1), 62 (2). See C Honorati and M Keyes, 'Parental Responsibility, Custody and Access' in Paul Beaumont and Jayne Holliday (eds), *A Guide to Global Private International Law* (Hart, 2022) 474. The HC96 Chapter III contains applicable law provisions. BIIa does not contain applicable law provisions. As such, applicable law is not a matter 'governed' by BIIa and its provisions could be engaged in relation to children who have their habitual residence on the territory of a Member State (N Lowe and M Nicholls, *The 1996 Hague Convention on the Protection of Children* (LexisNexis, 2012) 1.46).

dimension.[49] The implementation period ended at 11 p.m. on 31 December 2020.[50] For care proceedings issued after this date, the HC96 is now the relevant PIL instrument where a case has an international element.[51]

Although Brexit may have altered the legal frameworks surrounding care proceedings with an international dimension, BIIa and the HC96 perform broadly the same functions in these proceedings. As will be outlined in Chapter 2, which tracks the development of PIL in this area, many of the provisions of BIIa were drawn from the HC96. There has been a further change in the field of EU PIL concerning children as BIIa has undergone a further revision. Brussels II ter applies between the EU Member States (except Denmark) from 1 August 2022.[52] Whilst the UK will not be impacted by this change, the evolving legal environment surrounding transnational child protection issues is of significance. It is argued in this book that – generally – private international law instruments concerning children are capable of furthering the interests of children (and this is their stated intention) if they are used in the right way, however, the approach in England and Wales to care cases with an international element has been hampered by attempts to 'comply' with judicial guidance on their operation, which has in turn marginalised the individual interests of children with transnational connections.

The law and legal discussion in this book is correct at 30 October 2024, but the practices observed in the case sample relate to the law at the date of the relevant sample cases (heard between January 2015 and January 2018) when the UK was a member of the EU and BIIa was in force.

Structure and Methodology

This chapter sets out the context for the book and the methodology adopted for its underlying empirical study, addressed below. Chapter 2 continues with an analysis of the history of the HC96 and BIIa and their application to public law measures of child protection. It is suggested that whereas the HC96 developed with a strong child protection imperative, its impact in this regard was marginalised by BIIa which was formulated in a distinct political context (one where child protection issues were not a priority in the regulation of cross-border migration).

[49] European Union (Withdrawal) Act 2018 s 1, s 1A; European Union (Withdrawal Agreement) Act 2020 s 39.

[50] European Union (Withdrawal Agreement) Act 2020 s 39.

[51] Care proceedings issued before 11 p.m. on 31 December 2020 but, concluding after this date, may still engage with BIIa. The recognition and enforcement of any orders made in proceedings issued before the end of the implementation period (but concluding after this date) are governed by BIIa (Agreement on the withdrawal of the United Kingdom of Great Britain and Northern Ireland from the European Union and the European Atomic Energy Community 2019 OJ C/384I Art 67(2)(b)).

[52] Council Regulation (EU) 2019/1111 of 25 June 2019 on jurisdiction, the recognition and enforcement of decisions in matrimonial matters and the matters of parental responsibility, and on international child abduction, [2019] OJ L178/1 Art 105.

There follows, in chapter 3, an analysis of the interaction between jurisdictional decisions and child welfare. A core function of BIIa and the HC96 is to determine which forum is competent to decide a case concerning a child, and a court must consider jurisdictional issues at the outset of care proceedings with an international element.[53] A determination as to the competent forum can have a significant, even life-changing, impact on a child, in both the short term and the long term.[54] However, the extent to which a court considers this impact when making a jurisdictional decision varies considerably, and the role of the best interests of a child has been debated in this context. An analysis is therefore given of the interplay between jurisdictional decisions and best interests, including in a similar or parallel category of cases: international child abduction.

The way in which care proceedings with an international element fit within the general practice and policy of care proceedings in England is analysed in chapter 4. PIL instruments support cross-border co-operation and provide a framework for the mutual recognition of judgments between different States. These functions can be seen as corresponding to aspects of the practice of care proceedings generally. For example, cross-border co-operation is a means of gathering evidence and providing relevant information across borders where children have international connections playing a role in safeguarding and ultimately identifying what is in the best interests of a child. The mutual recognition of court judgments is relevant to the means of securing legal permanence for a child to live with kin or a parent overseas – the quest for permanence for children being a core component of care proceedings practice. Chapter 4 therefore outlines how care proceedings practice operates generally, and the place of international issues in this landscape.

Against this background, the remainder of this book in chapters 5, 6, 7 and 8 presents the findings of an empirical study of care proceedings with an international element. A core objective of the empirical study was to illuminate the way that these cases were handled throughout the life of the case, rather than focusing solely on outcome, disputes or unusual cases, with a view to creating a profile of care cases with an international element. This was a mixed methods study, incorporating a quantitative and qualitative case file analysis of 100 care cases with an international dimension heard in England between January 2015 and January 2018. Fifty of the cases involved countries where there was an applicable internationally or regionally agreed framework of PIL (BIIa or HC96) and 50 involved states where BIIa/HC96 did not apply in relation to the UK (termed 'non-Contracting States' in this book). The data from this analysis was contextualised through

[53] *Re E (A Child) (Care* Proceedings: *European Dimension)* [2014] EWHC 6 (Fam); [2014] 1 WLR 2670; FPR 2010 PD 12 A.

[54] R Lamont, 'Care Proceedings with a European Dimension under Brussels IIa: Jurisdiction, Mutual Trust and the Best Interests of the Child' (2016) 28 *Child and Family Law Quarterly* 67; 70. *Re N (Children) (Adoption: Jurisdiction) (AIRE Centre and others intervening)* [2016] UKSC 15, [2017] AC 167.

qualitative interviews with 17 professionals with experience of care proceedings with an international element.

It should be noted that the sample of cases analysed for the purposes of the quantitative and qualitative case file analysis is not a random sample and is not representative of the population of care proceedings with an international element at a national level. At the time of writing, and indeed at the time that the empirical study was conducted, there was no mechanism by which it was possible to take a representative sample of care proceedings with an international element using existing administrative datasets.[55]

For this reason, the sample of 100 cases were taken from a dataset, constructed in collaboration with CFAB (Children and Families Across Borders), which was then linked to electronic court case files held by Cafcass.

CFAB is the UK Branch of International Social Services (ISS) network. It is a national charity which receives referrals from local authorities seeking co-operation with overseas authorities in care cases (and in child protection matters outside of court proceedings). CFAB works with partners in other countries to support children with international connections in this context. Some of its partners are other ISS members, some are statutory child protection authorities, some are Central Authorities designated by BIIa / HC96 and others are independent social workers or NGOs. Constructing a dataset from the cases CFAB has dealt with enabled a sample to be taken of care cases in England where there was a request for co-operation within a certain period and permitted cases to be captured involving non-Contracting States, so that comparisons could be drawn as to the role of PIL in this field.

The Cafcass Electronic Case Management System (eCMS) records demographic and case processing data on all public law cases issued in England and has formed the basis of several representative studies of care proceedings in England. Cases with an international element were not – at the time of taking this sample – identifiable in the eCMS.[56] It was therefore first necessary to construct a dataset of *known* cases with an international dimension and link that dataset with case records to permit an analysis of what happened in the cases. A random sample of 100 cases meeting the inclusion criteria (see Figure 1) was taken from CFAB's

[55] The lack of available data capable of secondary analysis on care proceedings with an international element in the UK has been noted at a European level. In Fenton-Glynn's study for the EU PETI Committee on adoption without consent across the EU, she noted the lack of available data to permit a statistical analysis of the adoption of overseas nationals and recommended that 'more extensive disaggregated data be compiled, in particular concerning the frequency with which children from other EU member states are taken into public care, and the rate at which they are placed for adoption' (C Fenton-Glynn, 'Adoption without Consent' (Policy Department for Citizens' Rights and Constitutional Affairs, European Parliament 2015, 47).

[56] In particular, the eCMS does not record variables on parties' nationalities. It should be acknowledged that the international elements in a case can arise in a variety of ways other than through nationality, and further that many international cases concern children with British nationality. Thus, the use of nationality as an indicator of a case's international character may in any event be insufficient.

database. The cases which met the inclusion criteria were then linked to Cafcass electronic case files to permit an analysis of the processing of the cases. The documents analysed are outlined in Figure 2.

Figure 1 Quantitative Sample: Inclusion Criteria

Quantitative Sample: Inclusion Criteria

- 'Outgoing case' (co-operation with a partner outside of the UK)
- Referred to CFAB between 1 January 2015 and 1 January 2018
- N=50 concern a BIIa / HC96 Contracting State
- N=50 concern a non-Contracting State
- Referred to in the context of care proceedings in England

Figure 2 Key Sources of Data from Cafcass E-Case Files

Most of the data for this phase of the study was collected from the following sources:

- Form C110A – Application for a Care / Supervision Order. Application form filed by the local authority to initiate proceedings.
- SWET – Social Worker's Initial Statement of Evidence
- Social Work Chronology and Genogram
- Initial / Final Care Plan – Local authority's plan for the child, required by s31A CA 89, contains information prescribed by The Care Planning, Placement and Case Review (England) Regulations 2010 Reg 5
- Court Orders – Case Management Orders and Standard Directions Orders (which follow a prescribed template)
- Guardian's Initial Analysis / Final Analysis – Report by children's guardian ad litem
- Assessments (including overseas assessments from Central Authority / CFAB)

Occasionally the following documents were also available.

- Position Statements and (rarely) Skeleton Arguments
- Parties' statements of evidence
- Email correspondence containing information from other sources e.g., ICACU, Embassies, CFAB
- (Rarely) judgments

The 'index child' method was used to gather quantitative data; data was gathered in relation to one child who is the subject of proceedings, rather than gathering data in relation to all children in each case.[57] This avoids duplication of information from cases with more than one child. Generally, the index child was the child whose care had precipitated the application.[58] Where there was a sibling group and not all the children had international connections, the index child was the child with a connection overseas.

The variables recorded in the quantitative study were taken in part from the quantitative study of Masson *et al* of the operation of the Public Law Outline 2014 in care proceedings, adjusted to account for the issues raised in case law, and the procedural requirements of the PLO 2014 in cross-border cases, so that there could be some analysis of how this guidance operated in practice.[59] The quantitative data was extracted from Cafcass' electronic case and analysed using descriptive statistics, with some crosstabulations where there were sufficient cases to permit this. In addition, a qualitative case file analysis of the 100 cases from the sample was conducted.[60] Chapters 5, 6, 7 and 8 contain pen-pictures of some of the cases (which have been anonymised and pseudonymised) to illustrate the issues raised in the quantitative and qualitative analyses conducted. Appendix I to this book contains a description of the sample to contextualise the findings in Chapters 5, 6, 7 and 9, providing a snapshot of the characteristics of families which comes before courts where care cases have an international element.

The findings from the sample of 100 cases with an international dimension are placed within a broader context through a thematic analysis of semi-structured qualitative interviews with 17 professionals who had experience of care proceedings with an international element (local authority lawyers and social workers, as well as social workers from CFAB and a social worker and lawyer from the International Centre for Adoption (IAC)).

The empirical study conducted received ethical approval from the University of Bristol Research Ethics Committee, Cafcass Research Governance Ethics Committee, and approval from the President of the Family Division. It was also subject to rigorous data protection procedures due to the sensitivity of the information contained in the cases. It was funded through a four-year ERSC post-graduate studentship. This study would not have been possible without the assistance and co-operation of Cafcass and CFAB, and the author thanks these two organisations

[57] J Hunt, A Macleod and C Thomas, The Last Resort: Child Protection, the Courts and the 1989 Children Act (Stationary Office, 1999).

[58] See J Masson et al, *Care Profiling Study* (Ministry of Justice, 2008) 8.

[59] J Masson et al, *Child Protection in Court: Outcomes for Children* (School of Law, University of Bristol and the Centre for Research on Children and Families, University of East Anglia, 2019).

[60] For examples of this method in studies of family law in practice, see J Hunt, A Macleod and C Thomas, *The Last Resort: Child Protection, the Courts and the 1989 Children Act* (Stationary Office, 1999); J Masson et al, *Care Profiling Study* (Ministry of Justice, 2008). See also J Pearce and J Masson, *Just Following Instructions? The Representation of Parents in Care Proceedings* (University of Bristol, 2011).

for their willingness to engage in this study, and to the time and assistance they provided.

The lack of available, disaggregated data on care proceedings with an international dimension constitutes a barrier to a representative quantitative study of the issue, and a limit on the possibilities for socio-legal research in this area. However, the empirical study which forms the basis of this book adopted a variety of methods to analyse multiple sources of data, to provide a rich and in-depth analysis of a sample of cases, which is not representative but which will capture issues relating to the way that cases courts, local authorities and those who work within them handle care proceedings with an international dimension. The topic of this book is large, and the aim of its empirical study was to shed light on some of the issues which the cases present – issues which may not be apparent from the reported case law. Having drawn out some of the core issues associated with the practice of care proceedings with an international element, this book concludes in Chapter 9 with some practice recommendations which direct attention to the way the cases operate at a national and international level.

2

Private International Law and the Regulation of State Child Protection Measures

PIL is concerned with determining which country's laws govern a relationship between private individuals.[1] However, the internationally and regionally agreed PIL frameworks considered in this book (BIIa and HC96) apply in relation to child protection measures initiated by the state. Such measures are usually considered to fall with the scope of public law (concerning a state-individual relationship) rather than private law (concerning the relationship between individuals). Tracing BIIa and HC96 back to their roots, it is apparent that the quandary of fitting public law measures into an internationally or regionally agreed framework of PIL has arisen in different ways at different times, as the instruments have adapted to increased transnational movement, and developments and changes in state responses to child maltreatment. This chapter places the interface between public law child protection measures and PIL in a broader context, examining the development of the instruments considered in this book.

In the first place, however, it should be noted that the public / private law divide in relation to state measure of child protection in England is not necessarily clear-cut. Care proceedings issued under Children Act 1989 Part IV are public law proceedings in the sense that they involve a relationship between the state (in the form of a local authority) and individuals. There is a threshold for state intervention embodied in statute, and local authorities' interventions in a family must be lawful, necessary and proportionate.[2]

However, care proceedings often occupy what Bainham has termed a 'hybrid' position between public and private law.[3] Whilst a local authority's application under CA 89 s 31 is for a care order (which would give a local authority parental responsibility for a child) or supervision order (which would empower a

[1] K Lipstein, 'The Hague Conventions on Private International Law, Public Law and Public Policy' (1959) 8 *The International and Comparative Law Quarterly* 506, 512.

[2] CA 89 s 31 (2); European Convention on Human Rights Article 8; *Re B (A Child)* [2013] UKSC 33; [2013] 1 WLR 1911 [67] Lord Wilson.

[3] A Bainham, 'Private and Public Children Law: An Underexplored Relationship' (2013) 25 *Child and Family Law Quarterly* 138, 139.

local authority to supervise and monitor a child for a specified period of time), in practice the proceedings may conclude with a private law order (e.g. a Child Arrangements Order that the child will live with a parent, a Special Guardianship Order for the child to live with a kinship carer).[4] These forms of 'legal permanence' by way of private law orders are discussed later in this chapter.[5] Public law issues may also arise in a private law context. A court in private law proceedings may, for example, direct the preparation of a report under CA 89 s 37 and ask a local authority to consider whether they should apply for a care order – and can also make an interim care order of its own motion when making this direction.[6]

Secondly, there will be significant variation in the extent to which child protection measures taken in different countries emanate from state-based interventions through a legalised procedure. Several writers have assessed different state responses to child maltreatment and have developed conceptual frameworks to illustrate and explain these variations.[7] For example, Gilbert et al have identified that different states may take a narrow or broad approach to state responsibility for children's upbringing or education which is 'related to how the child welfare system defines responsibility between the private and the public spheres, and to cultural views on children and the family'.[8] They identified three child maltreatment orientations through their comparative study, which explain the different relationships between the state and a child and family: child focus, family service and child protection. These orientations have developed and changed over time, in response to various factors; high profile child protection 'atrocity tales', expansion of child welfare systems, changing approaches to out-of-home care and changing legislative contexts including the cementing of children's rights through the incorporation of the UN Convention on the Rights of the Child 1989 (hereafter 'UNCRC') in many countries.[9] The state response to child maltreatment in England and Wales is generally seen as part of an Anglo-American/ liberal approach which is legalistic and where intervention is targeted towards protecting children.[10] This may stand in contrast to approaches in other countries which may have a more general aim of supporting a family unit or enhancing individual child wellbeing, and which are less adversarial, instead working in partnership with families or

[4] *Ibid.* See CA 89 s 8, s 13.

[5] Legal permanence refers to the legal frameworks which govern a child formally leaving care. See M Skivenes and J Thoburn, 'Pathways to permanence in England and Norway: A critical analysis of documents and data' (2016) 67 *Children and Youth Services Review* 152.

[6] CA 89 s 38 (1).

[7] For a comprehensive summary see N Parton, 'Addressing the Relatively Autonomous Relationship Between Child Maltreatment and Child Protection Policies and Practices' (2020) 3 *International Journal on Child Maltreatment* 19.

[8] N Gilbert, N Parton and M Skivenes, 'Introduction' in N Gilbert, N Parton and M Skivenes (eds), *Child Protection Systems: International Trends and Orientations* (Oxford University Press 2011) 6.

[9] N Gilbert, N Parton and M Skivenes, 'Changing Patterns of Response and Emerging Orientations' in N Gilbert, N Parton and M Skivenes (eds), *Child Protection Systems: International Trends and Orientations* (Oxford University Press 2011) 243–255.

[10] See N Parton, 'Addressing the Relatively Autonomous Relationship Between Child Maltreatment and Child Protection Policies and Practices' (2020) 3 *International Journal on Child Maltreatment* 19.

individual children.[11] It should also be noted that there are a number of countries where the primary child protection mechanisms are community-based and are not formalistic.[12] In this way it can be seen that there are variations in state responses to child maltreatment and the extent and prevalence of public law measures of protection as part of these responses.

Overall, therefore, the binary classification of state child protection measures as solely occupying a public law space (in contrast to private law measures) is not necessarily accurate, at least in England and Wales, and public law protective measures can in any event vary considerably in their nature and extent between different countries. Although national responses to child protection may not always look like public law measures, there have been historic difficulties and questions as to whether BIIa and the HC96 apply in situations where states have intervened to protect children or safeguard their welfare.

The Boll Case and the 1902 Guardianship Convention

The difficulties of fitting public law child protection measures into an internationally agreed PIL framework can be traced back to the earliest work of the Hague Conference of Private International Law (hereafter 'HCCH') and the Convention du 12 Juin 1902 Pour Régler la Tutelle des Mineurs (hereafter the '1902 Guardianship Convention') which was prepared following discussions at the second and third meetings of the HCCH.[13] The 1902 Guardianship Convention was concerned with allocating jurisdiction in relation to the narrow issue of guardianship and, influenced by the theories of the Italian jurist Pasquale Mancini, the child's nationality determined the law to be applied in relation to their guardianship.[14] Lipstein (writing in 1959) identified that at the time of drafting the 1902 Convention, the 'modern trend' of legislation directed towards the protection of children 'for the general interests of society' had not yet emerged.[15] The 1902 Guardianship Convention was ratified by 13 states.[16]

[11] *Ibid.*

[12] See for example MG Wessels et al, 'The Disconnect Between Community-Based Child Protection Mechanisms and the Formal Child Protection System in Rural Sierra Leone: Challenges to Building an Effective National Child Protection System' (2012) 7 *Vulnerable Children and Youth Studies* 211.

[13] P Nygh, 'The Hague Convention on the Protection of Children' (1998) 45 *NILR* 1; K Lipstein, 'One Hundred Years of Hague Conferences on Private International Law' (1993) 24 *ICLQ* 553.

[14] A Nussbaum, 'The Rise and Decline of the Law-of-Nations Doctrine in the Conflict of Laws' (1942) 42 *Columbia Law Review* 189; KH Nadelmann, 'Mancini's Nationality Rule and Non-Unified Legal Systems: Nationality versus Domicile' (1969) 17 *The American Journal of Comparative Law* 418; H Thue, 'Connecting Factors in International Family Law' in N Lowe and G Douglas (eds), *Families Across Frontiers* (Kluwer Law International, 1996) 55, 61.

[15] K Lipstein, 'The Hague Conventions on Private International Law, Public Law and Public Policy' (1959) 8 *ICLQ* 506, 511.

[16] N Lowe and M Nicholls, The 1996 Hague Convention on the Protection of Children (LexisNexis, 2012) 3.

The scope of the 1902 Convention was considered by the International Court of Justice ('ICJ') in Case Concerning the Application of the Convention of 1902 Governing the Guardianship of Infants (Netherlands v Sweden)[17] (also known as and referred to hereafter as 'the Boll case'). The case, heard by the ICJ in 1958, is considered in some detail here, as its factual matrix is a familiar cross-border situation which could just as easily occur today. The case also illustrates the difficulties in taking a narrow approach to the scope of PIL instruments concerning children – excluding public law child protection measures from their scope may lead to unequal treatment for children who have an experience bridging the public / private law divide.

Marie Boll was a Dutch national, the child of a Dutch father and Swedish mother, living in Sweden with her parents. Her mother died and, under Dutch law, her father automatically became her guardian. However, the Swedish Child Welfare Board placed Marie under a 'regime of protective upbringing' pursuant to Swedish legislation, and its decision was ratified by the Swedish court.[18] Marie was living, under this regime, with her grandparents in Sweden. A court in the Netherlands then discharged Marie's father as her guardian (with his consent), appointed another guardian and directed that Marie be entrusted to her care in the Netherlands. However, the measures taken by the Swedish court prevented Marie from being handed over to her guardian in the Netherlands. The Swedish and Dutch authorities had therefore arrived at conflicting decisions relating to Marie Boll.

The Netherlands submitted to the ICJ that the Swedish court had failed to comply with the 1902 Guardianship Convention. It was argued that the Netherlands, as the state of the child's nationality, had resolved Marie's guardianship, and accordingly the Swedish courts were prevented from taking measures which interfered with the exercise of those guardianship rights.

However, the ICJ did not consider that the measures of state protection taken by the Swedish authorities fell within the scope of the 1902 Guardianship Convention. The court accepted that these measures impacted upon what we would now understand as the exercise of parental responsibility by Marie's Dutch guardian.[19] It also recognised that guardianship and protective upbringing had common purposes.[20] However, the court characterised the child protection measures taken in Sweden as being directed towards a more 'general' purpose associated with the good of society, as follows:

> Protective upbringing contributes to the protection of the child, but at the same time, and above all, it is designed to protect society against dangers resulting from improper upbringing, inadequate hygiene, or moral corruption of young people. The 1902 Convention recognizes the fact that guardianship, in order to achieve its aim of

[17] *Case Concerning the Application of the Convention of 1902 Governing the Guardianship of Infants (Netherlands v Sweden)* 25 ILR 242.

[18] *Ibid* 63.

[19] *Ibid* 66.

[20] *Ibid* 69.

> individual protection, needs to be governed by the national law of the infant; to achieve the aim of the social guarantee which it is the purpose of the Swedish Law on the protection of children and young persons to provide, it is necessary that it should apply to all young people living in Sweden.[21]

Marie Boll's situation illustrated that nationality as a primary jurisdictional ground could not survive in a society where families were impacted by migration. Where families have experienced transnational movement, their nationality may not coincide with their habitual residence.[22]

The case also demonstrated the need for PIL instruments concerning children to adapt to evolving national approaches to child protection. Lowe and Nicholls describe the 1902 Convention as having become 'emasculated' by the Boll ruling.[23] However, at the time of the ICJ's judgment, child protection measures were seen as serving a very distinct purpose – securing 'the physical and moral welfare of the child' for the wider benefit of society.[24] The majority of the ICJ did not consider that such measures could fall within the scope of an internationally agreed PIL instrument such as the 1902 Convention. Lipstein's analysis of Boll at the time of the ICJ's judgment identified that PIL determine the private (not public) law applicable to a dispute and governs relationships between individuals.[25] The general consensus amongst PIL theorists at that time was that measures of an 'administrative, procedural or criminal character' were not recognised and enforced in other countries – the proposition being 'foreign public laws are not applied'.[26] According to Lipstein, public law child protection measures were not concerned with the maintenance or strengthening of family ties but rather the removal of a child by or under the supervision of administrative authorities.[27] Lipstein's view (and the view taken by the majority in the ICJ) may have reflected the nature of the relationship between the state and the child in need of protection in the post-war period. In light of the atrocities committed against children in WW2, coupled with issues of international displacement and the orphaning of children on an unprecedented scale, the focus was on international minimum standards for the protection of children, and human rights for all, rather than a focus on children as individual and specific rights holders (an approach which was not truly cemented until the widespread ratification of the UNCRC).[28]

[21] *Ibid.*

[22] H Thue, 'Connecting Factors in International Family Law' in N Lowe and G Douglas (eds), *Families Across Frontiers* (Kluwer Law International, 1996) 55; R Lamont and C Fenton-Glynn, 'Cross-Border Public Care and Adoption Proceedings in the European Union' (2016) 38 *Journal of Social Welfare and Family Law* 94, 95.

[23] N Lowe and M Nicholls, The 1996 Hague Convention on the Protection of Children (LexisNexis, 2012) 3.

[24] K Lipstein 'The Hague Conventions on Private International Law, Public Law and Public Policy' (1959) 8 *ICLQ* 506, 513.

[25] *Ibid.*

[26] *Ibid.*

[27] *Ibid.*

[28] e.g., the Universal Declaration of Human Rights 1948; European Convention on Human Rights 1950; Declaration on the Rights of the Child 1959. See A Dyer, 'The Internationalization of Family Law' (1997) 30 *University of California, Davis*, 625, 633.

However, following the Boll decision, the HCCH Members decided there was a need to update the 1902 Convention in light of the societal changes that had occurred in many Contracting States following two World Wars: the movement of populations across borders, the increase in the use of foreign labour and the stationing of troops abroad, the larger number of transnational families and higher rates of divorce.[29] These changes, and many others, meant that 'the cases in which children do not enjoy the normal protection of their parents (became) more and more frequent'.[30]

The Convention Concerning the Powers of Authorities and the Law Applicable in Respect of the Protection of Infants 1961

The Convention Concerning the Powers of Authorities and the Law Applicable in Respect of the Protection of Infants (hereafter the '1961 Convention') sought to address some of the difficulties highlighted by Boll. In particular, the Convention used habitual residence rather than nationality as the primary connecting factor for determining jurisdictional competence – albeit that the state of the child's nationality could override any measures taken by the state of their habitual residence.[31]

The 1961 Convention was also broader in its scope – it was not limited to issues relating to the guardianship of children but encompassed 'measures directed to the protection of his person or property'.[32] The aim of this change was, according to Dyer, to 'straddle the difference between private law measures, such as the attribution of custody rights, and the taking of a child into public care'.[33] The 1961 Hague Convention referred to a child's best interests being considered in the context of measures being taken for the protection of their person or property. This reference, though brief, may reflect the fact that children's rights were emerging as a matter of international concern. Whilst Dyer notes this innovation in the 1961 Convention, to a modern reader, the singular reference to a child's interests seems at odds with the Convention's overall purpose.[34]

[29] M W de Steiger, 'Rapport Explatif: Convention du 5 octobre 1961 concernant la compétence des autorités et la loi applicable en matière de protection des mineurs' (1960) HCCH.

[30] *Ibid* 8 (unofficial translation).

[31] 1961 Convention Art 1, Art 4. The possibility of competing jurisdictions between the state of the child's nationality and habitual residence was identified as one of the principal problems with the 1961 Convention and was addressed in the drafting of the 1996 Hague Convention (see P Lagarde, Explanatory Report on the 1996 Hague Child Protection Convention, Proceedings of the Eighteenth Session (1996), Tome II, Protection of Children (The Hague, SDU, 1998) [5]–[6], hereafter 'Paul Lagarde 'Explanatory Report' (1996) HCCH').

[32] 1961 Convention Art 1.

[33] A Dyer, 'The Internationalization of Family Law' (1997) 30 *University of California, Davis*, 634, 734.

[34] *Ibid* 634.

Ultimately, however, the 1961 Hague Convention was not a success, primarily because its reliance on both habitual residence and nationality as connecting factors gave rise to a risk of conflicts of jurisdiction.[35]

The 1996 Hague Convention

By contrast, the HC96 reflects the 'fundamental change of emphasis' which has occurred in relation to children's rights in the light of the UNCRC.[36] The UNCRC has as its 'bedrock' the concept that the best interests of the child must be a primary consideration in all actions concerning children.[37] This is the case 'whether undertaken by public or private social welfare institutions, courts of law, administrative authorities or legislative bodies'.[38]

The UNCRC provides an 'essential backdrop' for the development of modern international children's law.[39] Both the 1993 Hague Intercountry Adoption Convention and 1996 Hague Child Protection Convention contain an expressed commitment to upholding the rights of the child as embodied by the UNCRC.[40] The preamble to the HC96 also reflects a desire 'to improve the protection of children in international situations' and a recognition of the 'importance of international co-operation for the protection of children'. Nygh considers that the preamble, whilst not binding, 'must not be seen as superfluous' as it reflects the stated aims of the Convention.[41]

The influence of the UNCRC on the HC96 is also evident in its specific provisions and terms used. For example, the HC96 refers to 'parental responsibility' – a term which was not widely used by individual Contracting States at the time that the Convention was drafted but which was drawn from the UNCRC and used in preference to 'the relationship subjecting the infant to authority' from the 1961 Convention'.[42] The HC96 also contains frequent references to the need to consider

[35] N Lowe and M Nicholls, *The 1996 Hague Convention on the Protection of Children* (LexisNexis, 2012) 3. The UK did not become a Contracting Party to the 1961 Hague Convention for this reason: P Torremans (ed), *Cheshire, North & Fawcett, Private International Law* (Oxford University Press, 2017) 1101.

[36] P Nygh, 'The Hague Convention on the Protection of Children' (1998) *NILR* 1, 8.

[37] J Zermatten, 'The Best Interests of the Child Principle: Literal Analysis and Function' (2010) 18 *International Journal of Children's Rights* 483, 484; UNCRC Art 3 (1).

[38] UNCRC Art 3 (1).

[39] A Dyer 'The Internationalization of Family Law' (1997) 30 *University of California, Davis*, 634, 645.

[40] A Marvel, 'The U.N. Convention on the Rights of the Child and the Hague Conference on Private International Law: The Dynamics of Children's Rights Through Legal Strata' (1996) 6 *Transnational Law & Contemporary Problems* 271, 294. Whilst the 1980 Hague Child Abduction Convention predates the UNCRC, it contains a commitment in its preamble to the best interests of children as a paramount consideration in matters relating to their custody.

[41] P Nygh, 'The Hague Convention on the Protection of Children' (1998) *NILR* 1, 8.

[42] HC96 Art 1 (2); UNCRC Art 8, 27; Paul Lagarde, 'Explanatory Report' (1996) HCCH) [534]; P Nygh 'The Hague Convention on the Protection of Children' (1998) *NILR* 1, 11.

a child's best interests in the context of jurisdiction,[43] applicable law,[44] mutual recognition of measures[45] and cross-border placements of children in alternative care.[46]

The HC96 is the broadest children's convention in its scope.[47] It encompasses 'measures of protection' in relation to children, of which matters of parental responsibility are one.[48] Children fall within the scope of the HC96 from birth up until the age of 18 – it does not apply to unborn children.[49] The term 'measures of protection' is not defined, but examples listed within the instrument demonstrate that the term includes both private and public law protective measures in relation to children.[50] Dyer explains that the purpose of this wide term was to 'broaden the attractiveness' of the HC96 (compared to its 1961 predecessor which had only been ratified by ten states) by ensuring that it could be compatible with a variety of different legal systems.[51] The inclusion of kafala as a measure of protection under the HC96 is illustrative of this.[52] Kafala is a form of guardianship used in legal systems influenced by or applying Islamic law.[53] Its inclusion was proposed by the Moroccan delegation to the HCCH Special Commission, and Morocco is a Contracting State to the Convention.[54]

Importantly for the purposes of this book, state measures of protection are specifically within the scope of the Convention: 'the placement of the child in a foster family or in institutional care, or the provision of care by kafala or an analogous institution' and 'the supervision by a public authority of the care of a child by any person having charge of the child' are both given as examples of matters within scope.[55] Lowe and Nicholls explain that the latter provision was inserted at the request of the Australian delegation to the Hague Conference to cover situations where children live with alternative carers under the supervision of the state but not as a result of a state placement.[56] The HC96 is also drafted in such a way that it can apply in countries where protective measures in relation to children

[43] HC96 Art 8, 9 and 10.

[44] HC96 Art 22.

[45] HC96 Art 23 (2) (d), Art 28.

[46] HC96 Art 33 (2).

[47] P Torremans (ed), *Cheshire, North & Fawcett, Private International Law* (Oxford University Press, 2017) 1022.

[48] HC96 Art 1.

[49] HC96 Art 2; N Lowe and M Nicholls, *The 1996 Hague Convention on the Protection of Children* (LexisNexis, 2012) 22.

[50] For example, 'the … restriction of parental responsibility'; 'the placement of the child in a foster family or in institutional care, or the provision of care by kafala or an analogous institution'; 'the supervision by a public authority of the care of a child by any person having charge of the child' (HC96 Art (e), (a), (f)).

[51] A Dyer 'The Internationalization of Family Law' (1997) 30 *University of California, Davis*, 634, 635.

[52] HC96 Art 3 (f).

[53] P Lagarde 'Explanatory Report' (1996) HCCH [23].

[54] *Ibid.*

[55] HC96 Art 3 (e), (f).

[56] N Lowe and M Nicholls, *The 1996 Hague Convention on the Protection of Children* (LexisNexis, 2012) 27.

are taken by administrative as well as judicial authorities – including the types of measures initially taken in relation to Marie Boll by the Swedish Welfare Board.[57] Importantly, for the purposes of this book, adoption and measures preparatory to adoption are outside of the scope of the HC96.[58]

Chapter II of the HC96 contains its jurisdictional provisions. Art 5 sets out the child's habitual residence as the primary basis upon which a Contracting State will have jurisdiction to make decisions about a child, dealing with the difficulties inherent in the 1961 Hague Convention whereby the courts of a child's nationality could override a jurisdiction exercised on the basis of a child's habitual residence.[59] Habitual residence is not defined in the Convention, although the Practical Handbook to the Convention confirms that it must be given an autonomous meaning.[60] That said, the interpretation and approach to a child's habitual residence has been considered extensively in case law from both the courts of England and Wales and the CJEU in the context of BIIa and the 1980 Hague Child Abduction Convention, which has in turn informed discussion of its interpretation under the HC96. This is discussed further in chapter 3.

It is, however, clear that in contrast to the approach to habitual residence under BIIa Art 8 (discussed below), jurisdiction under HC96 Art 5 is based on the child's 'current' habitual residence (rather than their habitual residence at the point that a court is seised).[61]

The HC96 contains subsidiary jurisdictional grounds, including a prorogued jurisdiction based on the existence of divorce, separation or annulment proceedings (Art 10), a continuing jurisdiction in cases of wrongful removal or retention (Art 7) and jurisdiction based on presence for children whose habitual residence cannot be ascertained, including refugee children (Art 6).[62]

The HC96 also permits the taking of measures in cases of urgency based on the presence of the child (or the child's property) on the territory of a Contracting State, pursuant to HC96 Art 11. These measures have extra-territorial effect and are capable of recognition and enforcement under HC96 Chapter VI.[63] Art 11 measures must not be taken in such a way as to 'overstep' a foreign court's substantive jurisdiction to protect a child, and the measures taken must ensure the child's

[57] E.g., HC96 Art 5 'The judicial or administrative authorities of the Contracting State of the habitual residence of the child have jurisdiction to take measures directed to the protection of the child's person or property'.

[58] HC96 Art 4.

[59] N Lowe and M Nicholls, *The 1996 Hague Convention on the Protection of Children* (LexisNexis, 2012) 39.

[60] Hague Conference on Private International Law, Practical Handbook on the Operation of the 1996 Hague Child Protection Convention (The Hague, 2014) 4.5.

[61] L Collins and J Harris (gen eds), *Dicey, Morris and Collins, The Conflict of Laws* (Sweet & Maxwell, 2022) 20-007.

[62] *Ibid* 4.13.

[63] N Lowe and M Nicholls, *The 1996 Hague Convention on the Protection of Children* (LexisNexis, 2012) 41; Hague Conference on Private International Law, *Practical Handbook on the Operation of the 1996 Hague Child Protection Convention* (The Hague, 2014) 6.12.

protection but assist the foreign court in its task of making a final decision.[64] Art 11 measures will lapse when the Contracting State of the child's habitual residence has taken a measure required by the situation, or in the case of a child habitually resident in a non-Contracting State, when a measure taken in that state is recognised in the Contracting State where the Art 11 measures were taken.[65]

A concurrent jurisdiction may also be exercised, based on presence, to take provisional measures of protection (without the requirement of urgency) under HC96 Art 12. These measures are limited to the territory upon which they were taken, although the Practical Handbook confirms that they can be recognised and enforced under the HC96 Chapter IV.[66] Art 12 measures cannot be used in cases of wrongful removal of a child (in contrast to Art 11 measures – see HC96 Art 7 (3)). The use of urgent protective measures under Art 11 to provide a 'soft landing' for a child returning to the Contracting State of their habitual residence after a wrongful removal or retention is discussed further in chapter 3.[67]

Finally, to avoid conflicts of jurisdiction there is a lis pendens provision (HC96 Art 13) and there is also a degree of flexibility in the jurisdictional provisions as jurisdiction can be transferred to a Contracting State better placed to deal with the case, where this is in a child's best interests, and they have a substantial connection to that Contracting State (Art 8 and 9).[68] As is discussed in greater detail in chapter 3, the jurisdictional provisions of the HC96 (and BIIa) were crafted with an intention to safeguard and promote the best interests of children generally.

The HC96 was novel in that it contained applicable law provisions, in Chapter III. The general principle underpinning the HC96 is that the authorities of a Contracting State exercising jurisdiction under Chapter II of the Convention apply their own law.[69] This principle subsisted under the 1961 Convention to facilitate the taking of measures by authorities with jurisdiction as they would be able to 'apply the law which (they) know best'.[70] Furthermore, the HC96 provides that where a child's habitual residence changes from one Contracting State to another Contracting State, the new Contracting State is responsible for the 'conditions of application' of any measure taken in the Contracting State of the child's former habitual residence.[71]

[64] L Collins and J Harris (eds), *Dicey, Morris and Collins, The Conflict of Laws* (Sweet & Maxwell, 2022) 20-013; C Honorati and M Keyes, 'Parental Responsibility, Custody and Access' in P Beaumont and J Holliday (eds), *A Guide to Global Private International Law* (Hart, 2022) 469.

[65] 96 HC Art 11 (2), (3).

[66] *Practical Handbook on the Operation of the 1996 Hague Child Protection Convention* (The Hague, 2014) 7.7.

[67] See also P Torremans (ed), *Cheshire, North & Fawcett, Private International Law* (Oxford University Press, 2017) 1104; *Re J (A Child)* [2015] UKSC 70 [31] Lady Hale; *AO v LA* [2023] EWHC 83 (Fam).

[68] L Collins and J Harris (eds), *Dicey, Morris and Collins, The Conflict of Laws* (Sweet & Maxwell, 2022) 20-038–20-039.

[69] HC96 Art 15 (1).

[70] Paul Lagarde 'Explanatory Report' (1996) HCCH [86]. See also L Collins and J Harris (eds), *Dicey, Morris and Collins, The Conflict of Laws* (Sweet & Maxwell, 2022) 20-048.

[71] HC96 Art 15 (3), Art 14, *Practical Handbook on the Operation of the 1996 Hague Child Protection Convention* (The Hague, 2014) 9.3–9.8. This rule does not apply if the child becomes habitually resident in a non-Contracting State.

However, the HC96 Art 15 (2) provides that authorities of Contracting States may 'exceptionally apply or take into consideration the law of another State with which the situation has a substantial connection.' The Explanatory Report to the HC96 explains that this provision is based 'not [on the] principle of proximity (the closest connection), but on the best interests of the child' – i.e. that it may be in the child's best interests to order the sale of a property belonging to them, situated in a Contracting State other than their habitual residence, and in such circumstances the court might apply the law of that Contracting State to facilitate the sale.[72] Art 15 (2) might also be used to apply the terminology for a particular family law used in another jurisdiction – an example is provided in the Practical Handbook in a child relocation context whereby the authorities of a Contracting State use the terminology for contact / access arrangements used in the Contracting State in which the child will be living, pursuant to Art 15 (2).[73] It is, however, clear that this provision therefore would also permit a Contracting State to consider the law of a non-Contracting State where the case has a connection to that State.[74]

There are also specific applicable law provisions in HC96 Chapter III Arts 16–18 dealing with the attribution and extinction of parental responsibility by operation of law, agreement, or a unilateral act (and not judicial or administrative measures).[75] In relation to such measures, the law of the child's habitual residence at the time that the act or agreement takes effect is the law applicable to the attribution or extinction of parental responsibility.[76] Furthermore, parental responsibility which exists in one Contracting State subsists after a change of a child's habitual residence to a new Contracting State.[77] The aim of this provision is to 'secure continuity in parent-child relationships.'[78] There is a general provision in HC96 Art 22 which provides that the application of the applicable law through Chapter III may only be refused if this would be contrary to public policy taking into account the child's best interests.[79]

[72] P Lagarde 'Explanatory Report' (1996) HCCH [89]; See also P Torremans (ed), *Cheshire, North & Fawcett, Private International Law* (Oxford University Press, 2017) 1117.

[73] *Practical Handbook on the Operation of the 1996 Hague Child Protection Convention* (The Hague, 2014) 9.2. See also the discussion in L Silberman, 'The 1996 Hague Convention on the Protection of Children: Should the United States Join?' (2000) 34 *Fam. L.Q.* 239.

[74] N Lowe and M Nicholls, *The 1996 Hague Convention on the Protection of Children* (LexisNexis, 2012) 4.1.

[75] For a full discussion see *Ibid* at 4.7–4.38. These provisions are discussed in less detail in this book because it is more likely that parental responsibility will be attributed to a relative in care proceedings by way of a court order (a 'measure of protection') which would be capable of recognition under HC96 Chapter IV. *Practical Handbook on the Operation of the 1996 Hague Child Protection Convention* (The Hague, 2014) 7.7.

[76] HC96 Art 16 (1) and (2).

[77] HC96 Art 16 (3).

[78] Hague Conference on Private International Law, *Practical Handbook on the Operation of the 1996 Hague Child Protection Convention* (The Hague, 2014) [9.14].

[79] See N Lowe and M Nicholls, *The 1996 Hague Convention on the Protection of Children* (LexisNexis, 2012) 4.6; L Collins and J Harris (eds), *Dicey, Morris and Collins, The Conflict of Laws* (Sweet & Maxwell, 2022) 20-051.

The HC96 is a 'double' convention which deals with jurisdiction, and recognition of measures taken arising out of the exercise of jurisdiction, meaning that, in principle, measures of protection taken in one Contracting State shall be recognised 'by operation of law' in all other Contracting States (HC96 Art 23).[80] The Explanatory Report to the HC96 states that '(r)ecognition by operation of law means that it will not be necessary to resort to any proceeding in order to obtain such recognition …' provided that there is written evidence of the measure – e.g. a court order.[81] It is, however, possible for an 'interested person' to seek a decision on recognition from the authorities of a Contracting State under HC96 Art 24. This can include 'advance recognition' whereby an overseas competent authority is asked to decide on the issue of recognition before a child actually moves.[82] The Practical Handbook to the HC96 explains that this provision may avoid the difficult situation where there is a dispute as to the recognition or non-recognition of a measure taken in another Contracting State which is only brought to light when the measures is actually invoked.[83] Advance recognition may therefore avoid the 'inconvenience, hardship or insecurity' associated with waiting for a ruling as to a measure's recognition.[84]

Measures may also be enforced once they have been declared enforceable / registered for enforcement (HC96 Art 26). There is a requirement that the procedure for obtaining a declaration of enforceability be 'simple and rapid'.[85] The recognition and enforcement procedure is governed by national law.[86]

There are six grounds upon which a Contracting State may refuse to recognise a measure of protection or make a declaration of enforceability.[87]

a) if the measure was taken by an authority whose jurisdiction was not based on one of the grounds provided for in (HC96) Chapter II;
b) if the measure was taken, except in a case of urgency, in the context of a judicial or administrative proceeding, without the child having been provided the opportunity to be heard, in violation of fundamental principles of procedure of the requested State;[88]

[80] Peter Nygh, 'The Hague Convention on the Protection of Children' (1998) 45 *NILR* 23.

[81] P Lagarde, 'Explanatory Report' (1996) HCCH [120].

[82] HC96 Art 24; P Lagarde 'Explanatory Report' (1996) HCCH [129].

[83] Hague Conference on Private International Law, *Practical Handbook on the Operation of the 1996 Hague Child Protection Convention* (The Hague, 2014) 108.

[84] N Lowe and M Nicholls, *The 1996 Hague Convention on the Protection of Children* (LexisNexis, 2012) 5.6.

[85] HC96 Art 26 (2).

[86] HC96 Art 24, Art 26 (1).

[87] The grounds for non-recognition are discretionary, not mandatory – a court does not have to refuse recognition even if one of the grounds is established (L Collins and J Harris (eds), *Dicey, Morris and Collins, The Conflict of Laws* (Sweet & Maxwell, 2022) 20-059; C Honorati and M Keyes, 'Parental Responsibility, Custody and Access' in Paul Beaumont and Jayne Holliday (eds), *A Guide to Global Private International Law* (Hart, 2022) 472.

[88] In *NG v OG* [2014] EWHC 4182 (Fam), [2015] All ER (D) 59 (Jan) the court refused to recognise an order made in Russia under HC96 Art 23 (2) (b) as the child had not been given an opportunity to be heard.

c) on the request of any person claiming that the measure infringes his or her parental responsibility, if such measure was taken, except in a case of urgency, without such person having been given an opportunity to be heard;
d) if such recognition is manifestly contrary to public policy of the requested State, taking into account the best interests of the child;
e) if the measure is incompatible with a later measure taken in the non-Contracting State of the habitual residence of the child, where this later measure fulfils the requirements for recognition in the requested State;
f) if the procedure provided in (HC96) Article 33 has not been complied with.

Importantly, a Contracting State considering the recognition or enforcement of a measure taken in another Contracting State may not review the judgment as to its merits.[89] The means of enforcing a measure of protection are governed by national law 'taking into account the best interests of the child'.[90]

Finally, it is apparent from the co-operation provisions of the HC96 that the instrument was specifically geared towards the protection of children in cross-border situations. Cross-border co-operation between Contracting States became an integral part of the work of the Hague Conference from 1960 onwards.[91] The aspiration of co-operation was present in the 1961 Convention but without a practical means of ensuring that it occurred successfully.[92]

Central Authorities were first used in Hague instruments dealing with the international service of documents,[93] and taking of evidence,[94] although in the beginning their role was for the 'one-way' receipt of documents and onward transmission.[95] The French Central Authority then began to operate as both the sending and receiving authority for both Conventions, and this innovation resulted in the model of Central Authorities seen today – as agencies that both send and receive information.[96] The 'two-way' model was used to support the 1980 Hague Child Abduction Convention.[97]

[89] HC96 Art 28.

[90] HC96 Art 28, Lowe and Nicholls note the requirement to consider the child's best interests in the context of the practicalities of enforcement that may 'dilute the powers of enforcement' (N Lowe and M Nicholls, *The 1996 Hague Convention on* the *Protection of Children* (LexisNexis, 2012) 5.15).

[91] PH Pfund, 'The Developing Jurisprudence of the Rights of the Child – Contributions of the Hague Conference on Private International Law' (1997) 3 *ILSA International Journal of International and Comparative Law* 665.

[92] P Lagarde, 'Explanatory Report' (1996) HCCH [541]. For example, Article 10 of the 1961 Convention on the Protection of Minors envisaged that a Contracting States would not take measures in respect a child who was already the subject of measures in another Contracting State child 'save after an exchange of views'.

[93] Convention of 15 November 1965 on the Service Abroad of Judicial and Extrajudicial Documents in Civil or Commercial Matters, Art 2.

[94] Convention of 18 March 1970 on the Taking of Evidence Abroad in Civil or Commercial Matters, Art 2.

[95] C S. Bruch, 'The Central Authority's Role under the Hague Child Abduction Convention: A Friend in Deed' (1994) 28 *Family* Law *Quarterly* 35.

[96] *Ibid* 38.

[97] *Ibid* 35.

As such, Central Authorities became not only a vital piece of infrastructure to ensure the effectiveness of the HCCH's Conventions, but they also signified the beginnings of a 'general mission of co-operation and information' between Central Authorities and, by association, Contracting States.[98] An entire chapter of the HC96 is devoted to co-operation between Central Authorities. In contrast to BIIa (discussed below), several co-operation provisions in the HC96 are specific to child protection scenarios. The clearest example of this is HC96 Art 36, which provides that 'in any case where the child is exposed to a serious danger, the competent authorities of the Contracting State where measures for the protection of the child have been taken or are under consideration, if they are informed that the child's residence has changed to, or that the child is present in another State, shall inform the authorities of that other State about the danger involved and the measures taken or under consideration.' This provision is novel as it applies in relation to non-Contracting States, evidencing an effort to secure the protection of children who move across borders at a global scale.[99]

The Development of Brussels IIa

The work of the HCCH in drafting the HC96 was influential in the development of the EU Regulation, Brussels IIa (BIIa) which represented a harmonisation of PIL in family law matters within the EU.

However, it is important to note that BIIa is an instrument which sought to achieve the political aims of the European Union. BIIa was a revision of a previous regulation which had governed matrimonial matters and matters of parental responsibility concerning children born to a marriage (Brussels II).[100] The Brussels II Regulation was significant in that it represented the EU's first real attempt to harmonise PIL between Member States in family law matters by way of a regulation with direct effect – the beginnings of a 'Europeanisation' of family law.[101]

[98] P Lagarde 'Explanatory Report' (1996) HCCH [591].

[99] Other examples of co-operation provisions with a child protection orientation include Article 33 (which relates to transborder placements of children in foster care, *kafala*, institutional care or analogous institutions), Article 34 (obtaining background information on the situation of a child) and Article 31 (c) (assistance in discovering the whereabouts of a child who may need protection in a Contracting State).

[100] Council Regulation (EC) No 1347/2000 of 29 May 2000 on jurisdiction and the recognition and enforcement of judgments in matrimonial matters and in matters of parental responsibility for children of both spouses [2000] OJ L160/19. See A Borrás. 'Explanatory Report on the Convention, drawn up based on Article K.3 of the Treaty on European Union, on Jurisdiction and the Recognition and Enforcement of Judgments in Matrimonial Matters' [1998] OJ C221/04, para 9 (hereafter 'Borrás Explanatory Report' [1998]').

[101] C McGlynn, 'The Europeanisation of Family Law' (2001) 13 *Child and Family Law Quarterly* 35; M Ní Shúilleabháin 'Ten Years of European Family Law: Retrospective Reflections from a Common Law Perspective' (2010) 4 *ICLQ* 1021. The Brussels II Regulation was preceded by a Brussels II Convention [1998] (*OJ C221/27*) which had in fact not entered into force. Prior to this, the 1968 Brussels Convention on jurisdiction and the enforcement of judgments in civil and commercial matters [1972] (OJ L299/32)

It had become apparent that European economic integration had a knock-on effect on individuals and families.[102] The regulation of family law matters by an EU Regulation in the form of Brussels II reflected an awareness, as Martiny states, that the diversity of family law systems within the EU 'can to a certain degree be considered a barrier to the free movement of persons'.[103] There was therefore a political imperative to support free movement through the harmonisation of EU PIL concerning children and families, and a mandate, enshrined in the Treaty of Amsterdam (1997), for the Council to adopt 'measures in the field of judicial cooperation in civil matters having cross border implications … insofar as necessary for the proper functioning of the internal market'.[104] These measures would support one of the EU's core policy objectives – the creation of an Area of Freedom, Security and Justice.

The Brussels II Regulation was very narrow in scope and was criticised as it led to an inequality of treatment between children of married and unmarried spouses.[105] This spurred the need for revision, leading to the BIIa Regulation discussed in this book.

An examination of the HC96 and BIIa side by side reveals that there is significant overlap between two instruments both in terms of its structure and substantive provisions – many of its terms are nearly identical. Furthermore, several EU Member States were active in the drafting of the HC96 – individuals involved in the Working Party to re-draft the Brussels II Regulation also representing their country at the HCCH meetings to discuss the HC96.[106] This raised the question as to whether there was a need for BIIa – the HCCH was already working on a further Convention and the EU was involved in this process. However, in producing an EU specific instrument dealing with many of the same matters which appear in the HC96, McEleavy suggests that the EC may have been 'staking a claim … possibly for both internal political motives and reasons of future external competence'.[107]

had provided a framework for recognition of civil measures between Member States – including maintenance. However, family law measures were expressly excluded from the scope of the 1968 Brussels Convention. For a fuller discussion of the instruments which preceded Brussels IIa see C McGlynn (*Ibid*) 38–39; Nigel Lowe 'The Growing Influence of the European Union on International Family Law: A View from the Boundary' (2003) 56 *Current Legal Problems* 439; M Ní Shúilleabháin (ibid) 1021.

[102] N Lowe, (*ibid*) 444 citing the Borrás Explanatory Report [1998] para. 1.

[103] D Martiny, 'The Impact of the EU Private International Law Instruments on European Family Law' in JM Scherpe (ed) *European Family Law Vol 1* (Elgar, 2016) 265.

[104] See Treaty Establishing the European Community (Consolidated version 2002) Art 65 [2002] OJ C325/1.

[105] M Ní Shúilleabháin, 'Ten Years of European Family Law: Retrospective Reflections from a Common Law Perspective' (2010) 4 *ICLQ* 1021, 1024; K Trimmings *Child Abduction within the European Union* (Hart Publishing, 2013) 8–9.

[106] Peter McEleavy, 'The Brussels II Regulation: How the European Community has Moved into Family Law' (2002) 51 International and Comparative Law Quarterly 883, 893. See also Costanza Honorati and Mary Keyes, 'Parental Responsibility, Custody and Access' in Paul Beaumont and Jayne Holliday (eds), *A Guide to Global Private International Law* (Hart, 2022).

[107] *Ibid* 894.

In this regard, BIIa reflects two policy objectives that EU stakeholders sought to achieve over and above the HC96. First, it had been agreed at the European Council in Tampere in 1999, and in further detail in 2001, that a programme of measures would be implemented to achieve the automatic recognition and enforcement of decisions between EU Member States, including in family matters.[108] In particular, France had in 2000 presented an initiative for an EU Regulation providing for the mutual enforcement of rights of access in relation to children.[109] Secondly, building on the French proposal, there was a move spearheaded by the EC to place intra-EU child abduction on the agenda (notwithstanding the existence of the 1980 Hague Child Abduction Convention) – in particular the issue of children being wrongfully retained in another country after a period of agreed contact.[110] The inclusion of child abduction provisions in BIIa was a controversial issue, with a number of states (led by the UK and Germany) objecting on the grounds that this would create unnecessary complexity and further litigation.[111] Ultimately the negotiations led to the inclusion of child abduction provisions under BIIa which were intended to complement the 1980 Hague Child Abduction Convention and bolster its provisions in intra-EU cases.[112]

Thus, the BIIa in its final form represents something of a hotchpotch of different interests and ideas about what cross-border problems the EU should be seeking to regulate through a regionally agreed PIL framework. Public law / state-based child protection measures were not a part of these discussions and negotiations.

Like the HC96, BIIa contains provisions dealing with jurisdiction, mutual recognition and co-operation. However, it does not contain applicable law provisions. The jurisdictional grounds are similar to those found in the HC96. The primary jurisdictional basis is the child's habitual residence (BIIa Art 8), although unlike the HC96, BIIa is based on perpetuatio fori, and habitual residence is considered at the time the court is seised of proceedings, rather than jurisdiction being based on the child's 'current' habitual residence.[113] There are subsidiary grounds for jurisdiction based on prorogation of jurisdiction (unlike the HC96, not limited to there being contingent divorce, separation or annulment proceedings) (BIIa Art 12), continuing jurisdiction to deal with rights of access after a

[108] 'Tampere European Council 15 and 16 October 1999 Presidency Conclusions' (1999) European Council; Draft Programme of measures for implementation of the principle of mutual recognition of decisions in civil and commercial matters [2001] OJ C12/1; McEleavy (*ibid*); N Lowe, 'The Growing Influence of the European Union on International Family Law: A View from the Boundary' (2003) 56 *Current Legal Problems* 439, 446.

[109] Initiative of the French Republic of 3 July 2000 with a view to adopting a council regulation on the mutual enforcement of judgments on rights of access to children [2000] OJ C234/7; BIIa Recital (4); K Trimmings *Child Abduction within the European Union* (Hart Publishing, 2013) 9–10.

[110] For a detailed discussion of the events which led to child abduction being placed on the agenda for the revised Brussels II Regulation, see Trimmings (*ibid*) Chapter 2.

[111] Trimmings (*ibid*) 20.

[112] E.g., BIIa Art 10, Art 11, Art 40 (1) (b), Art 42.

[113] BIIa Art 8; P Torremans (ed), *Cheshire, North & Fawcett, Private International Law* (Oxford University Press, 2017) 1097.

lawful relocation to another Member State (BIIa Art 9) and presence (BIIa Art 13). BIIa also contains jurisdictional provisions which provide for a continuing jurisdiction after a wrongful removal or retention (BIIa Art 10) and, pursuant to BIIa Art 11 (6)–(8), provisions which facilitate the making of an order for a child's return notwithstanding an order for non-return made in another Member State pursuant to the 1980 Hague Child Abduction Convention Art 13.[114] Jurisdiction can also be transferred to another Member State 'better placed' to deal with the whole or part of proceedings where this is in a child's best interests under BIIa Art 15 (discussed further in chapter 3).

The mutual recognition provisions of BIIa are also similar to the HC96. Judgments should be recognised 'without any special procedure being required' pursuant to BIIa Art 21 (1). It is nonetheless possible for a decision on recognition (or non-recognition) to be sought by any interested party (BIIa Art 21 (3)).

Judgments can only be enforced once they have been declared enforceable / registered for enforcement (BIIa Art 28). However, there is the ability under BIIa for certain orders to be directly enforced (without the requirement of exequatur) where they are accompanied by the appropriate certificate, namely access orders[115] and orders for the return of a child made pursuant to BIIa Art 11 (8).[116] For all other judgments, a court may only refuse to make a declaration of enforceability or refuse to recognise a judgment based on one of the BIIa Art 23 grounds. These are similar to those found in the HC96, namely:

> that recognition would be contrary to public policy in the relevant state where recognition / enforcement is sought, taking into account the best interests of the child (BIIa Art 23 (a));[117]
>
> that the child was not given an opportunity to be heard (except in cases of urgency) (BIIa Art 23 (b));[118]
>
> the judgment was given in default of appearance by a person who was not serve[d] with a document instituting proceeding in sufficient time to enable them to prepare a defence (unless it can be proved that they accepted the judgment unequivocally) (BIIa Art 23 (c));[119]
>
> the judgment infringes someone's parental responsibility, and they did not have an opportunity to be heard (BIIa Art 23 (d));

[114] For a full discussion of the BIIa Art 11 (6)–(8) procedure see P Beaumont, L Walker, and J Holliday, 'Conflicts of EU courts on child abduction: the reality of Art 11(6)–(8) Brussels IIa proceedings across the EU' (2016) 12 *Journal of Private International Law* 211.

[115] BIIa Art 42.

[116] BIIa Art 41.

[117] The CJEU confirmed that the public policy exception to recognition should only be engaged 'taking into account the best interests of the child, recognition of the judgment given in another Member State would be at variance to an unacceptable degree with the legal order of the State in which recognition is sought, in that it would infringe a fundamental principle' *P v Q* (C-455/15 PPU) EU:C:2015:763, [2016] Fam Law 165 [39].

[118] See *Re D (a child) (Recognition of a Foreign Order)* [2016] EWCA Civ 12, [2016] Fam Law 311.

[119] Considered extensively by the Court of Appeal in *Re D (A Child) (Recognition of Foreign Order)* [2016] EWCA Civ 12, [2016] Fam Law 311.

the order is incompatible with a later judgment in the Member State in which recognition is sought (BIIa Art 23 (e));

the order is irreconcilable with a later judgment in [sic] by a non-Member State (BIIa Art 23 (f));

the consent procedure under BIIa Art 56 was not complied with (BIIa Art 23 (g)).

Importantly, a judgment / measure of protection must not be reviewed as to its 'merits' or 'substance' in the context of mutual recognition.[120]

Like the HC96, BIIa contains a chapter on co-operation, and Central Authorities are designated for the purposes of the Regulation. However, the lack of attention given to state child protection measures in BIIa is apparent in this context, when compared with the co-operation provisions of the HC96. Whilst BIIa included equivalent provisions to those found in the HC96 relating to the cross-border placement of children in foster or institutional care,[121] and co-operation to obtain information on the 'situation of the child',[122] there are no equivalent co-operation provisions for tracing children at risk or protecting children at risk who cross borders.[123] The work of the EU in legislating to deal with children at risk has, as highlighted by Stalford, and by Lamont and Fenton-Glynn, focused on tackling exploitative and criminal practices which impacted children, rather than child maltreatment within the family.[124] Whilst the 'placement of a child in a foster family or in institutional care' is expressly within the scope of BIIa, the regulation repeatedly refers its application to 'civil matters'.[125] This reflected in the mandate for the EU to legislate relation to civil matters with a cross-border element by the Treaty of Amsterdam as set out above.

A further impact of BIIa in relation to the EU Member States concerned their competence to sign and ratify the HC96. As a result of case law concerning the external competence of the EU (known as ERTA case law)[126] when the EU legislates in an area, it assumes competence as a whole to enter into any further

[120] BIIa Art 26, HC96 Art 28.

[121] BIIa Art 56.

[122] BIIa Art 55 (a) (i).

[123] cf HC96 Art 31 (c) and Art 36 *supra*. This has been rectified to an extent by Council Regulation (EU) 2019/1111 of 25 June 2019 on jurisdiction, the recognition and enforcement of decisions in matrimonial matters and the matters of parental responsibility, and on international child abduction [2019] OJ L178/1 (hereafter 'Brussels II ter') Art 80 which brings the co-operation provisions more in line with those found in the HC96 (see also Proposal for a Council Regulation on jurisdiction, the recognition and enforcement of decisions in matrimonial matters and the matters of parental responsibility, and on international child abduction (recast) COM/2016/0411).

[124] H Stalford, *Children and the European Union: Rights, Welfare and Accountability* (Oxford: Hart Publishing, 2012) 175; R Lamont and C Fenton-Glynn, 'Cross-Border Public Care and Adoption Proceedings in the European Union' (2016) 38 *Journal of Social Welfare and Family Law* 94, 95. For the EU *Aquis* on the Rights of the child see – 'Annex to the EU Strategy on the Rights of the Child: EU Aquis and Policy Documents on the Rights of the Child' (2021) European Commission.

[125] BII Art 56; BIIa Recital (1) and (2).

[126] From Case 22/70 *Commission v Council (ERTA)* ECLI:EU:C: 1971:32, [1971] ECR 263. See N Lowe and M Nicholls, *The* 1996 *Hague Convention on the Protection of Children* (LexisNexis, 2012) 1.22–1.23.

agreements which regulate relationships with non-Member States in that area.[127] It was therefore necessary for the EU to authorise the Member States to sign and ratify/accede to the HC96 in the interests of the EC.[128] The practical impact of this was that the majority of EU Member States – including the UK – experienced the entry into force of BIIa before they had experienced the operation of the HC96.[129]

Against this background, it is perhaps unsurprising that confusion arose as to whether public law measures taken to protect a child could fall within the scope of BIIa. In echoes of the Boll case concerning the 1902 Guardianship Convention, and the question as to whether it could encompass public law measures, the CJEU has had to adjudicate this issue.

In Case C-435/06 Proceedings Brought by C, the CJEU was asked to rule on whether a public law decision by a Swedish Welfare Board to place a child in foster care fell within the scope of BIIa.[130] The Swedish government argued that it was 'difficult to imagine a decision arising more manifestly from the exercise of public powers than a decision requiring a child being taking into care which could, in certain circumstances, even result in that child being deprived of his liberty'.[131] The CJEU rejected this argument, holding that 'civil matters' had to be interpreted autonomously, and in light of the spirit and objectives of BIIa. Excluding public law measures from its scope would lead to unequal treatment between children within the EU. Further, as observed by Beaumont and Trimmings, BIIa covers all decisions on parental responsibility 'including measures for the protection of the child'.[132] The CJEU noted that BIIa governed matters of parental responsibility, and

[127] For a discussion on external competence in this context see G De Baere and K Gutman, 'The impact of the European Union and the European Court of Justice on European family law' in J M Scherpe (ed), *European Family Law Vol 1* (Elgar, 2016) 5, 22–27; P McEleavy, 'The Brussels II Regulation: How the European Community has Moved into Family Law' (2002) 51 *ICLQ* 883, 906–907; M Ní Shúilleabháin, 'Ten Years of European Family Law: Retrospective Reflections From a Common Law Perspective' (2010) 49 *ICLQ* 1021, 23.

[128] Council Decision of 5 June 2008 authorising certain Member States to ratify, or accede to, in the interest of the European Community, the 1996 Hague Convention on Jurisdiction, Applicable Law, Recognition, Enforcement and Cooperation in respect of Parental Responsibility and Measures for the Protection of Children and authorising certain Member States to make a declaration on the application of the relevant internal rules of Community law – Convention on Jurisdiction, Applicable Law, Recognition, Enforcement and Cooperation in respect of Parental Responsibility and Measures for the Protection of Children [2008] OJ L 151/36.

[129] The HC96 provides that only sovereign states may ratify it and it was therefore not possible for the European Community as a whole to ratify or accede to the HC96 (though the European Community became a HCCH member by virtue of the Council Decision 2006/719/EC of 5 October 2006 on the accession of the Community to the Hague Conference on Private International Law [2006] OJ L297/1). Some EU Member States had ratified or acceded to the HC96 before becoming members of the European Community.

[130] ECLI:EU:C:2007:714; [2007] ECR I-10141.

[131] Ibid [43].

[132] P Beaumont and K Trimmings, 'Court of Justice of the European Union's Case Law on Family Law Matters under Brussels IIa and Maintenance' in P Beaumont, M Danov, K Trimmings and B Yüksel (eds), *Cross Border Litigation in* Europe (Hart, 2017); BIIa Recital 5.

that actions by the state in relation to a child can impact upon parental responsibility in the same way as actions by a private individual.[133]

Similarly, in the context of transferring jurisdiction in public law proceedings between Member States pursuant to BIIa Art 15, the CJEU has held that the Regulation applies notwithstanding the practical difficulties associated with transfer. A transfer of jurisdiction may require fresh public law proceedings to be issued commenced by the relevant public authority in the receiving state.[134] Furthermore, differences in thresholds for state intervention between different Member States 'may lead the court of that other Member State to take account of factual circumstances that differ from those which might have been taken into account by the court initially having jurisdiction' when considering the fresh proceedings.[135] Despite these complexities, the CJEU held that transfer provisions of BIIa apply to public law child protection proceedings. The fact that these issues required a referral to the CJEU to assist with interpretation of the BIIa demonstrates that the challenge of fitting public law measures into a private international law framework – illustrated by the Boll case discussed above – continued to trouble national courts over fifty years later.

In summary, therefore, BIIa had its roots in supporting the internal market, incorporating several areas which certain stakeholders considered priorities for EU legislation. The introduction of BIIa marginalised the impact of the HC96 within the EU. By legislating in this area, the EU restricted individual Member States' freedom to ratify or accede to the HC96. BIIa also limited the practical impact of the HC96 when it eventually entered into force in the individual Member States as a result of BIIa's disconnection clause.[136] This provision stated that BIIa took priority over the HC96 in relation to children with their habitual residence on the territory of a member state in relation to matters governed by the Regulation.[137] This meant – in practice – that children habitually resident in the UK could not benefit from many of the terms of the HC96 (e.g. in relation to transfers of jurisdiction) even if they had strong connections to Contracting States outside of the EU.[138]

Although there is undoubtedly a private law dimension to many care proceedings, it would seem (as will be discussed in chapter 3) that there was a lack of

[133] Case C-435/06 *Proceedings Brought by C* ECLI:EU:C:2007:714; [2007] ECR I-10141 [46]–[53]. See also R Lamont and C Fenton-Glynn, 'Cross-Border Public Care and Adoption Proceedings in the European Union' (2016) 38 *Journal of* Social *Welfare and Family Law* 94.

[134] Case C-428/15 *Child and* Family *Agency v J. D* EU:C:2016:819; [2017] Fam 248.

[135] Ibid [37].

[136] BIIa Article 61 (a); 62 (1).

[137] For a discussion of the disconnection rules in BIIa and the problems they can cause in their interaction with the HC96, see T Kruger and L Samyn, 'Brussels II bis: Successes and Suggested Improvements' (2016) 12 *Journal of Private International Law* 132, 151–154.

[138] See *West Sussex County Council v H* [2014] EWHC 2550 (Fam) and, more recently, the discussion in *Re X (Children) (Article 61 BIIa)* [2021] EWCA Civ 1305. The restriction on transfers of jurisdiction between BIIa Member States and HC96 Contracting States has been addressed in Brussels II ter Art 97 (2) (b).

awareness in England and Wales as to how international PIL instruments may impact care cases. This might be influenced by the fact that the first international PIL instrument governing the state measure of child protection came in the form of BIIa rather than the HC96 – because BIIa is an instrument which had its roots in supporting free movement within the EU, and a range of other policy priorities, which did not include cross-border child protection issues. The situation is further complicated by the fact that domestic legislation in England and Wales governing care proceedings does not set out their jurisdictional basis.

The Family Law Act 1986 (FLA 1986) (which was amended following the entry into force of BIIa and the HC96 respectively) is the 'controlling Act' determining the jurisdictional basis for family law applications which fall within its scope.[139] The Act provides, for example, that a court shall not make an order under CA 89 s 8 (except for an order varying or discharging the same) unless it has jurisdiction pursuant to BIIa or HC96, failing which there are jurisdictional provisions under national law.[140] As such, the jurisdictional basis for the majority of private law applications concerning children is derived from BIIa/HC96. However, the FLA 1986 does not expressly apply to care proceedings under CA 89 Part IV.[141] Judges have held that, notwithstanding the scope of the FLA 1986, the same jurisdictional rules should apply to public law proceedings as to private law ones.[142] However, it took the judgment of Munby P in Re E (A Child) (Care Proceedings: European Dimension) at the end of 2014 to bring home the impact of BIIa in care proceedings.[143] More recently, and particularly following the loss of BIIa following Brexit, case law has considered the operation of the HC96 and its jurisdictional provisions in care proceedings concerning children with connections to non-Contracting States, particularly as the HC96 has no equivalent of BIIa Art 14, which provided that where there was no jurisdiction under the regulation, national jurisdictional rules would apply. Despite this, it has been held that the jurisdictional provisions of the HC96 apply to proceedings in the UK which are within its scope, even where the case involves a non-Contracting State.[144] Overall, the

[139] R White et al (eds), *Clarke Hall & Morrison on Children* (Butterworths, 2022) [921], FLA 1986 Part 1.

[140] See FLA 1986 s 2 (1), (3); s 1 (1) (a), s 3. The FLA 1986 has since been amended because of Brexit, and the end of the implementation period on 31 December 2020, to exclude references to BIIa (see The Jurisdiction and Judgments (Family) (Amendment etc.) (EU Exit) Regulations 2019 (SI 2019/519), reg. 1(1), Sch. para. 15(2)(a)).

[141] See R Lamont, 'The Development of Child Protection Across International Borders for Children at Risk of Harm' in G Douglas, M Murch and V Stephens (eds), *International and National Perspectives on Child and Family Law* (Cambridge University Press, 2018) 239–242 for a discussion of the evolution of jurisdictional rules in public law proceedings in England and Wales.

[142] *Re R (Care Orders: Jurisdiction)* [1995] 1 FLR 711; *Warrington Borough Council v W (Care Proceedings: Jurisdiction)* [2021] EWFC 68.

[143] *Re E (A Child) (Care Proceedings: European Dimension)* [2014] EWHC 6 (Fam); [2014] 1 WLR 2670.

[144] *Hackney London Borough Council v P* [2022] EWHC 1981 (Fam); *Warrington Borough Council v T* [2021] EWFC 68, R White et al (eds), *Clarke Hall & Morrison on Children* (Butterworths, 2022) [917.1].

picture created is that the impact of BIIa/HC96 in the context of care proceedings was not something that was really thought about until issues and complications arose through the cases themselves.

Conclusion

The aim of the discussion in this chapter has been to illustrate the roots of HC96 and BIIa and their connection to state measures of child protection. Children's transnational connections are undoubtedly more complex than they were at the turn of the twentieth century, when the first Hague Convention dealing with PIL in children's matters was drafted. 'Problems' in private international law increase as populations become more diverse.[145] However, questions around the scope of the instruments, and the recognition of public law measures between different countries, have arisen in various forms since at least the Boll case in 1958. The HC96 sought to ensure that a broad spectrum of children's issues is regulated, including both private and public law issues, in a manner consistent with the UNCRC and with a clear child protection orientation. By contrast, BIIa did not develop with the same impetus to regulate state child protection measures. The case law discussed in this book demonstrates that the interface between state child protection measures and private international law continues to arise in a wide variety of situations concerning children with transnational connections.

[145] D Henrich, 'Family Law Across Frontiers: Facts, Conflicts, Trends' in N Lowe and G Douglas (eds), *Families Across Frontiers* (Kluwer Law International, 1996) 41.

3

Forum Issues in Care Proceedings

This chapter will focus on one of the core functions of internationally and regionally agreed PIL frameworks concerning children – determining the forum competent to make decisions about a child – and will consider how this function interacts with considerations of a child's best interests.

As discussed in chapter 2, the HC96 was influenced by the approach to children's rights as embodied by the UNCRC. Both HC96 and BIIa contain an express commitment to the best interests of the child pursuant to the UNCRC Art 3.1 and, in the case of BIIa, the Charter of Fundamental Rights of the European Union Article 24.[1] Furthermore, BIIa states that the grounds of jurisdiction contained in the regulation are 'shaped in the light of the best interests of the child'.[2]

The early PIL instruments concerning children discussed in chapter 2 saw the child's nationality as the dominant basis for a court's jurisdiction – a rigid criterion which could fix jurisdiction in a state with which a child had little connection.[3] The development of international agreements on PIL by the HCCH led to the use of habitual residence as a 'global connecting factor'.[4] Habitual residence was seen as a more 'modern, fact-centred' connecting factor than nationality.[5] Lamont notes that a habitual residence is focused on the child's connection to the state in question, rather than that of their parents, which is consistent with the development of child rights and autonomy as enshrined in the UNCRC.[6] Furthermore, a child's participation in proceedings is more practical and possible if the child is well integrated into the applicable forum, another way in which this jurisdictional ground may promote children's rights.[7]

The HC96 and BIIa both include subsidiary grounds for jurisdiction including presence (for children whose habitual residence cannot be ascertained),[8]

[1] BIIa Art 33; HC96 Preamble.

[2] BIIa Recital 12.

[3] See A Dyer, 'The Internationalization of Family Law', (1997) 30 University of California, Davis 625; Peter Nygh, 'The Hague Convention on the Protection of Children' (1998) 45 *NILR* 1.

[4] SL Gössl and R Lamont, 'Connecting Factors' in P Beaumont and J Holliday (eds), *A Guide to Global Private International Law* (Hart, 2022) 49. See BIIa Art 8, HC96 Art 5.

[5] A Dyer, 'The Internationalization of Family Law', (1997) 30 *University of California, Davis* 625, 632.

[6] R Lamont, 'Habitual Residence and Brussels II Bis: Developing Concepts for European Private International Family Law' (2007) 3 *Journal of Private International Law* 261, 267.

[7] H Stalford, Children and the European Union Rights, Welfare and Accountability (London: Hart 2012) 108.

[8] BIIa Article 13, HC96 Article 6.

prorogation[9] and continuing jurisdiction after a wrongful removal or retention.[10] These instruments also contain mechanisms for the transfer of jurisdiction to another BIIa Member State or HC96 Contracting State, which may be better placed to hear the case where this is in a child's best interests.[11] However, the primacy of the child's habitual residence in this jurisdictional scheme reflects a way of thinking about children as independent of their parents, with multiple connections of varying strength.[12] Other jurisdictional grounds are exceptions to the general principle that habitual residence is the primary connecting factor.[13]

Fiorini describes how this flexibility, and in particular the existence of alternative grounds for jurisdiction, enables parties or courts to 'modulate the application of the instrument(s) in order to achieve a better protection of the best interests of the children in question'.[14] If these instruments operate effectively, they will lead to the identification of an appropriate forum, which is well placed to decide what is in children's best interests. It is therefore possible to ensure that children do not fall into a lacuna where there is no forum available to protect them and uphold their welfare in the short or long term.[15] Cross-border co-operation and the mutual recognition of judgments can be seen as ancillary, supportive mechanisms to facilitate forum identification and assist the relevant state to assess and determine a child's best interests.[16] In this way, the jurisdictional schemes in both HC96 and BIIa could be described as seeking to meet the best interests of children *generally*.[17]

However, in care proceedings, jurisdictional decisions are made about *individual* children. If a court considers itself competent (or fails to address the issue of

[9] BIIa Art 12, HC96 Art 10.

[10] BIIa Art 10, HC96 Art 7.

[11] BIIa Art 15, HC96 Art 8 and 9.

[12] AL Estin, 'Transjudicial Child Welfare: Local Governments and International Law' (2013) 22 *Transnational Law & Contemporary Problems* 595. Habitual residence forms the basis of three of the primary conventions concerning children produced by the HCCH; the HC96, the 1980 Hague Child Convention and the HCA 1993. See N Lowe, 'The 1996 Hague Convention on the Protection of Children – A Fresh Appraisal' (2002) 14 *CFLQ* 191.

[13] SL Gössl and R Lamont, 'Connecting Factors' in P Beaumont and J Holliday (eds), *A Guide to Global Private International Law* (Hart, 2022) 50.

[14] A Fiorini, 'The Protection of the Best Interests of Migrant Children – Private International Law Perspectives' (May 1, 2016). Available at SSRN: https://ssrn.com/abstract=2862361 25.

[15] This idea was considered in *Re B (A Child) (Reunite International Child Abduction Centre intervening)* [2016] UKSC 4; [2016] AC 606. Lord Wilson at [42] interpreted the interplay between best interests and the criterion of proximity as reflected in BIIa Recital 12 as follows; "where interpretation of the concept of habitual residence can reasonably follow each of two paths, the courts should follow the path perceived better to serve the interests of children … if interpretation of the concept of habitual residence can reasonably yield both a conclusion that a child has an habitual residence and, alternatively, a conclusion that he lacks any habitual residence, the court should adopt the former.' This interpretation operates to ensure that, all things being equal, a forum is available to determine a child's best interests.

[16] A Fiorini, 'The Protection of the Best Interests of Migrant Children – Private International Law Perspectives' (May 1, 2016). Available at SSRN: https://ssrn.com/abstract=2862361 22.

[17] United Nations Committee on the Rights of the Children, General comment No. 14 (2013) on the right of the child to have his or her best interests taken as a primary consideration (art. 3, para. 1) (29 May 2013 CRC/C/GC/14) [19].

jurisdiction at all), certain long-term consequences will flow from the application of national law, both in terms of the range of options available to the court and the ultimate outcome of proceedings for the child.[18] Despite this, the extent to which a court is entitled to consider a child's best interests as part of a jurisdictional decision will vary depending on the type of decision being made. This may feel counter-intuitive when these decisions are made in the context of care proceedings, where the child's best interests are the court's paramount consideration.[19]

The Welfare Impact of Jurisdictional Decisions

As outlined in chapter 1, the controversy around practice in care proceedings with an international element focused particularly on cases where there were plans to place a foreign national child for adoption in England and Wales, which highlighted the diversity of approaches to child protection and adoption within the EU.[20] If the courts of England and Wales have jurisdiction to determine care proceedings concerning a child with international connections, this may mean that the child is ultimately placed for adoption.[21] A jurisdictional decision can therefore define the ambit of any welfare enquiry by determining the forum competent to make decisions about a child.[22] It is perhaps understandable, therefore, that challenges to the court's jurisdiction in care proceedings may be brought by parents who are aware that, if successful, this may mean that their children cannot be placed for adoption in England.

Yüksel and Trimmings frame this issue as a choice of law problem arising from the determination that English law concerning non-consensual adoption is the applicable law in relation to foreign national children with links outside of the jurisdiction.[23] Thus, for example, in *Re N (Children) (Adoption: Jurisdiction)* Munby P conducted an extensive analysis of adoption law, concluding that non-consensual adoption of foreign national children was lawful but that a child's

[18] R Lamont, 'Care Proceedings with a European Dimension under Brussels IIa: Jurisdiction, Mutual Trust and the Best Interests of the Child' (2016) 28 *Child and Family Law Quarterly* 67, *Re N (Children) (Adoption: Jurisdiction) (AIRE Centre and others intervening)* [2016] UKSC 15, [2017] AC 167.

[19] CA 89 s 1 (1).

[20] R Lamont, 'Care Proceedings with a European Dimension under Brussels IIa: Jurisdiction, Mutual Trust and the Best Interests of the Child' (2016) 28 *CFLQ* 67, 82–83. See also N Gilbert, N Parton and M Skivenes (eds), *Child Protection Systems: International Trends and Orientations* (OUP, 2011); K Burns, T Pvsv, and M Skivenes (eds), *Child Welfare Removals by the State: A Cross-Country Analysis of Decision-Making Systems* (Oxford Scholarship Online, 2016).

[21] See C Fenton-Glynn, 'Adoption without Consent: Update 2016' (Policy Department for Citizens' Rights and Constitutional Affairs, European Parliament 2016); J Masson, 'Recognition of Adoption Orders: A Problem for the Courts of England and Wales?' (2016) 46 *Family Law* 1113.

[22] R Lamont, 'Care Proceedings with a European Dimension under Brussels IIa: Jurisdiction, Mutual Trust and the Best Interests of the Child' (2016) 28 *CFLQ* 67, 82–83.

[23] B Yüksel and K Trimmings, 'Choice of Law Aspects of Non-Consensual Adoption of Eastern European Children in England and Wales' (2017) 3 *International Family Law* 202.

international connections are an integral part of any welfare analysis as to whether adoption will be in their best interests as a matter of English law.[24] This includes consideration of foreign law insofar as it may give rise to a 'limping adoption' – where an adoption order is not recognised in the state of the child's nationality. Interestingly, however, *Re N* was primarily a case about jurisdiction, namely the proper approach to the best interests of the child when considering whether to transfer jurisdiction in care proceedings under BIIa Art 15. It traversed into a discussion about the legality of the adoption of foreign nationals because a potential outcome of the court refusing to request a transfer of jurisdiction was the application of domestic law – a decision which eventually resulted in the two children of Hungarian nationality, who were the subject of the care proceedings, being placed for adoption. Whilst the judgment did not conclude that the courts of England and Wales could apply foreign law in relation to the adoption of foreign nationals, the Court of Appeal's judgment in *Re N* was clearly intended to address some of the controversy and criticism levelled at the English court's approach to foreign national children.[25]

Lamont has considered the issues outlined above with reference to the jurisdictional framework in BIIa and the principle of mutual trust which underpins the regulation.[26] National systems of family law remain diverse.[27] There are significant differences between state child protection systems across the EU and further afield, and the legal frameworks regulating these systems also vary considerably.[28] Accordingly, a decision that the family court has jurisdiction in care proceedings opens the door to the application of English law, which could ultimately lead to the child's placement for adoption. This outcome may be avoided if that court lacks jurisdiction or if jurisdiction is transferred to a state where non-consensual adoption is rare or unheard of.[29] Lamont observes that the principle of mutual trust within the EU 'effectively shields domestic law on child protection from assessment by another Member State court, indirectly limiting the scope of any assessment of

[24] *Re N (Children) (Adoption: Jurisdiction)* [2015] EWCA Civ 1112; [2016] 2 WLR 713, Adoption and Children Act 2002 s 1 (4).

[25] C Fenton-Glynn, 'Re N – Conflict and Confluence of Adoption Law in Europe' (2015) 45 *Family Law* 1433. The Court of Appeal's judgment in *Re N* was overturned by the Supreme Court although the judgment focused primarily on the issue of transfers of jurisdiction under BIIa Art 15 rather than the legality of adoptions of foreign citizens – see *Re N (Children) (Adoption: Jurisdiction) (AIRE Centre and others intervening)* [2016] UKSC 15, [2017] AC 167.

[26] R Lamont, 'Care Proceedings with a European Dimension under Brussels IIa: Jurisdiction, Mutual Trust and the Best Interests of the Child' (2016) 28 *CFLQ* 67.

[27] For a discussion of the harmonisation of family law within the EU see K Boele-Woelki (ed), *Perspectives for the Unification and Harmonisation of Family Law in Europe* (Intersentia, 2003).

[28] N Gilbert, N Parton and M Skivenes (eds), *Child Protection Systems: International Trends and Orientations* (OUP, 2011).

[29] C Fenton-Glynn C, 'Adoption without Consent' (Policy Department for Citizens' Rights and Constitutional Affairs, European Parliament 2015); C Fenton-Glynn, 'Adoption without Consent: Update 2016' (Policy Department for Citizens' Rights and Constitutional Affairs, European Parliament 2016); R Lamont and C Fenton-Glynn, 'Cross-Border Public Care and Adoption Proceedings in the European Union' (2016) 38 *Journal of Social Welfare and Family Law* 94.

the child's best interests'.[30] Limiting the scope of a best interests assessment in this way is a counter-intuitive step in care proceedings, where the child's best interests are paramount, and an analysis of how those best interests are met, may involve 'an element of comparison between legal systems'.[31] The impact of the principle of mutual trust is such that 'the child's best interests are never going to be a primary consideration in a system where the potential future outcomes for that child cannot be assessed'.[32] This is one reason why – according to Lamont – the BIIa regime may present difficulties in care proceedings.[33]

The principle of mutual trust is a fundamental element in the EU's imperative to establish an Area of Freedom, Security and Justice within the European Union, and is an essential part of the proper functioning of BIIa.[34] The loss of BIIa, and application of the HC96 in its place because of Brexit, does not necessarily avoid the challenge associated with the principle of mutual trust identified by Lamont. Mutual trust is an underpinning concept in global private international law (albeit one that is qualified by provisions which permit states to protect their vital interests).[35] In the context of the HC96 it is particularly relevant to the mutual recognition of measures of protection, as Contracting States can only refuse to recognise such measures on limited grounds, which include the 'safety valve' of the public policy exception (recognition may be refused if it would be 'manifestly contrary to public policy of the requested State, taking into account the best interests of the child').[36]

The application of the common law principle of comity in this context can also indirectly limit the scope of an assessment of a child's best interests. The family courts have been anxious to ensure respect for comity when determining forum issues under national law in cases where there is no internationally or regionally agreed framework of PIL.[37] The principle of comity has been interpreted as being wide-ranging enough to encompass 'administrative, judicial and social services' in family law cases with an international dimension.[38] Early jurisdiction decisions from the High Court in care proceedings emphasised the importance of comity when considering whether another BIIa Member State would be better placed

[30] R Lamont, 'Care Proceedings with a European Dimension under Brussels Ila: Jurisdiction, Mutual Trust and the Best Interests of the Child' (2016) 28 *Child and Family Law Quarterly* 67, 86.

[31] *Ibid.*

[32] *Ibid* 85.

[33] *Ibid.*

[34] Brussels IIa Recital (1), (21). K Lenaerts, 'The Best Interests of the Child Always Come First: The Brussels II *bis* Regulation and the European Court of Justice' (2013) 20 *Jurisprudence* 1302, 1304.

[35] J Holliday and P Beaumont, 'Introduction' in P Beaumont and J Holliday (eds), *A Guide to Global Private International Law* (Hart, 2022), 6.

[36] HC96 Art 23 (d); Art 27; J Holliday and P Beaumont, 'Introduction' in P Beaumont and J Holliday (eds), *A Guide to Global Private International Law* (Hart, 2022), 6; M Weller, 'Mutual Trust: In Search of the Future of European Union Private International Law' (2015) 11 *Journal of Private International Law* 64, 73.

[37] See, for example, V M (A Child) (Stranding: Forum Conveniens: Anti-Suit Inunction) [2019] 4 WLR 38 at [35(iii)].

[38] *Warrington Borough Council v TN* (Care Proceedings: Comity) [2020] EWFC 79 [26].

to hear a care case – and comity in this context referred to respect for foreign state child protection systems as well as judicial authorities.[39] This approach has survived the UK's departure from the European Union. For example, in *Warrington Borough Council v TN (Care Proceedings: Comity)* MacDonald J noted that the principle of comity does not derive from the UK's membership of the EU and survives as a common law principle 'based on courtesy, respect and reciprocity'.[40]

Jurisdictional decisions can have a range of consequences for a child.[41] In the short term, they may entail an international move and a change of placement (and the losses and gains associated with this).[42] In the long term, a jurisdictional decision can be 'strongly determinative of the eventual outcome for the child'.[43] Adherence to principles of comity or mutual trust may restrict the extent to which a court can enter into a comparative evaluation of the long-term impact of a forum decision on a child's future. Approaching a jurisdictional decision in a narrow way, which does not evaluate the short and long-term impact of the court's decision on the child's welfare, will meet the interests of actors who wish to avoid England and Wales becoming or remaining the competent forum to determine the child's best interests. As such, it is important to consider to what extent are an *individual* child's best interests considered by courts when these decisions are made.

The next section of this chapter frames the primary jurisdictional decisions which may arise in care proceedings by reference to Eekelaar's concepts of 'direct' and 'indirect' best interests.[44] In this way, it is possible to build a foundation for exploring how the different jurisdictional provisions of BIIa/ HC96 operate in practice and the impact that they have on children in care proceedings.

[39] In *Nottingham City Council v LM and others* [2014] EWCA Civ 152 [2014] WLR (D) 092 Ryder LJ said at [19] that the starting point in relation to a transfer of jurisdiction under BIIa Art 15 was the principle of comity. See also *Re T (A Child) (Care Proceedings: Request to Assume Jurisdiction)* [2013] EWCA Civ 895; [2014] 2 WLR 1204.

[40] *Warrington Borough Council v TN* (Care Proceedings: Comity) [2020] EWFC 79 [26].

[41] See *Re N (Children) (Adoption: Jurisdiction) (AIRE Centre and others intervening)* [2016] UKSC 15, [2017] AC 167 in relation to the short- and long-term consequences of a transfer of jurisdiction.

[42] See *Re CK (Children) (Care Proceedings: Habitual Residence: Article 15)* [2015] EWHC 2666 (Fam) [81] where Moylan J observed that whilst it is possible to transfer jurisdiction to another BIIa Member State and for that Member State to then decide whether or not the child should move there, there would be 'considerable potential problems' with this approach, particularly as the sending court would only have jurisdiction to take provisional measures under BIIa Article 20. However, some more recent, incoming, cases from Ireland, the English court has accepted a transfer of jurisdiction pursuant to BIIa Article 15, but the child has remained in their placement in Ireland pending a substantive welfare decision. See *Child and Family Agency v M* [2018] EWHC 1581 (Fam); [2019] Fam 199. In *Re S (No 2) (Care Proceedings) (Article 15: Second Application for Second Transfer)* [2019] EWFC 12; [2019] 1 WLR 5045, the child remained in Ireland throughout the transferred proceedings, which concluded with an order confirming the child's placement there.

[43] R Lamont, 'Care Proceedings with a European Dimension under Brussels IIa: Jurisdiction, Mutual Trust and the Best Interests of the Child' (2016) 28 *CFLQ* 67, 69.

[44] J Eekelaar, 'The Role of the Best Interests Principle in Decisions Affecting Children and Decisions about Children' (2015) 23 *The International Journal of Children's Rights* 3.

Jurisdictional Decisions and Eekelaar's 'Direct' and 'Indirect' Welfare Paradigm

UNCRC Art 3.1 is the 'foundation of a substantive right' for individual children in relation to matters which concern them, and a 'fundamental, interpretive legal principle', guiding the way that decisions are made about a child.[45] But do jurisdictional decisions engage an obligation to consider their impact on an individual child's welfare? This raises the question as to whether jurisdictional decisions are 'about' children, or whether they can be seen as being simply about a forum, irrespective of their impact.

Eekelaar suggests a categorisation of decisions concerning children.[46] On the one hand, there are cases where the determination of an issue will indirectly affect a child. Here, the decision-maker should focus on the issue to be decided, rather than on what outcome would meet the child's best interests. The child's best interests are relevant insofar as they relate to the impact of the decision on the child, but the weight to be accorded to those interests will vary. The issue for determination is foregrounded in such cases. If the best solution to this issue has a detrimental impact on a child's best interests, 'it may need to be modified or even abandoned', but this is 'not inevitable because the nature of that outcome may be so important that it must be achieved notwithstanding its effect on the child's interests, or on other "primary" considerations'.[47]

In cases which directly 'concern' children, the child's best interests are foregrounded. Whilst other issues and interests may be relevant, the weight accorded to those other issues will vary, as the central focus will be on finding an outcome which promotes the child's best interests, following an open and holistic inquiry. Accordingly, care proceedings directly concern children's best interests.[48]

Eekelaar thought that jurisdictional decisions were about a forum, rather than directly concerning children, and therefore such cases fell into the 'indirect best interests' category. Eekelaar also classified decisions under the 1980 Hague Child Abduction Convention over whether or not to return a child to the state of their habitual residence after a wrongful removal or retention, as 'indirect best interests' decisions which were about a forum. This classification goes to the heart of a conflict which has arisen over the role of a child's welfare in decisions under the 1980 Hague Child Abduction Convention, a conflict which provides some context for the discussions in this part of the chapter.

[45] Jean Zermatten, 'The Best Interests of the Child Principle: Literal Analysis and Function (2010) 4 *The International Journal of Children's Rights* 483, 485; United Nations Committee on the Rights of the Children, General comment No. 14 (2013) on the right of the child to have his or her best interests taken as a primary consideration (art. 3, para. 1) (29 May 2013 CRC/C/GC/14).

[46] J Eekelaar, 'The Role of the Best Interests Principle in Decisions Affecting Children and Decisions about Children' (2015) 23 *The International Journal of Children's Rights* 3.

[47] *Ibid* 5.

[48] *Ibid* 8.

Schuz has rejected the suggestion that the decisions under the 1980 Hague Child Abduction Convention can be framed solely as forum decisions – a decision to return, or to refuse to return, a child to the state of their habitual residence may have 'fateful implications' for a child in the short and long-term, as it will lead to the court in that state making a fundamental decision about the child's future.[49] The gravity of decisions under the 1980 Hague Child Abduction Convention, as observed by Schutz, has led to extensive consideration of how courts can apply the Convention in a manner consistent with UNCRC Art 3.1 and European Convention of Human Rights (ECHR) Art 8, particularly through a line of case law from the ECtHR culminating in *Neulinger and Shuruk v Switzerland*.[50] The Grand Chamber in *Neulinger* said that an interpretation of the Convention consistent with UNCRC Arti 3.1 (and accordingly ECHR Art 8) required an 'in depth examination of (the child's) entire family situation'. This decision was controversial, as it was considered to undermine the effectiveness and aims of the Abduction Convention.[51]

McEleavy notes this jurisprudential development took place against a change in the profile of abducting parents. Initially, abducting parents were mostly non-custodial parents (usually fathers) who removed children across borders and separated them from their primary carers (usually mothers). Over time the typical profile changed to primary carers who were 'going home' with a child to a country they had a close connection to. Against this changing profile there may have been a 'greater temptation for courts to allow return proceedings to drift into a consideration of substantive custody issues.'[52] Drawing on McEleavy's observations, importing a more holistic inquiry into the best interests of the child in the context of a constrained forum decision may have represented an attempt to soften the impact of a blunt jurisdictional decision on a child's welfare.

According to Eekelaar, the Grand Chamber in *Neulinger* had erred in treating the issue to be determined as a direct best interests question. In fact, the case involved an issue of a forum, where the best interests of the child are indirectly relevant and fall to be considered through the exceptions to return embodied in the 1980 Hague Child Abduction Convention, particularly the 'grave risk' exception under Art 13 (b).[53] Subsequently, the ECtHR has endorsed an approach which

[49] R Schuz, 'Policy Considerations in Determining the Habitual Residence of a Child and the Relevance of Context' (2001) 11 *Journal of Transnational Law and Policy* 101, 102. See also R Schuz, 'Commentary on *RCB as Litigation Guardian of EKV, CEV, CIV and LRV v The Honourable Justice Colin James Forrest*', in H Stalford, K Hollingsworth, S Gilmore (eds), *Rewriting Children's Rights Judgments: From Academic Vision to New Practice* (Hart Publishing, 2017), 497.

[50] *Neulinger and Shuruk v Switzerland* (Application No 41615/07) (ECtHR, 6 July 2010).

[51] L Walker, 'The Impact of the Hague Abduction Convention on the Rights of the Family in the Case-Law of the European Court of Human Rights and the UN Human Rights Committee: The Danger of Neulinger' (2010) 6 *Journal of Private International Law* 649; LJ Silberman, 'The Hague Convention on Child Abduction and Unilateral Relocations by Custodial Parents: A Perspective from the United States and Europe-Abbott, Neulinger, Zarraga' (2018) 63 *Oklahoma Law Review* 733.

[52] P McEleavy, 'The European Court of Human Rights and the Hague Child Abduction Convention: Prioritising Return or Reflection?' (2015) 62 *NILR* 365, 402.

[53] J Eekelaar, 'The Role of the Best Interests Principle in Decisions Affecting Children and Decisions about Children' (2015) 23 *The International Journal of Children's Rights* 3, 18.

is more in line with Eekelaar's 'indirect best interests' approach. In *X v Latvia*, the court stated that the Convention could be harmoniously interpreted in line with the ECHR through appropriate and 'effective' (as opposed to 'in-depth') consideration of the exceptions to return and a fully reasoned decision.[54] These exceptions are focused on the potential impact of returning the child and, if established, the court has a wide discretion over whether or not to order their return to the state of their habitual residence.[55]

Transfers of Jurisdiction and Best Interests

The debate about the place of welfare in decisions under the 1980 Hague Child Abduction Convention has parallels with certain jurisdictional decisions taken under BIIa and the HC96 in care proceedings.

BIIa and HC96 contain several jurisdictional grounds, and the primary basis for a court having substantive jurisdiction in relation to a child is their habitual residence. However, as an exception to the general rules of jurisdiction, it is possible under both BIIa and HC96 for substantive jurisdiction to be transferred to another Member or Contracting State where the child has a connection, which may be better placed to hear the case.[56] The provisions in both instruments provide that a transfer of jurisdiction must be in the child's best interests.[57]

The specific transfer provisions contained in BIIa Art 15 and 96 HC Art 8 and 9 differ slightly and are therefore examined in greater depth, before they are discussed by reference to their engagement with an individual child's welfare interests.

BIIa Art 15 enabled jurisdiction to be transferred to a Member State with which a child has a 'particular connection'. In identifying whether a child has a 'particular connection', the provision contained an exhaustive list of factors which would satisfy this criterion, including the child's nationality. For a transfer of jurisdiction under the HC96 Art 8 or 9 there is a similar list of criteria which must be satisfied which relate to the child's connection to the other Contracting State, however, this includes the broad criterion of the child having a 'substantial connection' with the

[54] *X v Latvia* (Application No 27853/09) (ECtHR, 26 November 2013). P Beaumont et al, 'Child Abduction: Recent Jurisprudence of the European Court of Human Rights' (2015) 64 *International and Comparative Law Quarterly* 39, 43–45.

[55] 1980 Hague Child Abduction Convention Article 12 (settlement), 13 (2) (child's objections), 13 (b) (grave risk). *Re M (Children) (Abduction: Rights of Custody)* [2007] UKHL 55; [2008] AC 1288 [43] Lady Hale.

[56] BIIa Art 15, HC96 Art 8 and 9. Under BIIa Art 15 the child must have a 'particular connection' with the Member State in question as listed in BIIa Article 15 (3). Under HC96 Art 8, a child must have a 'substantial connection' with the other Contracting State, and some examples of connections which might meet this criterion are listed at HC96 Art 8 (2).

[57] BIIa Art 15 (1), HC96 Art 8 (4).

Contracting State in question, which may mean that the provision can be used in a wider variety of situations compared with BIIa Art 15.[58]

BIIa Art 15 permitted a transfer of the whole or 'a specific part' of a case to a better placed Member State. Whilst the HC96 Art 8 and 9 do not expressly mention a transfer of jurisdiction for a part of a case, the Practical Handbook for the Convention states that this is possible and would bring the HC96 in line with both BIIa and the 2000 Hague Protection of Adults Convention.[59]

BIIa Art 15 enabled a request for a transfer of jurisdiction to be made by one of the parties, by a court of its own motion or by the court of another Member State with which a child had a particular connection. However, where a request was made by a court, at least one of the parties needed to consent to the transfer of jurisdiction.[60] There is no requirement for the parties to consent to a transfer request made by another Contracting State, or sought by the court's own motion under HC96 Art 9. Under BIIa Art 15, both the sending and receiving court had to consider whether a transfer of jurisdiction is in the child's best interests, whereas under the HC96 Art 8 (4), only the receiving court is required to consider whether the transfer is in the child's best interests. Finally, under the HC96 there is no time limit provided for the receiving court to decide whether or not to accept a request for a transfer of jurisdiction, whereas a six-week time limit was imposed under BIIa Art 15.[61]

The transfer provisions of the HC96 were infrequently used in England and Wales, because BIIa took priority over the HC96 in relation to matters governed by the Regulation, where a child had their habitual residence on the territory of a BIIa Member State.[62] However, as a result of Brexit, and the loss of BIIa for proceedings issued after the end of the transition period (11 p.m., 31 December 2020), the transfer provisions of the HC96 will be more frequently considered, and the interpretation is comparable to that taken under BIIa.[63]

BIIa and the HC96 specifically require a court to consider whether it would be in a child's best interests for jurisdiction to be transferred.[64] However, Eekelaar considered that a potential transfer of jurisdiction under BIIa Art 15 is an

[58] HC96 Art 8 (2) (d).

[59] Hague Conference on Private International Law, *Practical Handbook on the Operation of the 1996 Hague Child Protection Convention* (The Hague, 2014) 5.5.

[60] BIIa Art 15 (2).

[61] BIIa Art 15 (5). Lowe and Nicholls also note that the transfer provisions under the HC96 contain what has been identified as an 'oversight' as Art 9 requests for a transfer of jurisdiction can only be made to a Contracting State of a child's habitual residence, whereas requests under Art 8 can also be made by Contracting States with jurisdiction based on the child' s presence under HC96 Art 6. The Explanatory Report to the HC96 has urged a purposive approach which permits an Art 9 request to be addressed to a Contracting State with jurisdiction under Art 6 N Lowe and M Nicholls, The 1996 *Hague Convention on the Protection of Children* (LexisNexis, 2012) 3.44.

[62] N Lowe and M Nicholls, The 1996 Hague Convention on the Protection of Children (LexisNexis, 2012) 3.51.

[63] P Torremans (ed), Cheshire, North & Fawcett, *Private International Law* (OUP, 2017) 1117.

[64] BIIa Article 15 (1), (3); HC96 Article 8(1), (4), 9(1); The ambit of the best interests assessments for the receiving court is discussed in *Re M (A Child) (Foreign Care Proceedings: Transfer)* [2013]

indirect 'best interests' question; 'it is a decision about the best place to make that decision'.[65]

Eekelaar's assessment was made in the light of early English case law on BIIa Art 15 transfers which took an approach to child welfare in this context which was 'attenuated' and 'limited to the issue of forum'.[66] In *Nottingham City Council v LM* and others, Ryder LJ described it as being akin to the approach to the best interests in relation to a prorogation of jurisdiction under BIIa Art 12 as set out in *Re I (A Child) (Contact Application: Jurisdiction)*.[67] It did not entail an 'profound investigation' as to what is in the child's best interests generally. Rather, the question to be answered was whether it was in a child's best interests for the case to be determined in another jurisdiction, informed by 'the sort of considerations which come into play when deciding upon the most appropriate forum'.[68] The starting point for this attenuated best interests inquiry was the principle of comity – it was to be assumed that the requested state would be able to protect a child and safeguard their welfare, adequately.[69]

This can be seen as an 'indirect best interests' approach as described by Eekelaar; the primary issue to be decided is the 'better placed' / forum question. There are parallels here with the approach taken in *forum non conveniens* cases, where a child's best interests are important, but not paramount, in deciding whether proceedings should be stayed in favour of a more convenient forum.[70] Although the Court of Appeal in *Re T (A Child) (Care Proceedings: Request to Assume Jurisdiction)* rejected an attempt by Mostyn J to import domestic *forum conveniens* principles into BIIa Art 15 transfer cases, both bodies of case law reflect an 'indirect' best interests approach to forum decisions; a child's best interests are a matter to be weighed in the balance but only with reference to the jurisdictional issue to be determined.[71]

However, the 'attenuated' approach to welfare in the context of a BIIa Art 15 transfer of jurisdiction was rejected by the Supreme Court in the 2016 case of *Re N*.[72] Delivering the judgment of the court, Lady Hale said that the focus of a best interests inquiry in the context of BIIa Art 15 was on the welfare impact of the

EWHC 646 (Fam); [2013] Fam 308, approved in *Re HJ (A Child) (Jurisdiction: Brussels II Revised)* [2013] EWHC 1867 (Fam); [2014] 1 FLR 430.

[65] J Eekelaar, 'The Role of the Best Interests Principle in Decisions Affecting Children and Decisions about Children' (2015) 23 *The International Journal of Children's Rights* 3, 12.

[66] *Nottingham City Council v LM and others* [2014] EWCA Civ 152 [2014] WLR (D) 092 [19] Ryder LJ.

[67] Ibid and *Re I (A Child) (Contact Application: Jurisdiction)* [2009] UKSC 10; [2010] 1 AC 319 [36] Lady Hale.

[68] *Ibid* Lady Hale.

[69] *Nottingham City Council v LM and others* [2014] EWCA Civ 152 [2014] WLR (D) 092.

[70] *Re S (Residence Order: Forum Conveniens)* [1995] 1 FLR 314; *Re D (Stay of Children Act Proceedings)* [2003] EWHC 565 (Fam) [2003], 2 FLR 1159.

[71] *Re T (A Child) (Care Proceedings: Request to Assume Jurisdiction)* [2013] EWCA Civ 895; [2014] Fam 130.

[72] *Re N (Children) (Adoption: Jurisdiction) (AIRE Centre and others intervening)* [2016] UKSC 15, [2017] A.C. 167.

transfer of jurisdiction. This may require an evaluation of the short- and long-term consequences of transferring jurisdiction for the child.

> … there is no reason at all to exclude the impact upon the child's welfare, in the short or the longer term, of the transfer itself. What will be its immediate consequences? **What impact will it have on the choices available to the court deciding upon the eventual outcome?** This is not the same as deciding what outcome will be in the child's best interests. It is deciding whether it is in the child's best interests for the court currently seised of the case to retain it or whether it is in the child's best interests for the case to be transferred to the requested court.[73] (emphasis added)

For the two children in *Re N*, conducting this kind of welfare evaluation would lead to a consideration of the impact of the jurisdictional decision on the children as individuals; in the short term, they would have to leave their home with their foster carers in England where they were settled, to an unknown foster placement in Hungary, a country unfamiliar to them. In the longer term, the forum making decisions about their future would be unable to consider as a possible outcome their long-term placement with those foster carers, 'whether through adoption, or through a special guardianship order, or through an ordinary residence order'.[74]

The CJEU subsequently affirmed that a best interests inquiry required a court to assess 'any negative effects that such a transfer might have on the familial, social and emotional attachments of the child concerned in the case or on that child's material situation'.[75] Lamont identifies the 'minimalistic' ambit of the best interests assessment envisaged by the CJEU – it is limited to identifying the negative consequences of a transfer of jurisdiction.[76] Furthermore, the CJEU said that it was impermissible to consider the substantive law of the requested Member State in the context of a best interests evaluation, as this would be in breach of the principles of mutual trust and the mutual recognition of judgments which underpin BIIa.[77] In this way, the CJEU's approach perpetuated the conflict, identified by Lamont, between the kind of expansive best interests inquiry required in care proceedings and the principle of mutual trust.[78] Lowe and Setright highlight the difficulty in reconciling the CJEU's decision with the Supreme Court's decision in *Re N*; how is a court to evaluate the 'impact (of transfer) on the choices available to the court' without considering the substantive law of the requested state?[79]

[73] *Ibid* [45] Lady Hale.

[74] *Ibid.*

[75] (Case C-428/15) *Child and Family Agency v J. D* EU:C: 2016:819, [2017] Fam 248 [59].

[76] R Lamont, 'The Development of Child Protection Across International Borders for Children at Risk of Harm' in G Douglas, M Murch and V Stephens (eds), *International and National Perspectives on Child and Family Law* (Cambridge University Press, 2018), 244.

[77] *Ibid.*

[78] R Lamont, 'Care Proceedings with a European Dimension under Brussels Ila: Jurisdiction, Mutual Trust and the Best Interests of the Child' (2016) 28 *CFLQ* 67.

[79] N Lowe and H Setright, 'Transferring the Problem – How Art 15 of the Revised Brussels II Regulation Operates in the Public Law Context' (2017) *International Family Law* 13. See also R Lamont, 'The Development of Child Protection Across International Borders for Children at Risk of Harm'

However, by focusing on the impact of transfer on the lived experience of an *individual child*, the Supreme Court's approach in *Re N* may narrowly avoid offending against the principle of mutual trust.

Although it may be difficult to reconcile the approaches taken by the Supreme Court and CJEU to the place of a child's best interests when considering a transfer of jurisdiction, courts in England and Wales subsequently take a far more expansive approach to best interests in the light of these decisions.[80] The European approach and interpretation of the transfer provisions – arising out of a 'more intense and more consistent' application of BIIa Art 15 – can inform the approach taken to the interpretation and application of the equivalent provisions under the HC96 Art 8 and 9.[81] It is now harder to reconcile Eekelaar's view that a transfer of jurisdiction is an 'indirect' best interests decision which is 'about' forum rather than being about an individual child. Trimmings notes Lady Hale's care in distinguishing the focus of a welfare enquiry in the context of a transfer of jurisdiction from an evaluation of what is in a child's best interests generally.[82] However, the approach to transfers of jurisdiction now sees the child's best interests operating as a separate criterion to be satisfied, with the focus of the inquiry being on the real-life impact of the forum decision on the child concerned, and as such might now be framed as a direct best interests approach.

Determinations of Habitual Residence and Best Interests

As set out at the beginning of this chapter, a child's habitual residence is the primary connecting factor under BIIa and HC96 which determines the competent forum to make welfare decisions about a child. Although determinative of the competent forum under these instruments, a decision over where a child is habitually resident does not entail an examination of the welfare impact of that decision.

Habitual residence is not defined in either the HC96 or in BIIa.[83] The CJEU has considered the interpretation of habitual residence under BIIa on several occasions, and stated that the concept is 'an autonomous one of EU law, which has to be interpreted in the light of the context of the provisions referring to that

in G Douglas, M Murch and V Stephens (eds), *International and National Perspectives on Child and Family Law* (Cambridge University Press, 2018).

[80] For example, Re A (Refusal of Article 15: Application for Transfer) [2017] 7 WLUK 307; Re D (Children art.15: Transfer of the Proceedings) [2017] EWHC 3078 (Fam); *Local Authority v MM* [2020] EWFC 65.

[81] C Honorati and M Keyes, 'Parental Responsibility, Custody and Access' in P Beaumont and J Holliday (eds), *A Guide to Global Private International Law* (Hart, 2022) 478.

[82] K Trimmings, 'Transfer of Jurisdiction and the Best Interests of the Child' (2016) 3 *CLJ* 471.

[83] L Collins and J Harris (general eds), *Dicey, Morris and Collins, The Conflict of Laws* (Sweet & Maxwell, 2022) 20-008.

concept and the objectives of (BIIa)'.[84] In particular, the CJEU has said that the concept must be interpreted in light of Recital 12 of BIIa (which states that the grounds of jurisdiction are shaped in light of the best interests of the child, in particular on the criterion of proximity). As such, ascertaining a child's habitual residence for the purposes of BIIa Art 8 required a factual enquiry as to the 'place which reflects some degree of integration by the child in a social and family environment'.[85] Certain factors will be relevant to national courts undertaking this enquiry, such as the 'duration, regularity, conditions and reasons' for the child's presence in a Member State and the child's nationality.[86] The habitual residence of a child's primary carer will be particularly relevant where the case concerns a young child or infant.[87] Gössl and Lamont identify that the CJEU's approach to habitual residence generally is factual, and the intention of the parties as to their habitual residence 'plays a subordinate – if any – role'.[88]

Similarly, and consistently with the tradition of the Hague Conference on Private International Law, habitual residence pursuant to HC96 Art 5 is not defined in the Convention itself.[89] The Practical Handbook to the HC96 states that habitual residence is an 'autonomous concept and should be interpreted in light of the objectives of the Convention rather than under domestic law constraints'.[90] Honorati and Keyes note the possibility for habitual residence to be interpreted differently under the 1980 and 1996 Hague Conventions.[91] For example, Schuz analysed the interpretation of habitual residence under the Abduction Convention in different jurisdictions, and identified different approaches categorised as a 'parental intention' model (which focusses on the subjective intention of the parents to determine where the child should live) and a 'factual model' (which focuses on the 'objective connections between the child and his environment').[92] More recently and influenced by the CJEU's approach to the concept as outlined above, national courts have applied a combined or hybrid approach to the interpretation of habitual residence under the 1980 Hague Child Abduction Convention

[84] Case C-523/07 *Proceedings brought by A* ECLI:EU:C:2009:225, [34]-[35]; (Case C-497/10) *Mercredi* EU:C:2010:829 [44]- [46]; (Case C-435/06) *Proceedings Brought by C*, EU:C:2007:714 [50]. See also P Torremans (ed), Cheshire, North & Fawcett, *Private International Law* (OUP, 2017) 1094.

[85] *Proceedings brought by A* (Case C-523/07) ECLI:EU:C: 2009:225; [2010] Fam 42, 44.

[86] *Ibid* [39], [44].

[87] (Case C-497/10) *Mercredi* EU:C:2010:829 [54]–[55].

[88] SL Gössl and R Lamont, 'Connecting Factors' in P Beaumont and J Holliday (eds), *A Guide to Global Private International Law* (Hart, 2022) 59.

[89] P Lagarde 'Explanatory Report' (1996) HCCH [40].

[90] Hague Conference on Private International Law, *Practical Handbook on the Operation of the 1996 Hague Child Protection Convention* (The Hague, 2014) 4.5.

[91] C Honorati and M Keyes, 'Parental Responsibility, Custody and Access' in P Beaumont and J Holliday (eds), *A Guide to Global Private International Law* (Hart, 2022) 470.

[92] R Schuz, 'Disparity and the Quest for Uniformity in Implementing the Hague Child Abduction Convention' (2014) 9 *Journal of Comparative Law* 7. See also T Kruger, 'Habitual Residence: The Factors that Courts Consider' in P Beaumont, M Danov, K Trimmings and B Yüksel (eds), *Cross Border Litigation in Europe* (Hart, 2017) for a discussion of the ways that national courts have drawn upon the CJEU's approach to habitual residence.

which sees parental intention as a relevant factor in assessing a child's connections to a particular state.[93]

The interpretation of a child's habitual residence in England and Wales was cemented by the decision of the UK Supreme Court, in the case of *A v A and another (Children: Habitual Residence) (Reunite International Child Abduction Centre and others intervening)*.[94] The court held that the 'English test' for habitual residence as set out in *R v Barnet London Borough Council, ex p Shah* should be abandoned.[95] The approach in *Shah* aligned habitual residence with 'ordinary residence' with a focus on 'a man's abode in a particular place or country which he has adopted voluntarily and for settled purposes as part of the regular order of his life for the time being, whether of short or of long duration'.[96] This placed a focus on the intention of a child's parents, whereas, according to the majority in the Supreme Court, this should be just one factor placed in the balance of a habitual residence evaluation.[97] The Supreme Court in *A v A* considered that the European test for habitual residence should be applied uniformly and consistently under the Hague Conventions and European Conventions.[98] Schutz considers this to be a 'combined' approach to habitual residence which sees parental intention as a relevant factor in the context of a factual enquiry into a child's objective intentions.[99]

As stated in the Practical Handbook to the HC96, there are different considerations which may be engaged with in the factual assessment of a child's habitual residence under the HC96 as to the 1980 Hague Child Abduction Convention.[100] However, thus far, in England and Wales the approach to the interpretation of habitual residence under the HC96 has remained consistent with the Supreme Court's decision in *A v A*.[101] Torremans considers that in this regard, the 'trend towards a uniform understanding of habitual residence appears to be a highly sensible one' to achieve legal certainty and predictability in cross-border children's cases.[102] There is, however, a significant difference in the approach to habitual residence under the HC96 and BIIa – the former instrument does not apply the

[93] *Ibid* 52.

[94] *A v A and another* (Children: Habitual Residence) (Reunite International Child Abduction Centre and others intervening) [2013] UKSC 60; [2014] AC 1.

[95] [1983] 2 AC 309 [343].

[96] [1983] 2 AC 309 [343] Lord Scarman.

[97] [2013] UKSC 60; [2014] AC 1 [37], [54] Lady Hale.

[98] *Ibid* [54].

[99] R Schuz, 'Disparity and the Quest for Uniformity in Implementing the Hague Child Abduction Convention' (2014) 9 *Journal of Comparative Law* 3.

[100] Hague Conference on Private International Law, *Practical Handbook on the Operation of the 1996 Hague Child Protection Convention* (The Hague, 2014) 4.6. See also P Beaumont and J Holliday, 'Recent Developments on the Meaning of "Habitual Residence" in Alleged Child Abduction Cases' in M Župan (ed), *Private International Law in the Jurisprudence of European Courts – Family at Focus* (University of Osijek, Croatia 2015).

[101] Re *J (A Child) (1996 Hague Convention: Morocco)* [2015] UKSC 70 [34].

[102] P Torremans (ed), *Cheshire, North & Fawcett, Private International Law* (OUP, 2017) 1104.

principle of *perpetuatio fori* and thus habitual residence under the HC96 means the child's 'current' habitual residence.[103]

Overall, however, the approach to ascertaining a child's habitual residence for the purposes either of BIIa or HC96 entails a factual inquiry into reasons for a child's presence in a country, and the practical extent of her integration in her social and family environment there. These markers are signs of stability and settlement within a particular state. Further, the Supreme Court held in *Re LC (Children) (Reunite International Child Abduction Centre Intervening)* that a child's state of mind may be relevant to an inquiry as to whether they have acquired habitual residence in a particular state.[104] Although the Supreme Court was careful to distinguish the child's state of mind in this context from their 'wishes', adding this dimension to the habitual residence inquiry can reflect a child's feelings about their social and family environment, and further the link between the concept of habitual residence and welfare.[105]

Whilst the use of a child's habitual residence as a primary basis for jurisdiction is designed to meet the best interests of children generally, a determination as to where a child is habitually resident does not take into account the best interests of the individual child in question – or require consideration of the potential impact of the finding upon them.[106] In fact, on one view, a court is prohibited from importing welfare considerations into a determination of jurisdiction in this way, as to do so would undermine this harmonised system of private international law and lead to exorbitant jurisdictional claims.[107] Lenaerts emphasises the importance of legal certainty in establishing jurisdiction under BIIa and the importance of 'clear cut rules' in PIL generally – stating that 'a case-by-case solution, which is difficult to predict, must be, if possible, avoided'.[108] Lamont identifies the diversity of approaches to the interpretation of a child's 'best interests' across the EU, and the uncertainty that could arise if best interests issues informed a court's decision as to whether it had substantive jurisdiction on habitual residence grounds.[109]

[103] L Collins and J Harris (general eds), *Dicey, Morris and Collins, The Conflict of Laws* (Sweet & Maxwell, 2022) 20.008; Hague Conference on Private International Law, *Practical Handbook on the Operation of the 1996 Hague Child Protection Convention* (The Hague, 2014) 4.10–4.11.

[104] *Re LC (Children) (Reunite International Child Abduction Centre intervening)* [2014] UKSC 1; [2014] AC 1038.

[105] See also, for a discussion of habitual residence under the Hague Children's Conventions, and the concept of 'belonging', AL Estin, 'Where (in the World) do Children Belong?' (2011) 25 *Brigham Young University Journal of Public Law* 217.

[106] R Lamont, 'Care Proceedings with a European Dimension under Brussels IIa: Jurisdiction, Mutual Trust and the Best Interests of the Child' (2016) 28 *CFLQ* 67. The CJEU confirmed this in Case C-393/18 PPU *UD v XB* ECLI:EU:C:2018:835.

[107] One of the problems with the 1961 Hague Convention on the Protection of Minors was that it permitted the state of the child's nationality to displace a jurisdiction founded on habitual residence if they considered that this would be in the child's best interests. This undermined the operation of this instrument and led to uncertainty. See P Lagarde 'Explanatory Report' (1996) HCCH [5]-[6].

[108] K Lenaerts, 'The Best Interests of the Child Always Come First: The Brussels II *bis* Regulation and the European Court of Justice' (2013) 20 *Jurisprudence* 1302, 1304.

[109] R Lamont, 'Care Proceedings with a European Dimension under Brussels IIa: Jurisdiction, Mutual Trust and the Best Interests of the Child' (2016) 28 *CFLQ* 67, 70. See also M Ní Shúilleabháin 'Surrogacy,

Overall, a determination of substantive jurisdiction on habitual residence grounds is neither a direct, nor even an indirect, best interests question – a child's best interests play no part in the decision. It is not suggested here that a child's best interests *should* play a part in a habitual residence determination. However, the disparity in approach as compared to transfers of jurisdiction discussed above is striking, particularly as from a child's point of view, there is little difference between these two categories of jurisdictional decision – they can have the same, significant, impact in the short and long term, for all the reasons discussed above.

Jurisdiction and Families Fleeing Care Proceedings

The uneasy place of welfare within the two categories of jurisdictional decision outlined above is apparent in the litigation of jurisdictional disputes in care proceedings.[110] For example, a number of groups have been established which advise parents to leave the country if social services have said that they will issue care proceedings and assist them with doing so.[111] A common destination for this has been Ireland, which has been perceived as less interventionist than England, with adoption from care being less likely.[112] In several reported cases, mothers who have travelled to Ireland to avoid care proceedings had previously experienced the removal of children through care proceedings, into foster care, long-term kinship care or through adoption.[113] Many travelled whilst pregnant, or within days of their baby being born, sometimes having been informed that the local authority would be seeking the removal of their baby once born under an interim care order,

System Shopping, and Article 8 of the European Convention on Human Rights' (2019) 33 *International Journal of Law, Policy and The Family* 104, 109–111.

[110] R Lamont, 'The Development of Child Protection Across International Borders for Children at Risk of Harm' in G Douglas, M Murch and V Stephens (eds), *International and National Perspectives on Child and Family Law* (Cambridge University Press, 2018).

[111] Examples include 'Forced Adoption' run by Ian Josephs and the Ectopia Network based in Ireland. For reporting on these networks, see 'Revealed: The Networks Helping Families Flee Social Services' (*Channel 4 News*, 20 July 2012) https://www.channel4.com/news/revealed-the-networks-helping-families-flee-social-services; N Balasundaram, 'British Families Flee to Ireland to Escape Threat of Social Services' (*Irish Post*, 19 August 2015) https://www.irishpost.com/news/british-families-flee-to-ireland-to-escape-threat-of-social-services-63574; E Miller, 'I Ran Away to France to Keep My Baby' (*BBC News*, 4 April 2019) https://www.bbc.co.uk/news/stories-47802296.

[112] See Balasundaram and the discussion of the 'Ectopia Network' based in Co. Wexford which sought to assist families who had fled social services in England (*ibid*).

[113] *Re HJ (A Child) (Transfer of Proceedings)* [2013] EWHC 1867 (Fam); [2014] 1 FLR 430; *Re M (A Child) (Foreign Care Proceedings: Transfer)* [2013] EWHC 646 (Fam); [2013] Fam 308; *Child and Family Agency v M* [2018] EWHC 1581 (Fam); [2019] Fam 199; (Case C-428/15 Child and Family Agency v J. D EU:C:2016:819; [2017] Fam 248); (Joined Cases C-325/18PPU and C-375/18PPU) *Hampshire County Council v CE (Child and Family Agency intervening)* EU:C:2018:739; [2019] 1 WLR 2091; Mothers who are 'repeat clients' of the family court constitute a sizeable population of mothers involved in care proceedings. See K Broadhurst et al, 'Vulnerable Birth Mothers and Recurrent Care Proceedings: Final Summary Report' (2017) *Nuffield Foundation.*

with a potential care plan for adoption.[114] In some cases parents have been candid about their reasons for leaving the country – to avoid the jurisdiction of the courts of England and Wales and the intervention of their local authority. In *Re M (A Child) (Foreign Care Proceedings: Transfer)* the mother reportedly told Cobb J that she had left 'purposely to avoid my child (i.e. the baby) being stolen' by the local authority who had taken proceedings in relation to her older three children.[115] Similarly in *Re HJ*, the Irish judge referred to a 'tactical decision' taken by parents that their baby be born in Ireland, after becoming aware that a care order would be sought in England after his birth.[116]

Lamont notes that care proceedings may involve difficult, or 'borderline', habitual residence determinations, as these cases often involve situations where a child's life has been 'fundamentally disrupted'.[117] Children who are in need of state protection may have experienced instability in their lives, which may have included cross-national movement – not necessarily deliberate transnational migration by their parents to avoid state intervention but migration associated with a parent not having firm roots or support systems in particular country.[118]

This observation is particularly apt in cases where children are removed before, or very shortly after, care proceedings are issued, or cases involving babies who are born after the mother has left the country, where jurisdictional challenges and disputes can be closely connected with the harm that children have been exposed to. In *Lancashire County Council v T & Others: Habitual Residence: Care Proceedings)* a father removed five children to Ireland in an unplanned manner, five days prior to care proceedings being issued.[119] The parents challenged the court's jurisdiction, arguing that the children had lost their habitual residence by the point when care proceedings were issued or, alternatively, that the proceedings should be transferred to Ireland under BIIa Art 15. Moylan J held that the children had not lost their habitual residence in England and Wales in such a short space of time, given that the move was not 'a genuine relocation to seek a better life in Ireland' but rather an attempt to avoid care proceedings.[120] The consequence of concluding that the court has jurisdiction to make welfare decisions about the

[114] This occurred in *Re HJ (A Child) (Transfer of Proceedings)* (ibid); *Re M (A Child) (Foreign Care Proceedings: Transfer)* (ibid); (Case C-428/15) *Child and Family Agency v D (R intervening)* (ibid); *Child and Family Agency of Ireland v A Mother, A Father, A Local Authority* [2018] EWHC 939 (Fam); (Joined Cases C-325/18PPU and C-375/18PPU) *Hampshire County Council v CE (Child and Family Agency intervening)* (ibid).

[115] *Re M (A Child) (Foreign Care Proceedings: Transfer)* [2013] EWHC 646 (Fam); [2013] Fam 308 [2].

[116] *Re HJ (A Child) (Transfer of Proceedings)* [2013] EWHC 1867 (Fam); [2014] 1 FLR 430 [4].

[117] R Lamont, 'Care Proceedings with a European Dimension under Brussels IIa: Jurisdiction, Mutual Trust and the Best Interests of the Child' (2016) 28 *CFLQ* 67, 71. See also R Schuz, 'Policy Considerations in Determining the Habitual Residence of a Child and the Relevance of Context' (2001) 11 *Journal of Transnational Law and Policy* 101.

[118] See, for example, *Re R (A Child)* [2015] EWCA Civ 674.

[119] *Lancashire County Council v T & Others: Habitual Residence: Care Proceedings* [2014] EWHC 3321 (Fam).

[120] *Ibid* [60].

children based on their habitual residence, in cases such as this, is that the court is empowered to order the children's return to England, and that order can then be enforced using the mutual recognition provisions of the relevant PIL instrument.

Given the prevalence of cases of this nature, the Irish court asked the CJEU to clarify in *Child and Family Agency v D* the extent to which a need to discourage 'forum shopping' in a child protection context may form part of a best interests assessment when considering whether to request a transfer of jurisdiction pursuant to BIIa Art 15.[121] The CJEU held that a parent's reasons for exercising their freedom of movement prior to proceedings being issued should not form part of the best interests analysis, unless these considerations are such that there might be 'adverse repercussions on the situation of the child'.[122] Nonetheless, in practice, it seems that in cases of families fleeing care proceedings to Ireland, it is common for care proceedings to be issued in Ireland, and a request to be made by the Irish court to transfer those proceedings to England (a request which is often accepted, even when the child has remained in Ireland following the transfer).[123]

Honorati and Keyes consider that whilst the transfer of jurisdiction provisions under HC96 facilitates parents' party autonomy, the 'strict requirements' that must be satisfied to engage the transfer provisions restrict the extent to which parents can elect to litigate in a particular jurisdiction.[124] However, the particular factual issues which may arise in care cases, as outlined above, may mean that such 'strict requirements' of the transfer provisions are necessary. Where proceedings are initiated by the state to protect a child, upholding the autonomy of parents who seek to avoid this litigation (or who seek to litigate in a jurisdiction which is not informed of the background concerns about the children) may conflict with a child's interests. Parents may seek a transfer of jurisdiction to avoid a child protection jurisdiction in England and Wales which they view as 'less favourable' (e.g., at a general level, due to the practice of non-consensual adoption, or at a specific level because they have been involved in care proceedings previously). In turn, courts may defeat attempts to evade a child protection jurisdiction through the operation of the transfer provisions, where this is considered to be in a child's best interests.

It is important to note that where a court has jurisdiction in this context, notwithstanding a desire by parent/s for proceedings to take place elsewhere (or not at all), there are a variety of legal routes which can be used to secure the swift return of a child who is removed overseas to avoid care proceedings. As set out

[121] Case C-428/15 *Child and Family Agency v J. D* EU:C: 2016:819, [2017] Fam 248 [22].

[122] *Ibid* [67].

[123] *Re M (A Child) (Foreign Care Proceedings: Transfer)* [2013] EWHC 646 (Fam); [2013] Fam 308; *Re HJ (A Child) (Transfer of Proceedings)* [2013] EWHC 1867 (Fam); [2014] 1 FLR 430; Case C-428/15 *Child and Family Agency v J. D* EU:C:2016:819, [2017] Fam 248; *Re S (A Child) (Care Proceedings: Jurisdiction)* [2008] EWHC 3013 (Fam); [2009] 2 FLR 550 (where the child remained in Ireland following the transfer of jurisdiction); *A Local Authority v M (Care Proceedings: Adoption)* [2018] EWHC 2840 (Fam).

[124] C Honorati and M Keyes, 'Parental Responsibility, Custody and Access' in Paul Beaumont and Jayne Holliday (eds), *A Guide to Global Private International Law* (Hart, 2022) 471–472.

above, if a court considers that it has substantive jurisdiction, an order may be made for the child's return, which may then (depending on the country the child has been taken to) be enforced using the mutual recognition provisions of BIIa / HC96. In some cases, however, where parents remove a child from the jurisdiction of England and Wales shortly after care proceedings have been issued, the local authority may have acquired parental responsibility for the child through the making of an ICO.[125] This may open the door to a local authority pursuing the return of the child under the 1980 Hague Child Abduction Convention, as the removal is wrongful, and in breach of the local authority's rights of custody.[126] The availability of this particular remedy will depend on whether the child has been removed to another Contracting State to the 1980 Convention. Even if a local authority has not yet acquired parental responsibility for a child during care proceedings, but court proceedings have been issued, there is also the possibility of rights of custody being vested in the court, and a return might nonetheless be pursued (usually by a local authority) under the 1980 Hague Child Abduction Convention.[127]

The cases discussed above represent attempts by parents to move across borders tactically, avoid proceedings and challenge the jurisdiction of the forum they are avoiding. The aim of the parents in these cases is a substantive welfare outcome – to keep their children in their care and sometimes to avoid the possibility of adoption. A successful challenge to a court's jurisdiction may achieve this, without there being an extensive investigation into whether this is the child's best interests. On one view, parents in these cases are exercising their autonomy for issues to be litigated in a particular jurisdiction. Gössl and Lamont argue that parental intention should play a more significant role in a habitual residence enquiry, rather than being just one of the factors considered in the context of a broad factual analysis. Affording greater weight to parental intention would reflect 'the autonomy of the people involved (in the case of children exercised by their parents) (and) the intention of the parties to settle at a certain place', and thus provide 'personal legal certainty'.[128] However, it is noted by Gössl and Lamont that this will be applicable in cases where 'third and vulnerable parties' are not involved, and the persons involved are the only parties to the dispute.[129] Consistent with this observation, in the reported cases discussed in this chapter, courts in England and

[125] Children Act 1989 s 33 (3).

[126] For example, (Joined Cases C-325/18PPU and C-375/18PPU) *Hampshire County Council v CE (Child and Family Agency intervening)* EU:C:2018:739; [2019] 1 WLR 2091 where the local authority could have pursued return of the children from Ireland under the 1980 Hague Child Abduction Convention but opted to pursue the enforcement of an order for the children's return under BIIa instead.

[127] L Collins and J Harris (gen eds), Dicey, Morris and Collins, The Conflict of Laws (Sweet & Maxwell, 2022) 20–088; P Torremans (ed), *Cheshire, North & Fawcett, Private International Law* (OUP, 2017) 1138; *Re H (Child Abduction: Rights of Custody)* [2000] 2 A.C. 291 (HL).

[128] SL Gössl and R Lamont, 'Connecting Factors' in P Beaumont and J Holliday (eds*), A Guide to Global Private International Law* (Hart, 2022) 56, 58.

[129] *Ibid* 49.

Wales have not been receptive to the jurisdictional challenges brought by parents fleeing care proceedings, and a finding that a court does not have jurisdiction in this context may have a significant impact on a child's welfare.

Jurisdiction in Care Proceedings which do not Engage Brussels IIa and 1996 Hague Convention

Finally, it should be noted that children with links to countries which are not BIIa Member States or HC96 Contracting States may have a different experience of jurisdictional decisions. It has been held that the HC96 provides a jurisdictional basis for care proceedings concerning children with links to both Contracting and non-Contracting States, provided that the subject matter of the case falls within the scope of the Convention.[130] If, however, a child is found to be habitually resident in a non-Contracting State, there may only be jurisdiction in the proceedings under national law.[131]

However, it is not possible to transfer jurisdiction to a country in which BIIa or the HC96 is not in force. This raises the question as to how to deal with cases where children are present in England but have strong connections to non BIIa/HC96 states.

In some cases, courts have considered arguments about jurisdiction in care proceedings in this context by reference to *forum conveniens* principles (as laid down in *Spiliada Maritime Corporation v Consulex*) [1997] AC 46). *Forum conveniens* principles have been considered in the context of private law proceedings concerning children, where it has been argued that England and Wales is not a convenient forum and that proceedings should be stayed in favour of another country (being one where BIIa or the HC96 does not apply). It has been held that where the *Spiliada* principles relating to *forum conveniens* are applied in children's cases, their best interests are an important – but not paramount – consideration.[132] There are few reported decisions where *forum conveniens* is considered in the context of care proceedings.[133] However, it is notable that the place of a child's welfare in the context of a *forum conveniens* decision aligns broadly with the 'old' case law on BIIa Art 15 transfers discussed above – the child's best interests are an

[130] *Warrington Borough Council v W (Care Proceedings: Jurisdiction)* [2021] EWFC 68.

[131] Hague Conference on Private International Law, *Practical Handbook on the Operation of the 1996 Hague Child Protection Convention* (The Hague, 2014) 4.11; *Hackney London Borough Council v P* [2022] EWHC 1981 (Fam), *Warrington Borough Council v T* [2021] EWFC 68; Richard White et al (eds), *Clarke Hall & Morrison on Children* (Butterworths, 2022) [917.1].

[132] *Re S (Residence Order: Forum Conveniens)* [1995] 1 FLR 314; *Re D (Stay of Children Act Proceedings)* [2003] EWHC 565 (Fam) [2003], 2 FLR 1159; *Warrington Borough Council v W (Care Proceedings: Jurisdiction)* [2021] EWFC 68.

[133] But see *Re NAA (a child: findings on death of parents: convenient forum)* [2017] EWFC B76 and *Warrington Borough Council v W (Care Proceedings: Jurisdiction)* [2021] EWFC 68 for examples of care cases where the issue has been raised.

'indirect' consideration. This disparity in the approach to a child's best interests between children 'caught' by PIL instruments and those who are not represents another area of complexity – and potential unfairness – in the operation of care proceedings with an international dimension.

This disparity is also evident in cases where children are moved from England to non-Member or Contracting States to avoid local authority intervention or care proceedings. In contrast to, for example, cases involving Ireland outlined above, the extent to which courts can 'retrieve' children who are removed to avoid child protection intervention may be limited by the absence of a PIL instrument facilitating a transfer of jurisdiction (as well as the absence of a framework for the mutual recognition of court orders which might facilitate the enforcement of an order for a child's return to England). However, there are cases where English courts have chosen to exercise jurisdiction on exceptional or novel grounds, where children have been removed to non-Contracting States against a background of child protection concerns. Examples may be found in cases involving children moved to the self-declared 'Turkish Republic of Northern Cyprus' (hereafter 'TRNC').[134] EU law has been suspended in the TRNC, and the HC96 and 1980 Hague Child Abduction Convention do not apply there.[135] As such the TRNC may have been 'seen as a safe haven for parents and families to take their children to evade UK social services, or other UK legal action'.[136] In *Leicester City Council v Chhatbar & Another*, parents moved from England to the TRNC with their child, who was the subject of a child protection plan.[137] Mostyn J considered that the parents' motivation in moving to the TRNC was to evade child protection interventions in England, as the parents had no pre-existing connections to the region. He found that the child had not lost his habitual residence in England in the five days between his removal and the local authority issuing wardship proceedings. The jurisdictional position was less clear-cut in *K and D (Wardship Without Notice Return Order)* as the children had been present in the TRNC for around four years. Macdonald J considered possible jurisdictional grounds under BIIa but ultimately decided that it was appropriate for the English court to exercise jurisdiction in wardship on the basis of the children's British nationality and order the children's return in wardship.[138] *Local Authority B v X (Mother) and others* concerned a child

[134] The TRNC is a self-declared state not recognised by any other state apart from Turkey. The term TRNC is used here as this is the term used in court judgments discussing legal relationships with the region of Cyprus where the government of the Republic of Cyprus does not exercise effective control.

[135] Act concerning the conditions of accession of the Czech Republic, the Republic of Estonia, the Republic of Cyprus, the Republic of Latvia, the Republic of Lithuania, the Republic of Hungary, the Republic of Malta, the Republic of Poland, the Republic of Slovenia and the Slovak Republic and the adjustments to the Treaties on which the European Union is founded – Protocol No 10 on Cyprus [2003] OJ L236/0955; *Local Authority B v X (Mother) & Ors* [2020] EWFC 37 [9].

[136] *Local Authority B v X (Mother) & Ors* [2020] EWFC 37 [9]; *Leicester City Council v Chhatbar & Another* [2014] EWHC 830 (Fam).

[137] [2014] EWHC 830 (Fam).

[138] The *parens patriae* jurisdiction concerning children emanates from a common law principle that an infant who is a British national 'owes a duty of allegiance to the Sovereign and so is entitled to

who was born in the TRNC, his mother having travelled there whilst pregnant to avoid care proceedings in England.[139] The mother was involved in criminal activity in the TRNC and UK, and the child had been placed in institutional care in both the TRNC and the Republic of Cyprus. The mother and child were eventually deported (with the child) to the UK and the local authority issued care proceedings. Cobb J found that, 'unusually' at the time that the local authority issued care proceedings, the child was without a habitual residence and the English court therefore had substantive jurisdiction to make decisions about him pursuant to BIIa Art 13.

The cases involving families fleeing local authority involvement to the TRNC illustrate the novel ways in which English courts have found or exercised jurisdiction concerning children to defeat attempts by parents to evade investigations of abuse or neglect in England. In the same way as for the Irish cases described above, the aim of the parents in leaving England with their children for the TRNC was to avoid the jurisdiction of the English courts, with an awareness that the TRNC is a region where it would be difficult to secure a child's return. In *K and D (Wardship Without Notice Return Order)* and *Local Authority B v X (Mother)*, the authorities in the TRNC were unwilling to take measures to protect the children in question, and the blunt impact of a finding that the English court lacked jurisdiction in these cases would effectively be to leave the children in a situation where there was no court which would intervene to protect their welfare.[140] Thus whilst a child's best interests may not always be capable of being a direct consideration when a court is arriving at a decision as to whether it has jurisdiction (particularly in the context of a habitual residence inquiry for the purposes of BIIa / HC96), there is nonetheless a welfare imperative in cases where families move children across borders to avoid child protection interventions to establish and exercise jurisdiction – particularly where the consequence of failing to do so is to leave a child in a detrimental situation, under the competence of a forum which is unwilling to take further steps to promote their welfare.

protection' *Re P (GE) (An Infant)* [1965] Ch 568 [587]. There remains a dispute, unresolved by the competing obiter views of Lord Wilson, Lady Hale and Lord Toulson on the one hand, and Lord Sumption and Lord Clarke on the other in *Re B (A Child) (Reunite International Child Abduction Centre Intervening)* [2016] UKSC 4, [2016] AC 606 – as to whether the *parens patriae* jurisdiction is only to be exercised in exceptional situations. Irrespective of these competing views, it remains a national residual ground of jurisdiction which can be exercised in a child protection context where a British national is overseas. The dangers of overstepping the reach of the *parens patriae* jurisdiction are that a British court may make an exorbitant jurisdictional claim which would offend against the principle of comity, particularly where there is a competent forum in another country with which the child has a connection.

[139] [2020] EWFC 37.

[140] In *K and D (Wardship Without Notice Return Order)* one child was in a children's home in the TRNC and the other was in a children's home in the Republic of Cyprus – both states had indicated they would not take any further measures in respect of the children and wished to facilitate their return to the UK. Similarly in *Local Authority B v X (Mother)*, both the TRNC and the Republic of Cyprus indicated they would not take measures to protect the child (who had been placed in a children's home in the Republic of Cyprus during the course of the mother's deportation to the UK).

Conclusion: Jurisdiction and Welfare

This chapter has focused on the two principal forum decisions which may arise in care proceedings engaging internationally and regionally agreed PIL instruments – decisions to transfer jurisdiction to a better placed forum, and decisions about whether a court has substantive jurisdiction based on a child's habitual residence. Whilst both BIIa and the HC96 are built on a foundation of a commitment to the best interests of children generally, the extent to which an individual child's best interests are considered varies between these two categories of jurisdictional decision. Eekelaar considered that forum questions fell into an 'indirect best interests' category. The focus of the decision is on the forum question, with a child's best interests being considered only insofar as they relate to the determination of that question. It has been demonstrated here that the two categories of jurisdictional decision which are most likely to arise in care proceedings are polarised in their approach to the best interests of the child, although the substantive impact of these decisions from a child's point of view may be the same. A decision to transfer jurisdiction to a better placed forum under BIIa Art 15 was initially conceived through case law as being an 'indirect' best interests question with an 'attenuated' welfare enquiry. This approach has evolved through case law, and the short- and long-term impact on a child of a decision to transfer jurisdiction is now a separate issue which a judge must consider.

By contrast, a decision that a court has substantive jurisdiction based on a child's habitual residence draws upon a factual inquiry which does not consider a child's best interests, even in an indirect way. However, the consequences that flow from such a decision may be the same as for a decision to transfer jurisdiction – a child may move across borders to the forum where their future will be decided or may remain in England and Wales and face the range of potential outcomes of care proceedings including placement for adoption or long-term foster care.

The welfare impact of jurisdictional decisions is apparent in cases where parents seek to avoid the exercise of jurisdiction in care proceedings in relation to their children by moving to another country – either with their children, or whilst pregnant with a child but aware that a local authority may seek the child's removal under an interim care order when they are born. These cases have been referred to as a form of 'forum shopping' by parents.[141] In deciding whether an English court has jurisdiction in these cases, a child's best interests are neither a direct or indirect consideration. However, case law has identified creative ways in which courts can exercise jurisdiction in such cases (including in cases where children are removed to non-BIIa/HC96 states), where a failure to do so may compromise a

[141] Case C-428/15 *Child and Family Agency v J. D* EU:C: 2016:819, [2017] Fam 248 [22].

child's welfare. Where this is not possible, the Irish cases discussed in this chapter illustrate the way that substantive jurisdiction can be transferred back to the English courts where this is in a child's best interests, defeating attempts at 'forum shopping' by another means. However, for children with links to non-Contracting States, there is a further disparity – the lack of an easily available mechanism to ensure that proceedings concerning them take place in the best placed forum, coupled with an approach to welfare in this context which has not evolved in line with case law on BIIa Art 15 transfers of jurisdiction.

4

Practice and Permanence in Care Proceedings with an International Element

This chapter considers care proceedings practice more generally, identifying areas relevant to children with transnational links, and the intersection between international / regional PIL frameworks and domestic care proceedings.

In the life of a care case, if a court has substantive jurisdiction in relation to a child with international connections, it will then go on to consider the local authority's application for a care order supervision order.[1] This will entail a determination as to whether the 'threshold criteria' are met as the child has suffered, or is at risk of suffering significant harm, and the outcome to the proceedings which would meet the child's best interests.[2] Where a child has connections overseas, there may be relevant background information held by agencies in other countries. This might include previous court proceedings, social services records, criminal or medical evidence. Where the child has familial connections overseas, it may be necessary for assessments to be conducted to inform a decision about the child's permanent placement. This chapter outlines *domestic* care proceedings practice, drawing out those issues of particular significance to children with transnational links. The discussion centres around the concept of permanence, as achieving permanence for children with a placement decision which is in their best interests is the aim of care proceedings in England.

Permanence

The concept of permanence – the long-term plan for a child's upbringing – is integral to the policy surrounding the practice of care proceedings in England.[3]

[1] CA 89 s 31.

[2] CA 89 s 31 (2).

[3] J Wade et al, *Investigating Special Guardianship: Experiences, Challenges and Outcomes* (Department for Education, 2014); J Dickens, Chris Beckett and Sue Bailey, 'Justice, Speed and Thoroughness in Child Protection Court Proceedings: Messages from England' (2014) 46 *Children and Youth Services Review* 103.

Dickens *et al* describe its rise to prominence in both the US and the UK against a background of concern about 'drift' across the care system, and psychological research which highlighted the harm that children can suffer if decisive action is not taken to protect abused or neglected children.[4] Permanence therefore speaks to children having a sense and experience of stability – it has an emotional and physical dimension – and achieving permanence is an 'underpinning framework for all social work with children and families'.[5] From a policy perspective, there has been a focus on *legal permanence* – the form of order which secures any permanent placement, and the way such an order affords parental responsibility to a carer and impacts on the parental responsibility of a parent.[6] The requirement to consider pathways to permanence is embodied in legislation in England and Wales. For example, local authorities must consider how they will achieve permanence for children from the day they become 'looked after' by them.[7] Care Plans must also contain permanence plans for a child's long-term care.[8]

What permanence looks like in practice will differ depending on what is appropriate for the child. It is also impacted by factors which are difficult to plan for – a lack of suitable placements or changes in court practice, placement breakdown or multiple changes of placement for some looked after children.[9] For many children, permanence is achieved by returning to or remaining with their birth families. A local authority is subject to a statutory duty to promote the upbringing of children in need with their families.[10] Furthermore, local authorities must plan for looked after children to live with a parent or person with parental responsibility unless this is impractical or inconsistent with their welfare.[11] However, for some children, permanence is achieved through a kinship placement with family or friends or an adoptive placement. It is also important to note that some

[4] Dickens et al (*ibid*); citing J Rowe and L Lambert, *Children Who Wait: A Study of Children Needing Substitute Families* (Association of British Adoption Agencies, 1973).

[5] Department for Education, 'The Children Act 1989 Guidance and Regulations. Volume 2: Care Planning, Placement and Case Review, July 2021' (DfE, 2015) 2.3.

[6] J Boddy, 'Understanding Permanence for Looked after Children: A Review of Research for the Care Inquiry' (2013) *University of Sussex. School of Education and Social Work*, suggests a disproportionate policy focus on legal permanence at the expense of examining the quality of the relationships that children form, noting that legal permanence is not appropriate for all children.

[7] CA 89 s 22 – a looked after child is a child who is in local authority care, or who is provided with accommodation by a local authority.

[8] CA 89 1989 s 31 (3B).

[9] J Masson et al, *Child Protection in Court: Outcomes for Children* (School of Law, University of Bristol and the Centre for Research on Children and Families, University of East Anglia, 2019)166; G Schofield et al, 'The Search for Stability and Permanence: Modelling the Pathways of Long-Stay Looked After Children' (2005) 37 *British Journal of Social Work* 619.

[10] CA 89 s 17; Department for Education, 'The Children Act 1989 Guidance and Regulations. Volume 2: Care Planning, Placement and Case Review, July 2021' (DfE, 2015) 2.4.

[11] CA 89 s 22C. For a discussion of the rehabilitation of looked after children to their parents in England compared to other jurisdictions see J Thoburn, 'Reunification of children in out-of-home care to birth parents or relatives: A synthesis of the evidence on processes, practice and outcomes' (2009) *Deutsches Jugendinstitut*; J Boddy et al, 'Beyond Contact? Policy approaches to work with families of looked after children in four European countries' (2014) 28 *Children & Society* 152.

children find permanence within the care system e.g., in a long-term foster care placement.[12]

Whilst the approach in England to forms of legal permanence may have evolved in recent years (as discussed further below), the emphasis on achieving permanence for children at the end of care proceedings has remained a policy priority. More recently, reforms have sought to avoid delay in care proceedings, and the current policy aim in care proceedings is to achieve a permanent placement for a child at the end of proceedings which will not exceed 26 weeks.[13]

Overall, a placement decision made at the end of care proceedings is intended to be permanent. Once proceedings have concluded, the onus falls on a parent to establish that it would be in a child's best interest to change that placement and for a child to return to their care, and displacing the form of legal permanence made at the end of care proceedings is likely to require a court application. Some forms of legal permanence are easier to reverse than others. For example, when a child is placed for adoption, there are significant hurdles for a parent to challenge that decision. An application for the revocation of a placement order (which authorises a local authority to place a child with prospective adopters) requires the court's leave, and the parent to establish a change of circumstances.[14] Leave is also required to oppose the making of an adoption order.[15] There have been cases where adoption orders have been revoked under the inherent jurisdiction of the High Court, but this is rare, and only possible in 'highly exceptional and very particular circumstances'.[16] Where a child is in long-term foster care, a parent will have to apply to discharge the care order and a court will need to be satisfied that this is in the child's best interests, encompassing an evaluation of risk and harm.[17] A kinship placement is usually intended to be permanent, particularly a special guardianship placement.[18] Any application by a parent to resume the care of their child who is placed in kinship care is likely to be heard in the context of private law proceedings (assuming that the kinship placement has not broken down, which may result in further care proceedings). In all cases, one of the matters which a court will consider in evaluating whether returning to parental care is in a child's best interests is the impact on the child of a change of circumstances.[19] Overall, therefore, once care proceedings conclude with a child's placement away from the care of their parents, any potential resumption of care by the parents is generally subject to a judicial procedure which scrutinises whether this would be in

[12] E.g., B Larsson et al, 'Planning and Supporting Permanence in Long-Term Foster Care' (2021) *Nuffield Foundation*.

[13] Children and Families Act 2014 s 14.

[14] Adoption and Children Act 2002 s 24.

[15] *Ibid* s 47 (5).

[16] *HX v A Local Authority* [2020] EWHC 1287 (Fam) [38].

[17] CA 89 s 39; *Re TT (Children)* [2021] EWCA Civ 742.

[18] Department of Health, *Adoption: A New Approach* (White Paper Cm 5017, 2009) 5.8.

[19] CA 89 s 1 (1) (3).

the child's best interests, having regard to all the circumstances that subsist at that time.

The approach to permanence in England may stand at odds to that taken in other jurisdictions.[20] Many jurisdictions focus state responses to child maltreatment on supporting parents to resume the care of their children. Keddell's study of a child protection agency in Aotearoa/New Zealand, for example, examined the ways that social workers constructed collaborative relationships with parents, at the same time maintaining an awareness of potential risks to a child in returning home. The children in Kendell's case studies had been placed away from the care of their parents for several years.[21] As illustrated by Boddy and others, in countries with a child-protection focused system (such as England), once a child has been kept safe (for example by becoming 'looked after), 'pressure on social services teams is relieved and work with parents and families can cease to be a priority'.[22]

At an international and regional level, there is also an emphasis on the importance of children being rehabilitated to the care of their parents. The UN Guidelines for the Alternative Care of Children require that states regularly review decisions to remove children from the care of their parents and children should be returned 'once the original causes of removal have been resolved or have disappeared.'[23] The European Court of Human Rights (ECtHR) has emphasised that care orders must be temporary measures, and that state parties to the European Convention on Human Rights are subject to a positive duty to reunite a child with their parents as soon as the circumstances permit.[24] Adoption precludes the possibility of reunification and as such must only be considered in exceptional circumstances, where the overriding best interests of the child require that they be adopted.[25] However, the case of *Strand Lobben v Norway* is an illustrative example of the ECtHR's approach, and an emerging discourse from the court on the issue of permanence. The case concerned the proposed adoption of a three-year-old boy by his foster carers. The child had not lived with his mother since he was a small baby, having been removed from her care under a care order made by the relevant County Social Welfare Board in Norway. The mother challenged the proposed adoption

[20] J Wade et al, *Investigating Special Guardianship: Experiences, Challenges and Outcomes* (Department for Education, 2014); J Dickens et al, 'Justice, Speed and Thoroughness in Child Protection Court Proceedings: Messages from England' (2014) *Children and Youth Services Review* 17; M Skivenes and J Thoburn, 'Pathways to Permanence in England and Norway: A Critical Analysis of Documents and Data' (2016) 67 *Children and Youth Services Review* 152; J Thoburn, 'Reunification of children in out-of-home care to birth parents or relatives: A synthesis of the evidence on processes, practice and outcomes' (2009) *Deutsches Jugendinstitut.*

[21] E Keddell, 'Going home: Managing 'risk' through relationship in returning children from foster care to their families of origin' (2011) 11 *Qualitative Social Work* 604.

[22] J Boddy et al, 'Beyond Contact? Policy approaches to work with families of looked after children in four European countries' (2014) 28 *Children & Society* 152, 159.

[23] UN General Assembly, 'Guidelines for the Alternative Care of Children' 24 February 2010 A/Res/64/142 [14].

[24] *Olsson v Sweden (no. 2)* (Appn no 13441/87) (ECtHR, 27 November 1992); *Strand Lobben v Norway* (Appn no 37283/13) (ECtHR, 10 September 2019), para 208.

[25] E.g., *Johansen v Norway* (Appn no 17383/90) (ECtHR, 7 August 1996) para 78.

through the Norwegian courts but was unsuccessful. She alleged a violation of Article 8 of the ECHR on behalf of herself and her son. The Fifth Section of the ECtHR considered the impact on the child of being removed from a placement he had lived in for a long time. The court noted that

> When a considerable period of time has passed since the child was originally taken into public care, the interest of a child not to have his or her *de facto* family situation changed again may override the interests of the parents to have their family reunited.[26]

McEwan-Strand and Skivenes note the split in the judgments of the Fifth Section, with the majority of four taking an approach which elevated a child's best interests and the concept of permanence above the interests of their parents, and the minority of three focusing on the impact of severing biological links between a parent and a child through adoption.[27] The approach taken by the majority in the Fifth Chamber aligns more easily with the approach to permanence in England. However, when the case reached the Grand Chamber of the ECtHR, the court found an Article 8 violation on a procedural basis – namely that the Norwegian courts had not received up to date evidence of the change in the mother's circumstance before refusing her challenge to her son's adoption.[28] Notably, the Grand Chamber affirmed the approach to reunification taken by the ECtHR previously, in particular stating that the 'positive duty to take measures to facilitate family reunification as soon as reasonably feasible will begin to weigh on the competent authorities with progressively increasing force as from the commencement of the period of care, subject always to its being balanced against the duty to consider the best interests of the child'.[29] Despite this, Breen and others note that the Fifth Chamber's approach in Strand Lobben, together with a similar approach to permanence in *S. S v Slovenia*,[30] signify a recognition that a child's best interests may be served by a permanent placement with their 'de facto family' (including a foster placement), even where there is still a prospect of reunification of the child with their parents.[31]

Establishing permanence for children with international links may feed into the diversity of approaches to the issue taken in different jurisdictions, and at a transnational level by the European Court of Human Rights. Put against this background, it is perhaps inevitable that adoption as a form of legal permanence for children with international links became a controversial practice, as discussed above in relation to the issue of jurisdiction. As case law surrounding jurisdiction

[26] *Strand Lobben v Norway* (Appn no 37283/13) (ECtHR, 30 November 2017), para 104.

[27] A McEwan-Strand and M Skivenes, 'A Child-Centred Court of Human Rights? Strand Lobben v Norway (30 Nov. 2017)' (Strasbourg Observers, 3 January 2018) https://strasbourgobservers.com/2018/01/03/a-child-centred-court-of-human-rights-strand-lobben-v-norway-30-nov-2017.

[28] *Strand Lobben v Norway* (Appn no 37283/13) (ECtHR, 10 September 2019).

[29] *Ibid* para 208.

[30] (Application no. 40938/16) (ECtHR, 30 October 2018).

[31] C Breen et al, 'Family Life for Children in State Care, An Analysis of the European Court of Human Rights' Reasoning on Adoption Without Consent' (2020) 1 *International Journal of Children's Rights* 1, 24.

in care proceedings with an international element has developed, courts have also paid closer attention to facilitating placements with kin overseas through mechanisms of cross-border co-operation. On one view, a placement of a child with kin in their country of origin can be seen as promoting a child's heritage, cultural identity, language and nationality – providing for a child all the things that an adoptive placement in the UK may not be able to offer. Furthermore, Daly has argued that kinship care may provide 'continuity in a child's upbringing' – an important factor for States to consider in providing alternative care for children pursuant to UNCRC Art 20.[32] It is arguable that international kinship care placements may also meet this obligation, as well as preserving a child's 'ethnic, religious, cultural and linguistic background'.[33] The exploration of international kinship care placements in care proceedings has emerged alongside changing approaches to legal permanence in England generally, which have seen a greater emphasis on kinship placements as opposed to adoption.

Changing Approaches to Permanence – Policy, Practice and Reforms

As outlined by Masson *et al*, there has been a disparity between the view taken of adoption by policy makers and by the courts in recent years.[34] There have been extensive efforts by the government to ensure that children for whom adoption is appropriate are placed for adoption without delay.[35] By contrast, courts expressed concerns that adoption was being recommended for children without an appropriate evidential basis and exploration of other permanence options.

Two judgments are particularly significant. In 2013, the Supreme Court, in the case of *Re B*, said that children should only be placed for adoption in 'exceptional circumstances and where motivated by *overriding requirements* pertaining to the child's welfare, in short, where nothing else will do.'[36] A few months later in *Re B-S (Children)*, the Court of Appeal re-stated this principle, and endorsed a previous judgment referring to the need for a 'global, holistic evaluation' of the potential permanence options for the child, before deciding which one meets the child's welfare interests.[37] Munby P emphasised the need for 'proper evidence both from the local authority and from the guardian (which addresses) *all* the options which

[32] A Daly, 'Submission to the UN Committee on the Rights of the Child for the Day of General Discussion: "Children's Rights and Alternative Care"' (September 2021).

[33] UNCRC Art 20 (3).

[34] J Masson et al, *Child Protection in Court: Outcomes for Children* (School of Law, University of Bristol and the Centre for Research on Children and Families, University of East Anglia, 2019) 15–18.

[35] *Ibid* 15–16; Explanatory Notes to the Children and Families Act 2014, para 8.

[36] *Re B (A Child) (Care Proceedings: Threshold Criteria)* [2013] UKSC 33; [2013] 1 WLR 191 [198] (Lady Hale).

[37] *Re B-S (Children) (Adoption: Leave to Oppose)* [2013] EWCA Civ 1146; [2014] 1 WLR 563 [44] (Munby P) quoting *Re G (A Child)* [2013] EWCA Civ 965 [49–50] (McFarlane LJ).

are realistically possible and must contain an analysis of the arguments for and against each option', deriding 'sloppy practice' by local authorities in this regard.[38]

Subsequent judgments have sought to clarify that *Re B* and *Re B-S* were intended to be restatements of the law, and not to discourage local authorities from recommending adoption where appropriate.[39] However, it is clear that *Re B* and *Re-B-S* significantly influenced practice in a number of ways, and were, as Masson describes, 'disruptive judgments' which forced through a change in the way care proceedings operate.[40] Masson *et al* found that fewer placement orders were made after the judgments, although the impact of *Re B-S* in this regard could not be isolated from the general procedural reforms though the Public Law Outline.[41] But local authority lawyers and social work managers, as well as Cafcass guardians and judges, have perceived a shift in emphasis away from adoption and towards kinship placements.[42] As a result there has been a change in practice: a greater need to justify a care plan for adoption, more extensive justification for not recommending a family placement as well as more assessments of kin.[43]

More specifically, there has been an increase in the use of special guardianship for children to live with relatives. Both Masson *et al* and Harwin *et al* have found a rise in the number of children placed under a Special Guardianship Order (SGO) at the conclusion of care proceedings, corresponding to a decline in the number of placement orders (approving adoption plans) made over the same period.[44] Special guardianship was introduced as a form of permanence for children, for whom adoption was not considered appropriate, for example as they were already living with wider family or in foster care, were older or where the child was from a culture where adoption would not be an option.[45] However, in 2015, the government initiated a review on the use of special guardianship. There was a concern that this form of legal permanence was being used far more frequently than was envisaged, for young children or babies (the subtext being that adoption may be a more

[38] Re B-S (Children) (Adoption Order) (ibid) [34], [48] (Munby P).

[39] *Re R (A Child) (Adoption: Judicial Approach)* [2014] EWCA Civ 1625; [2015] 1 WLR 3273; *Re M-H (A Child) (Placement Order)* [2014] EWCA Civ 1396; Masson *et al* consider that the judgments and the manner in which they were handed down and distributed indicate an intention to effect a 'more restrictive approach to adoption' (J Masson et al, *Child Protection in Court: Outcomes for Children* (School of Law, University of Bristol and the Centre for Research on Children and Families, University of East Anglia, 2019) 17).

[40] J Masson, 'Disruptive Judgments' (2017) 29 Child and Family Law Quarterly 401.

[41] J Masson et al, *Child Protection in Court: Outcomes for Children* (School of Law, University of Bristol and the Centre for Research on Children and Families, University of East Anglia, 2019) 31.

[42] *Ibid* 113–114.

[43] *Ibid* 143.

[44] J Masson et al, *Child Protection in Court: Outcomes for Children* (School of Law, University of Bristol and the Centre for Research on Children and Families, University of East Anglia, 2019) 140; J Harwin et al, 'A National Study of the Usage of Supervision Orders and Special Guardianship over Time (2007–2016)' (2015) *Nuffield Foundation* 4.

[45] J Wade et al, *Investigating Special Guardianship: Experiences, Challenges and Outcomes* (Department for Education, 2014) 18; Department of Health, *Adoption: A New Approach* (White Paper, Cm 5017, 2009) 5.8.

suitable permanence option for these children).[46] There was also a concern about the quality of assessments and the suitability of placements (discussed further below). The government review of special guardianship resulted in an amendment to the Special Guardianship Regulations 2005, which placed greater emphasis on assessing a special guardian's relationship with a child, ability to care for them permanently and the child's needs, noting that children who have suffered abuse and neglect are likely to require extra support in any permanent placement.[47]

These changes have taken place against a background of reforms to care proceedings generally. The Family Justice Review in 2011 found that care proceedings were the subject of unacceptable delays, which had a potentially detrimental impact on children's welfare and opportunities for permanence through adoption.[48] Reforms have sought to ease the pressure that these cases place on the family justice system and minimise delay, namely through the Public Law Outline and the Children and Families Act 2014.[49] There has been a focus on diverting cases from proceedings by various means, including through pre-proceedings work with families.[50] Another aspect of the reforms has been a 26-week time limit for the resolution of proceedings.[51] This time limit may be extended where this is necessary to resolve proceedings justly, and guidance has confirmed that cases with an international element may require extensions.[52] However, the 26-week time limit places a further pressure on local authorities to complete assessments of kin within court timescales.[53]

The evolving practice environment and changing approaches to permanence in care proceedings *generally* has implications for practice in care proceedings with an international element. A concern to ensure that adoption (particularly non-consensual adoption of looked after children) is a 'last resort' has become embedded in care proceedings practice. As discussed in chapter 3, the adoption of children with international connections or foreign nationality has been the subject of wider scrutiny. Balanced against this is a local authority's statutory obligation to

[46] S Bowyer et al, *Impact of the Family Justice Reforms on Front-line Practice Phase Two: Special Guardianship Orders* (Department for Education, 2015); Explanatory Memorandum to the Special Guardianship (Amendment) Regulations 2016 No 111.

[47] Special Guardianship (Amendment) Regulations 2016 SI 2016/111; S Bowyer et al, *Impact of the Family Justice Reforms on Front-line Practice Phase Two: Special Guardianship Orders* (Department for Education, 2015).

[48] Family Justice Review Panel, 'Family Justice Review: Final Report' (Ministry of Justice and Welsh Government, 2011) 13–14.

[49] FPR 2010 Practice Direction 12A.

[50] *Ibid*, J Masson et al, 'Partnership by Law: The Pre-Proceedings Process for Families on the Edge of Care Proceedings.' (2013) School of Law, University of Bristol and the Centre for Research on Children and Families, University of East Anglia.

[51] Children and Families Act 2014 s 14 (2).

[52] Children and Families Act 2014 s 14 (5); *Re S (A Child)* [2014] EWCC B44 (Fam); Family Justice Council Public Law Working Group, 'Recommendations to Achieve Best Practice in the Child Protection and Family Justice Systems: Special Guardianship Orders' (FJC, 2020) Annex A [6].

[53] J Dickens, C Beckett and S Bailey, 'Justice, Speed and Thoroughness in Child Protection Court Proceedings: Messages from England' (2014) 46 *Children and Youth Services Review* 103, 109.

promote the upbringing of children by their families, including kin who may live overseas.[54] Special guardianship placements overseas do not appear to have been within the government's contemplation when SGOs were devised.[55] But freedom of movement within the EU undoubtedly means that children who are the subject of care proceedings may have significant familial links to other countries.[56] Such links must be explored in the same way as they would be for a child who only has family in England.

In the following sections, closer attention is paid to the way that overseas kinship placements fit within domestic practice in care proceedings.

Kinship Care: Inadequate Assessments and Untested Placements

As care proceedings have been time limited to 26 weeks, and there has been an increase in the use of special guardianship as a permanence option for children, concerns have been raised about vulnerable children moving to 'risky' or untested placements with kin, based on incomplete or inadequate assessments.[57]

There have been a number of tragic cases where children have died, or have been abused, whilst in the care of special guardians; Serious Case Reviews have identified failings in the assessment process or criticised decisions to place children with carers with whom they had no pre-existing relationship.[58] Masson *et al* and Harwin *et al* found in their respective studies that a third of special guardianship placements were 'untested', meaning that the child was not living with the carer at the time the SGO was made.[59] This was not the intention behind SGOs, which were devised to provide permanence for children with existing relationships

[54] CA 89 s 17 (1).

[55] However, the relevant White Paper did refer to its potential use by relatives who would not wish to adopt for religious or cultural reasons, or for unaccompanied asylum-seeking children who may have strong familial connections overseas (Department of Health, *Adoption: A New Approach* (White Paper Cm 5017, 2009) 5.8).

[56] R Lamont and C Fenton-Glynn, 'Cross-Border Public Care and Adoption Proceedings in the European Union' (2016) 38 *Journal of Social Welfare and Family Law* 94; *Re E (A Child) (Care Proceedings: European Dimension)* [2014] EWHC 6 (Fam); [2014] 1 WLR 2670.

[57] Department for Education, 'Special Guardianship Review: Report on Findings Government Consultation Response' (DfE, 2015) 5–6.

[58] H Cleaver and W Rose, *Safeguarding children living with foster carers, adopters and special guardians: learning from case reviews 2007–2019* (Coram/Baaf, 2020); R Wate, 'Serious Case Review Shi-Anne Downer (Birth Name) AKA Keegan Downer' (Birmingham Safeguarding Children Board 2017) BSCB 2015-16/2; K Harrington, 'Child A and Child B: A Serious Case Review' (Oxfordshire Safeguarding Children Board 2017); D Byford, 'Serious Case Review Overview Report: Megan' (Gloucestershire Safeguarding Children Board 2020) 0215.

[59] J Harwin et al, 'A National Study of the Usage of Supervision Orders and Special Guardianship over Time (2007–2016)' (2015) *Nuffield Foundation*, 146; Judith Masson et al, *Child Protection in Court: Outcomes for Children* (School of Law, University of Bristol and the Centre for Research on Children and Families, University of East Anglia, 2019) 147.

with their prospective special guardians.[60] Harwin *et al* identified a practice of SGOs being accompanied by supervision orders (which require local authorities to 'advise, assist and befriend' a child for a period of at least one (and up to three) years). This occurred in cases where there were 'untested placements, or the special guardians were not known to the child, and pressure to complete the case in 26 weeks.'[61]

Arising from these concerns, in 2016, Keehan J circulated 'informal guidance' for judges suggesting that an SGO should not be made until a child has lived with a carer for an appreciable period.[62] This resulted in cases where children were placed under interim care orders and even final care orders to permit the testing of a placement. The Court of Appeal in *Re P-S (children)* rejected the concept of a 'short term care order' for the purposes of placement testing and called for authoritative guidance on SGOs based on empirical evidence. The resulting guidance issued by the Family Justice Council, informed by research and a consultation, confirmed the need for robust assessment of special guardians' parenting capacity, encompassing assessment of the relationship between the child and their prospective carer.[63] This assessment process should not be constrained by the 26-week time frame; in short, speed should not trump thoroughness when it comes to special guardianship assessments.[64] The guidance also emphasised the importance of relationship building between a child and special guardian, stating as follows:

> Where there is little or no prior connection/relationship between the child and the prospective SG, it is very likely to be in the child's best interests that the child is cared for on an interim basis by the prospective SG before any final consideration is given to the making of an SGO.[65]

Hunt's research on specialist social workers' experiences of kinship care identifies some of the deep-rooted complexities associated with establishing whether a placement with kin is in a child's best interests, and the ways that such placements can be properly supported.[66] Social workers were caught amid competing demands imposed by the court process and variations in 'thresholds of acceptability' for kinship care, both within local authorities and between courts.[67] Hunt's study also identified 'intrinsic and unique' challenges associated with assessing prospective kinship carers, in that a prospective carer will often need to be taken

[60] J Wade et al, Investigating Special Guardianship: Experiences, Challenges and Outcomes (Department for Education, 2014) 42; J Harwin et al (ibid) 147.

[61] J Harwin et al (*ibid*) 88.

[62] *Re P-S (Children) (Care Proceedings: Special Guardianship Orders) (Association of Lawyers for Children Intervening)* [2018] EWCA Civ 1407; [2018] 4 WLR 99 [42]–[55] Ryder LJ.

[63] Family Justice Council Public Law Working Group, 'Recommendations to Achieve Best Practice in the Child Protection and Family Justice Systems: Special Guardianship Orders' (FJC, 2020).

[64] *Ibid* 64.

[65] *Ibid* 33.

[66] J Hunt, 'Practising Kinship Care: The Perspectives of Specialist Social Workers' (2021) Cardiff University.

[67] *Ibid* 114.

on a 'reflective journey' in the assessment process, to understand a local authority's concerns about a child, appreciate their experiences and the magnitude of the task which may lie ahead in caring for them throughout their minority.[68] Navigating these challenges, alongside complying with the regulations and expectations of the English courts around kinship care placements, may be particularly challenging where a prospective kinship carer lives overseas.

Conclusion

In this study, the issue of permanence for children is analysed by reference to the legal frameworks available for children to live overseas with kin, and how those frameworks are used in practice. Rather than focusing on outcomes for children, the focus is on the operation of cases, bringing out the decisions and choices that are made in cases with an international dimension, and the impact of those decisions for the children involved. As will be explored in chapter 7 and chapter 8 of this thesis, the operation of BIIa/HC96 in the context of securing permanence for children to live overseas raises significant issues of complexity for professionals involved in the cases, who struggle to navigate domestic criteria for kinship assessments and the challenges associated with cross-border situations.

[68] *Ibid.*

5

Findings on the Operation of Jurisdictional Rules in BIIa/HC96 in Care Proceedings

Introduction

In the life of care proceedings, the first engagement with an internationally or regionally agreed private international law (PIL) framework will likely be in the context of considering whether the court has jurisdiction in relation to a child with international connections. This chapter presents the findings of the empirical study which forms the basis of the book insofar as they relate to the operation of the jurisdictional rules in BIIa/HC96 and their translation into domestic care proceedings through case law and guidance. In doing so it examines how jurisdictional issues are framed by national actors, and how their determination impacts on a child's welfare or distorts the approach to a child's best interests. In contrast to later chapters, which discuss gathering background information on a child, and planning for a child's future placement, the discussion in this chapter centres around experiences which are unique to children with international connections; a child who only has domestic connections will not be the subject of a jurisdictional argument or determination.

This chapter does not address separately the operation of the jurisdictional rules in BIIa/HC96 in relation to children with connections to non-Contracting States. Overall, the jurisdictional scheme operates in the same way, although the implications of a finding that the court lacks jurisdiction in relation to a child with links to a non-Contracting State are perhaps different, and, as discussed in chapter 3, there is no ability under either instrument to transfer jurisdiction to a non-Contracting State.

'Framing' a Case as Having an International Element

The development of case law in relation to care proceedings with an international element directed attention to the legitimacy of the court's power in relation to children with international connections, particularly foreign nationals.[1] An integral part of this was an examination of jurisdiction in care proceedings, raising the question of whether a court is empowered to make substantive decisions about a child, and, even if it is, whether it should relinquish this power in favour of a foreign court through a transfer of jurisdiction.[2]

The Public Law Outline 2014 (PLO 2014), and the standardised documents which support its operation, encourage early framing of care proceedings as having an international dimension, in order that the court can identify and consider any jurisdictional issues at the outset of proceedings. The PLO 2014 states that, within one day of proceedings being issued, the court must consider jurisdiction 'in a case with an international element'.[3] Foregrounding jurisdictional issues in this way aims to ensure that they are addressed, rather than being overlooked or considered at a very late stage in proceedings.[4] However, it is notable that the focus of the international frame is the court's jurisdiction rather than other international aspects of the case which could also be considered at an early stage (e.g. gathering relevant child protection information from overseas– see chapter 5). The PLO 2014 goes on to state that where there is an issue as to jurisdiction, an urgent case management hearing will be required to consider 'whether there is, or should be, a request to a Central Authority or other competent authority in a foreign state or consular authority in England and Wales …'.[5] In this way, guidance requires that jurisdictional issues be considered through liaison with overseas state bodies. Furthermore, it places responsibility for framing and identifying these issues on the local authority and the court.

In the sample of 100 cases analysed, the procedure for the early identification of jurisdictional issues was led by templates and precedents. A local authority filed with the court its application in form C110A, and the required supporting documents, including an initial statement from the allocated social worker (known as a 'SWET') and an interim care plan. Within a day or so of proceedings being issued, the court would make Allocation Directions dealing with standard matters – appointing a solicitor for the child, allocating the case to a particular level of judge, directions for the filing of documents and the listing of the first

[1] For cases where overseas state authorities intervened, made submissions or sought leave to intervene in care proceedings, see *Re B (Children)* [2012] EWCA Civ 1940; *Re T (A Child) (Care Proceedings: Request to Assume Jurisdiction)* [2013] EWCA Civ 895; [2014] Fam 130; *Re T (A Child) (Care Proceedings: Request to Assume Jurisdiction)* [2013] EWHC 521 (Fam) [2013] 2 WLR 1263; *Re MP (Fact-finding Hearing: Care Proceedings: Art15)* [2013] EWHC 2063 (Fam); [2014] 1 FLR 702; *Re E (A Child) (Care Proceedings: European Dimension)* [2014] EWHC 6 (Fam); [2014] 1 WLR 2670; *Re CK (Children) (Care Proceedings: Habitual Residence: Article 15)* [2015] EWHC 2666 (Fam); *Merton London Borough Council v B (Central Authority of the Republic of Latvia intervening)* [2015] EWCA Civ 888; [2016] Fam. 123; *Medway Council v JB*[2015] EWHC 3064 (Fam); [2016] 2 F.L.R. 1360.

[2] Re E (A Child) (Care Proceedings: European Dimension) [2014] EWHC 6 (Fam).

[3] FPR 2010 Practice Direction 12A.

[4] *Re E (A Child) (Care Proceedings: European Dimension)* [2014] EWHC 6 (Fam); [2014] 1 WLR 2670; *Leicester City Council v S* [2014] EWHC 1575 (Fam); [2014] CN 931.

[5] FPR 2010 PD 12 A.

Case Management Hearing (CMH). Allocation Directions – like all court orders in care proceedings under the PLO 2014 – follow a prescribed template issued by the President of the Family Division. The templates which were applicable at the time the analysis was undertaken required the local authority, when making an application for a care order, to identify (a) whether the case had an international element and (b) any potential jurisdictional issues under BIIa.[6] A standard paragraph on the template order for Allocation Directions – which could be deleted if not applicable – identified that there may be an issue as to jurisdiction and directed the local authority to liaise with overseas state authorities to obtain information relevant to this.

Although all the cases analysed had an international element, in 22% of valid cases (n=21) the local authority did not identify this in the documents filed at issue. It should be noted that in eight of these cases, the international element was not apparent at issue, as it arose purely from the child having a potential kinship carer overseas, who had not yet been identified for assessment. Furthermore, although the PLO 2014 requires a court to consider jurisdiction in all cases with an international element, in 52% of valid cases (n=39) the court did not consider jurisdiction at the allocation stage. There seemed to be no obvious link between a local authority identifying the case as having an international element in its application and the court considering jurisdiction at the allocation stage. The approach was more *ad hoc*. For example, in Case 2, which concerned a small baby, the local authority flagged in their application form that the parents' habitual residence was unclear, but at the allocation stage there was no reference to any jurisdictional issues, which were only actively considered when the parties appeared before the court at the first CMH. Similarly in Case 38, the local authority identified in its application that the children were probably habitually resident in a West African country and may have been trafficked. However, the Allocation Directions recorded that there were 'no issues of jurisdiction'. At the first CMH, the court directed the local authority to liaise with the relevant consulate on the issue of jurisdiction, and exercised jurisdiction based on the children's presence (BIIa Article 20).

Overall, placing responsibility on the local authority to frame a case as having an international element, and on the court to consider jurisdiction 'on the papers', did not take place as envisaged by the PLO 2014. There was also no practice evident in the cases analysed of courts specifically listing an early hearing to deal with jurisdiction. In all the cases sampled, the local authority was seeking an urgent interim order (n=95 interim care orders, n=4 interim supervision orders and n=1 case where the precise interim order could not be identified due to a lack of documentation). As such the first hearing was usually on the local authority's application for an interim order, with jurisdictional issues being considered at the same time – or sometimes later in proceedings. Guidance suggesting that there should

[6] The standard orders in the Study sample did not contain a reference to jurisdiction being established under the HC96. More recent precedents issued in 2021, following the end of the Brexit transition period, refer to both instruments.

be a discreet hearing on jurisdictional issues at the outset of proceedings does not appear to account for the fact that many care cases commence with some form of emergency intervention, requiring court approval, and there is limited availability of court time. More importantly, however, the data suggests that jurisdictional issues are not considered at the outset of proceedings in a consistent way, either by local authorities in their applications or by courts at the allocation stage. The discussion later in this chapter reveals the misidentification of jurisdictional issues in several cases. It is, therefore, unrealistic to expect that jurisdictional issues can be appropriately identified as part of an ex parte procedure at the outset of proceedings.[7]

Identifying and Exploring Jurisdictional Issues

In 19 of the cases analysed, a jurisdictional issue was explored in care proceedings. These included six cases where jurisdiction was contested and one where jurisdiction was resolved by consent. In 12 of the cases, jurisdiction was not actually a contested issue, but the court required further information to satisfy itself that it had jurisdiction.

There were cases where the court appeared anxious to investigate and establish jurisdiction even though children were clearly habitually resident in England, and no one was challenging jurisdiction. This may indicate an anxiety to 'comply' with guidance on the issue but with an incomplete understanding of the jurisdictional regimes in BIIa/HC96. The following case examples illustrate explorations of jurisdiction which were not grounded in law and served to add to the work of the local authority, and to complicate the case.

Case 40. This case concerned a baby who was born in the UK and who had not lived anywhere else. Her mother was British and lived in the UK. Her father was from a West African country and lived there.

Although the father's residence overseas had no impact on the court's jurisdiction, the court directed the local authority to file a statement which set out the jurisdictional basis for the care proceedings. The local authority's statement on jurisdiction also demonstrated confusion about jurisdictional rules – it said that as the West African country was not a BIIa/HC96 state, jurisdiction stemmed from the Family Law Act 1986.[8]

[7] *Re F (A Child) (Care Proceedings: Habitual Residence)* [2014] EWCA Civ 789 the Court of Appeal said that it was not appropriate for a court considering jurisdiction at the outset of care proceedings to make *ex parte* declarations of habitual residence without giving the other parties an opportunity to make submissions if they wished to. Provisional / interim declarations of jurisdiction are permissible.

[8] Although it has been held that whilst care proceedings (under Part IV CA 89) are not within the scope of the jurisdictional rules in the Family Law Act 1986 Part 1, and private law proceedings (Part II CA 89) are, there are strong policy reasons why the jurisdictional rules in the Act should apply

Case 95. At the first hearing in the care proceedings, the court was concerned that it did not have jurisdiction. Parties were required to consider the application of BIIa, and to liaise with several institutions about jurisdiction. The case concerned two children, one who was born in the UK and the other who was born in a HC96 Contracting State. However, the family had lived in the UK for two years before proceedings were issued and were clearly habitually resident in England. The court seemed to be concerned that the foreign nationality of the family would impact upon the court's jurisdiction. The order made at the first hearing was that there was a jurisdictional issue because of the parents and children's nationalities – the parents being citizens of the HC96 Contracting State, one of the children being a dual national and the other being born overseas.

There were other examples where court orders recorded a basis for the court's jurisdiction which did not correspond to the jurisdictional regime in BIIa/HC96:

- 'Parents' habitual residence' (1 case)
- 'Born in the UK, Parents British Ordinary Residence' (1 case)
- 'Child and Mother's Habitual Residence' (2 cases)
- 'Habitual residence and UK Citizenship' (2 cases)

Further, in the one case where BIIa Art 12 (prorogation of jurisdiction where a child is habitually resident in another BIIa Member State) was recorded as the basis for jurisdiction, the children were clearly habitually resident in England and Wales having lived in this country with their father for three years before proceedings were issued.[9]

Jurisdictional issues were also closely linked to ideas about comity and ensuring that overseas state authorities were aware of and involved with care proceedings concerning foreign nationals. In Case 88, the local authority was criticised by the court for failing to issue proceedings for seven months after the child (an EU national) was accommodated by a local authority, contrary to guidance in judgments about the use of CA89 s 20 in cases with an international element.[10]

to children involved in care proceedings in the same way (*Warrington Borough Council v W (Care Proceedings: Jurisdiction)* [2021] EWFC 68; *Re R (Care Orders: Jurisdiction)* [1995] 1 FLR 711).

[9] Court orders are usually drafted by the parties' legal representatives after a hearing, and incorrect recording of jurisdiction may therefore be attributable to lawyers rather than judges.

[10] E.g., *Nottingham City Council v LM and others* [2014] EWCA Civ 152; [2014] 2 FLR 1372; *Leicester City Council v S* [2014] EWHC 1575 (Fam); [2014] CN 931 which urge local authorities to issue proceedings promptly in cases with an international element where jurisdiction might be in issue. See also *Merton London Borough Council v B (Central Authority of the Republic of Latvia intervening)* [2015] EWCA Civ 888; [2016] Fam 123, the court stopped short of criticising the local authority in relation to the accommodation of the subject child under CA89 s 20. However, questions were raised over the use of s.20 in this case, as the child was accommodated for over a year before proceedings were

This apparent 'failure' to comply with judicial guidance may have led to the court taking a more fastidious approach to jurisdiction; listing a specific hearing to consider a transfer of jurisdiction under BIIa Art 15, even though no application for transfer was made. At the hearing, none of the parties pursued a transfer of jurisdiction – not least because the parents were unable to leave England due to their bail conditions, and so would not have been able to participate in any proceedings in the EU state in question if the transfer had taken place.

In a similar vein, in Case 87, a request from an overseas state authority to transfer jurisdiction was entertained by the court even though none of the parties wanted this:

> **Case 87.** A request for an assessment of a maternal aunt was sent via CFAB to their partner agency in an Eastern European State, which is also the Central Authority. Following the positive assessment, the overseas Central Authority said it sought a transfer of jurisdiction. When the application came to be determined, it was resisted by all the parties, including the parents. It was refused. The court would not have been empowered to transfer jurisdiction under Article 15 BIIa in these circumstances in any event, because at least one of the parties must consent to the transfer where a request comes from another Member State.

This case, and others discussed below, illustrate courts exploring jurisdictional issues at the behest of overseas state authorities rather than the parties to the care proceedings themselves (although in Case 21, below, the father raised a jurisdictional argument on the back of an intervention of the overseas court). This is consistent with the idea of jurisdictional issues being explored to establish the legitimacy of proceedings and to satisfy potential complaints by overseas state authorities. LA Lawyer 2 gave another example of a case involving an Eastern European state, where a child had lived in England for several years and her parents did not seek her return.

> There was no question of that child being placed back there – there was no one there who could care for her. It seemed obvious to me that she was habitually resident here, but the judge wanted to go through all the complicated processes before saying "yes she is habitually resident here". I do think the court can overcomplicate things sometimes although I do understand why it is done in that way. (L2)

Anxiety to prevent criticism by overseas state authorities was apparent in the qualitative interviews, where local authorities discussed jurisdiction alongside

issued, and during that time the mother requested the return of the child to her care to no avail. The Latvian government were critical of the local authority's actions in this case.

the issue of liaison with embassies. There was a sense that liaison was a necessary requirement to ensure the legitimacy of the local authority's intervention in relation to a family.

> I have a case with a chap that comes from Kabul … the chances of getting a response from (the Afghan embassy) are negligible but I will still do the request … at least I can say to the court that I have tried. And, if that jurisdiction at a later stage complains I can say, "well you knew about it". (L1)

> We had one case … just before we got a grip of jurisdiction cases and I think there was a care order … (the overseas state authority) intervened at the last minute and there was an appeal … nothing changed at the end of it, and I think there were faults on both sides. We thought "we need to make sure we get this right so that if anyone comes back to us, we can say we did contact you". (L1)

> Munby [Sir James Munby, the former President of the Family Division] was very clear that whilst we had to be sensitive to overseas jurisdictions ultimately if the child was here and according to Brussels II the case could be dealt with here, it was possible to place a child who wasn't a British national for adoption. But some countries are more proactive than others at leaping to the defence of their citizens. (L5)

There was a pattern in the cases analysed of transfer of jurisdiction being raised as an issue and propelled forward by overseas state authorities, following assessments of family members. In addition to Case 87 described above:

Case 2. Care proceedings concerned a baby born in the UK whose parents were nationals of an EU Member State. At the first hearing the parents agreed for proceedings to take place in England and did not want their baby to leave the country. However, the relevant overseas Central Authority sought a BIIa Article 15 transfer. They became aware of the care proceedings after receiving a request for an assessment of the child's maternal grandparents. Once the request was made by the overseas Central Authority, the parents then changed their position and supported a transfer of jurisdiction. Jurisdiction was transferred and the child moved to the interim care of the maternal grandparents.

Case 21. A court in an EU Member State sought a BIIa Art 15 transfer, but this time the application was triggered by a request by the paternal grandmother – who was not a party to the care proceedings in England but who sought to care for the child in her home country. The father then made a separate application to the English court for a transfer of jurisdiction. The application was determined at a contested hearing, at which representatives from the overseas Ministry of Justice attended. The court refused the transfer request. Following this, the relevant state applied for party status in the care proceedings. This application was again made by representatives of the relevant state and was unsuccessful. The case concluded with a kinship placement in England.

Whilst it is appropriate for the court's jurisdiction to be properly established, the data suggested that at times cases were overcomplicated through the exploration of jurisdictional issues. Courts and local authorities have sought to address a prior practice where jurisdiction was often overlooked, through considering jurisdictional issues scrupulously in collaboration with overseas state authorities. The danger with this approach is that a jurisdictional dispute becomes a spectacle, which marginalises the interests of the child.

Jurisdictional Arguments, Litigation Strategies, Decisions which Impact on Welfare

Jurisdictional arguments were used by parties in several cases to achieve a result which aligned with their interests in proceedings:

Case 47. The child had been living with both of her parents, however, the risk in the case related to the father. The mother wanted to separate from the father and return to her home country in East Asia with the child. She was able to achieve this result within a short timeframe – without undergoing extensive assessment – through a successful challenge to the court's substantive jurisdiction in the care proceedings.

Case 8. The parents had taken their children to EU State 1 after receiving notice from the local authority of an application for an interim care order, seeking the removal of their children into foster care. The local authority sought the children's return from EU State 1. In response, the parents challenged the court's jurisdiction, arguing the children had lost their habitual residence in England by the point when proceedings were issued, and, in the alternative, sought a Brussels IIa Article 15 transfer of jurisdiction to EU State 1. They were unsuccessful, but the purpose of deploying this litigation strategy was to keep the children beyond the reach of the English local authority. The parents went on to move the children again to EU State 2 after the child protection authorities in EU State 1 expressed concerns about the children (this case is discussed further in chapter 6 as an example of sharing child protection information under BIIa).

Local authority lawyers interviewed were conscious that a jurisdictional decision resulting in a child moving to another country brought about a particular result, namely that their local authority was no longer responsible for the child. LA Lawyer 6 commented that it might 'look' like this was a local authority's motivation in seeking a transfer of jurisdiction, but it was clear that she genuinely felt that it was often in a child's best interests for jurisdiction to be transferred to another country:

> It feels sometimes like you're trying to say, "send them back". But that's not the motivation for what you're doing. The motivation for what you're doing is the promotion of that child's welfare and promoting their UN Rights under Article 20 (L6)

LA Lawyer 1 was also conscious that a transfer of jurisdiction would result in a child no longer being the responsibility of her local authority:

> We had to do a bit of work about – you know how it all works – that you can't just send them back you have to meet the criteria. At the end of the day if we send them back, we are no longer paying for them so in a way it is a cost saving measure for us. Being in foster care for [the] long term is going to cost a lot more than sending the kid back. (L 1)

These quotes provide context for some of the litigation strategies deployed by local authorities in the cases studied:

Case 31. A family fled to an EU State to avoid care proceedings. There had been longstanding local authority involvement with the family and the younger children were exposed to a risk of grooming and child sexual exploitation. The allegations were very serious, and the family composition was such that the risk persisted after the family had moved to another country. When the children were located in the EU state, the local authority's position was that they sought their return to England and a collection order removing the children from their parent's care when they returned.

However, at a later hearing, the local authority changed its approach and applied for jurisdiction to be transferred to the overseas state pursuant to

BIIa Art 15. This request was supported by the Guardian and accepted by the court.

When the request was transmitted, the relevant overseas authority refused to accept the transfer of jurisdiction as it considered the case did not meet the threshold for child protection intervention. The local authority was then simply granted permission to withdraw their application and the proceedings in England came to an end, albeit on the basis that there was going to be some form of ongoing monitoring by the child protection agency in the overseas state.

The local authority's *volte-face* in Case 31 is difficult to understand given the seriousness of the allegations, and the fact that the overseas authorities did not consider that intervention was required. Furthermore, when the transfer of jurisdiction was refused, the local authority simply sought to withdraw the care proceedings rather than to pursue the protection of the children through an order for their return. The case raises questions about how far a local authority will go to protect a child at risk, taken overseas. There are often legal options to pursue the return of a child in these circumstances, but this pursuit will inevitably have a substantial cost.[11] In Case 8, for example, where the children were moved across borders twice to evade child protection interventions, the local authority ultimately did not seek to enforce the order for the children's return from EU State 2, and that case also ended with the local authority being granted permission to withdraw the proceedings.

The same occurred in Case 9, where a mother removed her child overseas to an EU State after care proceedings had concluded. The child had been made the subject of a care order, on the basis that they would live at home with the mother, but there were significant concerns, and the local authority was continuing to assess the mother's parenting capacity after proceedings concluded. The local authority was initially proactive in seeking the child's return from the EU state and issued proceedings under the 1980 Hague Child Abduction

[11] For example, if the local authority has parental responsibility for the children at the time of their removal it might pursue the children's return under the 1980 Hague Child Abduction Convention. Alternatively, the local authority might seek an order for a child's return and then seek the enforcement of that return order using a PIL instrument such as BIIa/HC96 (see, for example (Joined Cases C-325/18PPU and C-375/18PPU) *Hampshire County Council v CE (Child and Family Agency intervening)* EU:C:2018:739; [2019] 1 WLR 2091). Where a child has been removed to a non-Contracting State, securing their return may be more challenging – see *Local Authority B v X (Mother)* [2020] EWFC 37; [2020] 2 FLR 784.

Convention. However, after the mother continued to move the child between various countries, the local authority sought permission to withdraw proceedings on the basis that the relevant overseas state authorities would be responsible for the child.

These case examples, and perspectives from qualitative interviews, demonstrate that where there are competent authorities who can exercise a child protection function, the local authority has the option of relinquishing its protective functions in favour of another state. This might happen through a deliberate litigation strategy – a local authority might seek or support a transfer of jurisdiction to another state under a PIL instrument. It might also occur through happenstance, where parents evade the intervention of a local authority or court by moving children overseas and a local authority seeks to withdraw proceedings and leave the child protection authorities in that state to deal with the matter (e.g. in 'known flight' cases – see chapter 6).

The discussion above goes some way to illuminate the impact of jurisdictional decisions in care proceedings as foreshadowed in chapter 3 – a jurisdictional argument may bring about a particular result which meets a party's interests. In some instances, jurisdictional arguments can be deployed strategically to bring about a desired result. If a legal representative has enough knowledge to be able to advance these arguments, this provides them with added power in care proceedings. This will be particularly apparent where other parties' representatives are not familiar with jurisdictional issues. LA Lawyer 1 illustrated this power through her reflections on her practice. She was a 'repeat player' in care proceedings with an international element, and her expertise was such that other parties often agreed with her position – or their lawyers agreed even if their clients did not.[12]

> We always flag jurisdiction as an issue … At the CMH I would expect to do a position statement on jurisdiction. It might say, "oh actually this court has jurisdiction, we are best placed to hear it". Or it might be, "at the present time we are best placed to hear it but we will keep it under review" because of course you can transfer (jurisdiction) part way through proceedings which I think some Local Authorities miss … All the local practitioners who are regulars in these cases will be expecting that and half the time they don't bother doing position statements, they will just say, "what she says". Or "my client doesn't agree but this local authority is very experienced and we see the force of their argument". (L1)

As discussed in chapter 2, jurisdictional decisions can also have a significant impact on a child's welfare. LA Lawyer 7 spoke of a case where her local authority

[12] M Galanter, 'Why the "Haves" Come Out Ahead: Speculations on the Limits of Legal Change' (1974) 9 *Law and Society Review* 95; see also W Felstiner, R Abel, A Sarat 'The emergence and transformation of disputes: Naming, blaming, claiming …' (1980) 15 *Law and Society Review* 631.

had sought a transfer of jurisdiction but was concerned about the welfare impact of the transfer.[13]

> We asked the (EU State's) courts to accept jurisdiction which they did. But … when they accepted jurisdiction, we didn't like their care plan. But obviously at that point we couldn't … you know … she was a (EU State citizen) child, she was going back … we had no choice but to accept that was their decision to make. (L7)

LA Lawyer 7's comments highlight the paradox inherent in using a jurisdictional decision to bring about a substantive outcome for a child, specifically an overseas kinship placement. Children may be sent overseas into unknown placements, based on limited welfare evidence, or alternatively into situations which feel uncomfortable or troubling for professionals in this country. Despite this there was a visceral sense that it is the 'right thing to do' in many cases for another state to exercise jurisdiction, particularly in relation to a child with foreign nationality. LA lawyer 6 was conscious of this paradox but nevertheless felt that jurisdiction should be transferred to facilitate an overseas placement.

> My view is that if you are looking at moving a child abroad, you can't make a special guardianship order because there won't be an appreciable period necessary for making the order. So, what my approach in these circumstances would be is to simply transfer the proceedings … let (that state) deal with the finalisation of the final order. It would mean the right order, recognised over there, with the right support plan and the right services. If you have a very difficult situation where the placement falls apart … you may be in a very, very uncomfortable position whether the case then has to re-transfer and the children [have] to be moved internationally again. (L6)

A jurisdictional decision can result in a child moving to a different country, to an overseas family placement, without there being a welfare enquiry into whether this placement is in the child's best interests. The mother in Case 47, discussed above, successfully challenged jurisdiction and was able to secure the return of her child to her home country in her care, without the court considering whether this placement was in the child's best interests. Contrasting two cases with similar facts can illustrate the way that a welfare enquiry can be 'short circuited' by a jurisdictional decision.

Case 20. The child in this case was four years old when proceedings were issued, and usually lived with her mother, in England. Following extensive pre-proceedings involvement with the family which had not lessened

[13] This case pre-dated the Supreme Court's decision in *Re N (Children) (Adoption: Jurisdiction) (AIRE Centre and others intervening)* [2016] UKSC 15, [2017] AC 167 which decided that a court must consider the short- and long-term consequences for a child of transferring jurisdiction as part of the best interests inquiry under BIIa Art 15.

the concerns about the care of the child, the local authority issued care proceedings.

The child's paternal grandmother who lived in a European state wished to be assessed to look after her granddaughter. She was assessed though CFAB, but the assessment was brief. The paternal grandmother was then invited to the UK to undergo a further assessment by the social worker; the local authority funding her travel costs. During the assessment the PGM was able to spend time with her granddaughter. The social worker was thus able to observe their relationship and the child was able to form a stronger bond with her grandmother. A special guardianship assessment was conducted, and a special guardianship support plan was put together, which included a small fund to enable the paternal grandmother to apply for the recognition of the SGO in her home country. The support plan also enabled the PGM to contact the kinship team at the local authority for post-placement support. The case was conducted carefully, and the district judge was proactive in dealing with practical issues associated with the child being placed overseas. The case seemingly resulted in a positive outcome for the child after a comprehensive welfare assessment.

Case 2. This case was discussed briefly above. It concerned a baby born to parents who were from an EU State. The baby's maternal grandmother wished to care for her on a permanent basis. She was assessed through the Central Authority by way of a request for co-operation under BIIa Article 55. The assessment was very brief and focused on the MGM's care of another grandchild rather than her capacity to care for the baby. At the request of the local authority, further questions were put to the MGM through the Central Authority, resulting in another brief report which satisfied the local authority that she would not relinquish care of the child to the parents in the event of an overseas placement. The overseas Central Authority sought a BIIa Article 15 transfer of jurisdiction because the MGM had received a positive assessment. This request was supported by the parents. The court acceded to the request to transfer jurisdiction. It was unclear at the point that the court made the order whether the baby would be moving to the care of the MGM or to foster care in the EU State on transfer – the order referred to both possibilities – although the baby ultimately moved to live with her MGM.

The jurisdictional decision made in Case 2 resulted in the overseas placement of a baby with their grandmother, an outcome sought by her parents and the overseas Central Authority. The same outcome was achieved for the child in Case 20.

However, the child in Case 20 had the benefit of her placement decision being made after a comprehensive kinship assessment, the establishment of a relationship with her grandmother and a plan for post-placement support. By contrast, the baby in Case 2 did not have the experience of the placement option being explored and assessed. The jurisdictional decision was central in this case, with her placement with her grandparents an incidental product of that decision.[14]

As discussed further in chapter 7, it is notable that strenuous attempts are made by national actors to fit cross-border assessments into a domestic frame for kinship assessments, with varying degrees of success. By contrast, in a case such as Case 2, the international/ jurisdictional frame dominated, and domestic criteria for kinship assessments and placements were not a relevant consideration.

Case 2 was decided prior to the Supreme Court's decision in *Re N* (2016) which stated that courts must consider the impact of a transfer of jurisdiction under BIIa Art 15 on a child's welfare.[15] In some ways Case 2 demonstrates why the Supreme Court's judgment was necessary. However, contrasting Case 2 and Case 20 illustrates the way that a jurisdictional decision can bypass the conventional welfare enquiry for children in care proceedings and operate as an automatic route to placement overseas. Even post-*Re N*, the focus of any welfare enquiry would be on the impact of the decision to transfer jurisdiction, rather than the merits of any overseas placement.

It is notable that the context for discussions around transfers of jurisdiction under BIIa Art 15 in the cases analysed, and qualitative interviews conducted, was one where it was assumed that a successful transfer of jurisdiction would be accompanied by a child's physical move to the state in question.[16] However, it is possible for jurisdiction to be transferred to another Member or Contracting State pursuant to BIIa Art 15 or HC96 Art 8 and 9, and for a child to remain in the requesting state, which can continue to exercise jurisdiction to ensure their ongoing protection based on their presence (BIIa Art 20, or HC96 Art 11 or 12).[17] This structure may be appropriate in cases where there is some certainty that a child will be moving to an overseas placement at some stage, but the competent authorities

[14] That is not to say that the jurisdictional decision was wrong – or that the court's discretion was exercised incorrectly – and in any event discretion in jurisdictional decision making is limited by different factors compared to a substantive welfare decision (see Chapter 3).

[15] *Re N (Children) (Adoption: Jurisdiction) (AIRE Centre and others intervening)* [2016] UKSC 15, [2017] AC 167.

[16] *HSE Ireland v SF (A Minor)* [2012] EWHC 1640 (Fam).

[17] This was the mechanism used to resolve proceedings in *Re S (A Child) (Care Proceedings: Jurisdiction)* [2008] EWHC 3013 (Fam); [2009] 2 FLR 550; *Re S (No. 2) (Care Proceedings) (Article 15: Second Application for Second Transfer)* [2019] EWFC 12; [2019] 1 WLR 5045; *Re S (No. 3) (Care Proceedings) (Article 56 Placement in the Republic of Ireland)* [2019] EWFC 36) – the Irish court transferred jurisdiction to England, but the child remained in foster care in Ireland while the English court resolved proceedings. Ultimately, however, the child's placement in Ireland was confirmed and it may be preferable to use this structure in situations where there is a degree of certainty that a child will ultimately move to the requested state.

in the overseas state are better placed to finalise arrangements for that placement (e.g. facilitating any further assessments or training of prospective kinship carers, putting in place a legal framework for the placement and arrangements for post-placement support). As observed by LA Lawyer 6 in the quote above, a transfer of jurisdiction necessarily entails handing over responsibility for a child's welfare to another country, and there may be advantages to an English court relinquishing control to an overseas court which may be better placed to determine the precise arrangements for a child's placement in the country in question.[18]

Case 105 encapsulates many of the issues set out in this chapter. The court made a decision, supported by the Guardian, which ran contrary to the child's welfare interests and wishes and feelings. There were alternative options in this case, which were either not identified or not pursued:

> **Case 105**: The children (aged six and three) had been present in England for around two months before the proceedings were issued. They had travelled from an EU State to England in the care of a maternal relative, with the consent of their mother. Their father could not be located or identified. The elder child attended school, and the younger went to nursery in England. Proceedings were issued as a result of concerns that one of the children had suffered a non-accidental injury in the care of the maternal relative.
>
> It became apparent during proceedings that the children had been known to child protection services in the EU State because of concerns about neglect by the mother.
>
> The children were removed into foster care under police protection and the local authority then issued care proceedings. The court identified that there was an issue as to jurisdiction at the allocation stage and directed at the first hearing that the parties file submissions on the issue of jurisdiction. The Guardian's report in relation to the children had suggested that they had significant emotional needs but had settled into foster care over the last two months. They were reported to be happy, did not wish to return to the EU State and were refusing to speak the language of that country, despite being encouraged to do so.
>
> However, the Guardian's view was that the EU State was better placed to hear the case. The court determined that the children were not habitually resident in England at the time that proceedings were issued

[18] See also the comments of Pauffley J in *Re A and B (Children: Brussels II Revised: Article 15)* [2014] EWFC 40 whereby a transfer of jurisdiction was appropriate to facilitate the exploration of overseas placement options, as opposed to the cumbersome and intensely regulated process overseen by the English court.

and accordingly that it did not have jurisdiction in relation to them. The children were returned to the EU State and placed in institutional care.

If Case 105 had been a 'domestic' care case where it was not necessary to make a jurisdictional decision, the children would have undoubtedly remained in foster care whilst their family members were assessed. The court would have conducted a 'global holistic evaluation' into the placement which would meet their best interests, taking into account all the matters contained in the welfare checklist. A potential outcome would have been the children's placement in the EU State only if this was considered to meet the children's best interests. However, the court had to decide if it had jurisdiction to proceed with a full welfare evaluation. As a result of the finding that the court did not have jurisdiction, the children were returned to the EU State and into institutional care, pending a decision about long-term arrangements. It does not seem likely that it was in the children's short-term best interests to be moved again, when they were happy in foster care, had experienced significant disruption already and were going to an unfamiliar environment in institutional care. As discussed in chapter 3, the determination of the children's habitual residence was a factual question for the court, and the fact that it was not in the children's best interests to move into institutional care in the EU State was not relevant. Here (and in contrast to decisions about transfer of jurisdiction) a jurisdictional decision can completely bypass a welfare evaluation.

Drawing on the discussion earlier in this chapter about misunderstandings of the jurisdictional rules in BIIa/96 HC, there were alternative avenues in Case 105 which would have minimised the disruption to the children. If one of the parties to the proceedings had agreed, the English court could have submitted a BIIa Article 15 request for a transfer of jurisdiction from the relevant EU State to the UK, permitting the children to stay in their placement at least until a substantive decision was reached as to where, and with whom, they should live. If Case 105 had taken place after the end of the Brexit transition period, the English court could have requested that the relevant EU court transfer its substantive jurisdiction to the UK pursuant to HC96 Art 9 (2).

Another option might have been for the court to continue to exercise jurisdiction in relation to the children based on their presence (under BIIa Article 20), pending a more substantive welfare decision by the relevant overseas court.[19]

[19] This has taken place in cases involving Ireland and England, in order that children do not have to undergo the disruption of moving from foster care in England to a temporary foster placement pending a substantive welfare decision (e.g. *Re S (A Child) (Care Proceedings: Jurisdiction)* [2008] EWHC 3013 (Fam); [2009] 2 FLR 550; *Re S (No. 2) (Care Proceedings) (Article 15: Second Application for Second Transfer)* [2019] EWFC 12; [2019] 1 WLR 5045; *Re S (No. 3) (Care Proceedings) (Article 56 Placement in the Republic of Ireland)* [2019] EWFC 36).

In a post-Brexit legal environment, the HC96 Article 11 enables jurisdiction to be exercised based on a child's presence on the territory of a Contracting State, in cases of urgency.[20] Those measures (unlike the equivalent provision in BIIa) are capable of recognition and enforcement in other Contracting States under Chapter IV of the Convention as they can have extra-territorial effect.[21] This provision has been used in cases of international child abduction to ensure that a child has a 'soft-landing' when they are returned to the state of their habitual residence.[22] The same provisions may be used effectively to ensure a 'soft-landing' for a child who must ultimately return to a Contracting State of their habitual residence as a result of a jurisdictional determination in care proceedings.

In any event, the case illustrates the real-life impact of decisions about jurisdiction – decisions which are traditionally conceived of as occupying a legalised sphere. A factual determination of the child's habitual residence is (unavoidably) divorced from questions of welfare. However, the *impact* of a jurisdictional determination can have significant welfare implications, as Case 105 demonstrates. A better understanding of the jurisdictional scheme in the operative PIL instrument could have potentially softened the blunt impact of the jurisdictional determination.

Summary Conclusions: Jurisdiction in Care Proceedings

- Domestic guidance on the operation of jurisdictional rules under BIIa/HC96 has emphasised the importance of early identification of jurisdictional issues in care proceedings. The PLO 2014 envisages that framing a case as having an international element will lead to the court considering jurisdiction within one day of proceedings being issued. However, in the sample of cases analysed for this book, it seemed that jurisdictional issues were not effectively identified by way of an *ex parte* procedure by local authorities in their application, nor by courts considering matters at the allocation stage of proceedings.
- The way jurisdiction was spoken about in court documents revealed misunderstandings by courts and parties' legal representatives about

[20] HC96 Art 11. In cases involving a child with connections to a non-Contracting State, the measures will 'lapse in each Contracting State as soon as measures required by the situation and taken by the authorities of another State are recognised in the Contracting State in question' (Art 11 (3)). An Interim Care Order or Interim Supervision Order under CA 89 s 38 may be made pursuant to Art 11 or 12 of the HC96 – see The Parental Responsibility and Measures for the Protection of Children (International Obligations) (England and Wales and Northern Ireland) Regulations 2010, SI 2010/1898 Reg 5. It is suggested that HC96 Art 11 is of greater use in the context of care proceedings with an international dimension, due to its extra-territorial effect.

[21] Cf BIIa Art 20. See Case C-296/10 *Purrucker v Vallés Pérez (No 2)* EU:C:2010:665.

[22] P Torremans (ed), *Cheshire, North & Fawcett, Private International Law* (OUP, 2017) 1104; *Re J (A Child)* [2015] UKSC 70 [31] Lady Hale; *AO v LA* [2023] EWHC 83 (Fam).

the jurisdictional provisions of BIIa/HC96. This may have led to an over-fastidious approach to jurisdiction, with jurisdictional issues being explored unnecessarily in some cases. It may also mean courts and parties are not alive to potential options within the confines of the jurisdictional rules of BIIa/HC96 which might alleviate the blunt impact of a jurisdictional decision on a child's welfare (see below).

- The identification and exploration of jurisdictional issues was closely tied to ideas about comity and co-operation with overseas state authorities, and it seemed that national actors perceived the exploration of jurisdiction in this way as necessary to establish the legitimacy of a local authority's and court's intervention in the life of a child and their family.
- Jurisdictional arguments can be consciously deployed by parties to care proceedings to bring about a result which meets their interests. For example, a decision that an overseas court has jurisdiction may result in a child moving overseas, or a local authority being relieved of responsibility for a child.
- Jurisdictional decisions can have a significant impact on a child's welfare. A child who experiences a jurisdictional decision being made about them may find that they are moved across borders without a full enquiry as to whether this is in their best interests.

6

Findings on Requesting and Exchanging Child Protection Information in Care Proceedings

Introduction

The discussion about jurisdiction in chapter 5 focused on the operation of PIL rules in a procedural and substantive manner at the outset of care proceedings, including the way that jurisdictional arguments in care proceedings could impact upon children's welfare. However, if a court decides that it has jurisdiction to make welfare decisions about a child, where the child has connections overseas, there may be information from overseas which is relevant to any decisions the court must make and which may inform any assessment by a local authority of the need to safeguard a child in the short and long term.

The co-operation provisions of both BIIa and the HC96 put in place a system for the exchange of information concerning children between Central Authorities.[1] Both instruments contain general provisions encouraging central authorities to co-operate to support the operation of BIIa / HC96. BIIa Article 55 provided that Central Authorities 'cooperate on specific cases to achieve the purposes of (the) Regulation' (a provision reproduced with a similar wording in the revised BIIa regulation, BII ter Art 77) and HC96 Article 30 requires that Central Authorities 'co-operate with each other and promote co-operation amongst the competent authorities in their States to achieve the purposes of the Convention'. Beyond these general co-operation provisions, there are specific co-operation functions in both instruments, which are relevant to child protection situations.[2] These include;

- The collection and exchange of 'information on the situation of the child … on any procedures underway … or … on decisions taken concerning the child'

[1] BIIa Chapter IV; HC96 Chapter V.

[2] It should be noted that there are further co-operation provisions than those discussed in this chapter, which are less relevant to care proceedings. For example, BIIa, BII ter and the HC96 all contain co-operation provisions to support mediation or conciliation (BIIa Art 55 (e); HC96 Art 31 (b); BII ter Art 79 (g)). The HC96 contain provisions to support parents seeking to secure rights of access with a child, to request a report on their suitability to have such accesss from the competent authorities of their Contracting State (HC96 Art 35).

(BIIa Art 55 (i)–(iii)) or 'information relevant to the protection of the child' (HC96 Art 34 (1))[3]

- Co-operation to assist holders of parental responsibility with seeking the recognition and enforcement of judgments (BIIa Art 55 (b), Art 57) or the implementation of measures of protection (HC96 Art 35)[4]
- Co-operation to support the effective operation of the provisions for a transfer of jurisdiction (BIIa Art 55 (c); 86HC Art 31 (1))[5]
- Provisions requiring consultation in cases where the cross-border placement of a child is contemplated (BIIa Art 55 (d), Art 56, HC96 Art 33)[6] (discussed further in Chapters 7 and 8).

The HC96 also contains further, relevant provisions;

- *Permitting a competent authority to request that the competent authorities of another Contracting State assist in* discovering the whereabouts of a child who is present and in need of protection in another state (96 HC Art 31 (c))[7]
- Permitting a competent authority in a Contracting State with which the child has a substantial connection to request the Contracting State of the child's habitual residence or presence to provide a report on the child's situation and / or consider taking measures of protection in relation to a child;
- A *mandatory* duty on competent authorities to communicate with authorities in a state where a child is present, if that child was known to them as having been exposed to 'serious danger' and protective measures were taken or were being considered in relation to the child. This applies even if the child has travelled to a non-Contracting State. (HC96 Art 36).[8]

The exchange of relevant child protection information under the HC96 is subject to Art 37 which provides that requests should not be made where this would 'place the child's person or property in danger, or constitute a serious threat to the liberty or life of a member of the child's family' – this may be a particularly significant consideration for children who are seeking asylum in the UK, where initiating any contact with the child's country of origin may place the child or their family members at risk.[9]

[3] See also BII ter Art 80 (1).
[4] See also BII ter Art 97 (3) and Art 81.
[5] See also BII ter Art.
[6] See also BII ter Art 82.
[7] See also BII ter Art 80 (1) (c).
[8] See also BII ter Art 80 (2) albeit that this is limited to children who travel between Member States.
[9] Department for Education, 'Care of Unaccompanied Migrant Children and Child Victims of Modern Slavery: Statutory Guidance for Local Authorities' (DfE, 2017) 58.

In the sample of cases analysed for this study, the co-operation through Central Authorities occurred in two different contexts.

a) To commission assessments of prospective kinship carers overseas (discussed further in chapter 7)
b) To request or share background information about a child's life in another country including prior child protection interventions and court proceedings.

This chapter focusses on the latter function. In the cases analysed for this study, co-operation via Central Authorities to request or share background information occurred primarily through use of BIIa Art 55 because the sample of cases analysed pre-dated the UK's exit from the EU, and the loss of BIIa.

The importance of information sharing in a child protection context generally is well established. Since the first publication of the statutory guidance, 'Working Together to Safeguard Children' in 1999, there has been a focus on the importance of information sharing and inter-agency co-operation in the field of child protection social work.[10] Domestically, there has also been an emphasis on the need to ensure that data protection legislation does not impede the appropriate sharing of information to ensure a child's protection.[11]

However, there is a lack of guidance available to local authorities as to how information can be requested and exchanged across borders. Although one of the recommendations of the Climbié Inquiry was that local authorities should know how to request child protection information from other countries, there has been no equivalent guidance for local authorities from the Department for Education or the judiciary on this practice.[12]

The role of Central Authorities – and other institutions – in exchanging relevant child protection information can be seen as more than an administrative process. Lamont has argued that Central Authorities and the European Judicial Network have the potential to support the mainstreaming of children's rights (as embodied in the UNCRC and Article 24 of the CFREU) in EU Member States, as they occupy a transnational space but also exist as part of national legal systems. Of particular significance to this study, Lamont highlights the role of Central Authorities in safeguarding children involved in cross-border proceedings, by reference to

[10] Tony Morrison, 'Working together to safeguard children: challenges and changes for inter-agency co-ordination in child protection' (2000) 14 *Journal of Interprofessional Care* 363.

[11] Department for Education, 'Information sharing: Advice for practitioners providing safeguarding services to children, young people, parents and carers, July 2018' (2018, HM Government).

[12] W Herbert Laming, *The Victoria Climbié Inquiry: Report of an Inquiry by Lord Laming* (HMSO, 2003) 6.619. Save for guidance which has encouraged local authorities to make use of the co-operation provisions generally – see J Munby, 'President's Guidance of 10 November 2014: The International Child Abduction and Contact Unit' (2014).

Case C-523/07 Proceedings Brought by A.[13] In that case, the Central Authority's information sharing function was vital in effectively navigating a situation where Finnish authorities took urgent protective measures in relation to three children who were habitually resident in Sweden but present in Finland. Communication through Central Authorities could ensure that the authorities with substantive jurisdiction were made aware of the urgent measures taken in relation to the child who was present in another state.[14]

This chapter will focus on the application of the co-operation provisions of PIL frameworks to exchange information about a child who is the subject of care proceedings via Central Authorities. It will also consider how equivalent information is gathered in 'domestic' cases, where a child has no international links, or where a child has connections to a non-Contracting State, meaning that the co-operation provisions of HC96 cannot be used.

Information about Prior Child Protection Interventions Overseas

Although 70% of the children in the sample of cases analysed for this study were born in the UK, many had overseas connections which may have given rise to the existence of information overseas relevant to their welfare. For example, 30% of children had lived in another country at some point in their lives. Some 22% of children had one or more siblings overseas. Furthermore, three children had been the subject of public law proceedings overseas (see Appendix I).

In many cases, requests through the Central Authority operated to exchange relevant background information about the family. There were seven cases where there was a request by an English local authority for previous decisions or proceedings concerning a child with connections overseas. In two cases the Central Authority was asked to assist with tracing a parent resident overseas. The way the co-operation provisions operated varied depending on the circumstances of the case. It was possible to identify three broad categories of case which demonstrate this variation:

1. 'Known flight' cases: A family move across borders during an active intervention either by courts or state authorities, and it is possible to identify the country they had travelled to.
2. 'Unknown flight' cases: A family relocate against a background of active intervention by courts or state authorities but without that state knowing / identifying the country they have travelled to.

[13] R Lamont, 'Central Authorities and the European Judicial Network: Cross-border cooperation as a mechanism for advancing children's rights in Europe' in H Stalford and I Iusmen (eds), *The EU as a Children's Rights Actor: Law, Policy and Structural Dimensions* (Verlag Barbara Budrich, 2016).

[14] Case C-523/07 *Proceedings brought by A* ECLI:EU:C:2009:225, [2010] Fam 42 [64]–[65].

3. 'Planned Relocation' cases: A family relocates to another country, and there have been historic proceedings or quiescent child protection concerns.

Communicating Child Protection Concerns in 'Known Flight' Cases

In Category 1 'Known Flight' cases, BIIa Art 55 was used effectively in three cases for states to communicate proactively welfare concerns about a child who had been moved to another BIIa state during proceedings, or to evade scrutiny from state child protection services. In these cases, BIIa was used successfully by state authorities to communicate pre-emptively child protection concerns to the authorities in the country where the child was taken, with the aim of ensuring that there was some ongoing monitoring. Any attempt at evasion by parents of child protection interventions was therefore undermined through this process. However, this proactive communication using BIIa was only possible because the country that the family had travelled to was known.

Case 31. The local authority used BIIa Article 55 to trace the family after they left the country for an EU state, shortly before care proceedings were issued in England. The relevant overseas statutory agency conducted a welfare check on the children pursuant to this request. They did not have any concerns about the children's welfare.

Case 8: A child was removed from England to EU State 1 by her parents shortly before the local authority issued care proceedings, following very serious, and credible, allegations of abuse made by the child against her father. BIIa Article 55 was used by the local authority to transmit to the child protection authorities of EU State 1 information about the family via the Central Authority, and a request that a welfare check be undertaken. As a result, the state child protection authorities of EU State 1 became directly involved and were increasingly concerned about the conditions that the family were living in. As their concerns increased, the parents moved the child again from EU State 1 to EU State 2. Despite the parents' actions, BIIa Article 55 was effective in that the family were subject to a degree of monitoring by child protection authorities both in EU State 1 and EU State 2.

Case 75. The mother in this case had removed the child from the shared care of the authorities in an EU State, who had the equivalent of a supervision order for the child. The mother had not previously told the local authority, or the court, about the previous proceedings concerning the child. The authorities in the EU state used BIIa Article 55 to communicate this information, which was then disclosed into ongoing care proceedings in England.

The kind of proactive communication which is seen in 'known flight' cases, as outlined above, is a specific requirement under the HC96. Under HC96 Art 36, there is a *mandatory* duty on competent authorities (i.e. local authorities) to communicate with authorities in a state where a child is present, if that child was known to them as having been exposed to 'serious danger' and protective measures were taken or were being considered in relation to the child.[15] This provision requires pre-emptive action to communicate child protection concerns where a child travels overseas but will only be possible where competent authorities know the country that the child has travelled to.

Furthermore, HC96 Art 36 applies where a child exposed to danger is moved to a non-Contracting State.[16] Again, this can only operate effectively if a local authority knows the country that the child is taken to. Also, local authorities cannot use Central Authorities to communicate with non-Contracting States, and so they must identify which body to communicate with to comply with this provision. It is not possible to draw conclusions about the practical application of HC96 Art 36 based on the sample of cases analysed due to the small numbers of cases where HC96 was used rather than BIIa. However, it is notable that whilst there was no specific provision in BIIa which mirrors HC96 Art 36, BIIa was used to the same effect in 'Known Flight' cases. This might indicate that professionals involved with the protection of children sought out ways to ensure they were protected if they travelled overseas and identified BIIa as one possible route for doing so, without a specific provision requiring this action from the regulation itself.

Communicating Child Protection Concerns in 'Unknown Flight' or 'Planned Relocation' Cases

For cases in Categories 2 ('Unknown Flight') and 3 ('Planned Relocation'), the authorities of the state that the child has a connection with may not be able to

[15] HC96 Art 36 is subject to the Art 37 exception whereby information should not be transmitted if it would place the child or their family at risk.
[16] P Lagarde, 'Explanatory Report' (1996) HCCH [150].

proactively share relevant child protection information via the Central Authority, either because:

a) they do not know that the family have relocated, or
b) they do not know where they have travelled to.

In these cases, it becomes incumbent upon professionals in the *receiving* state to seek out relevant background information from overseas. In England, social workers may have to rely on a background as reported by parents unless they seek to verify that information with overseas authorities. It was clear from the sample of cases analysed that requests for background information were not made by local authorities in every case where a child or their siblings had previously lived overseas. There were also four cases in the sample where the existence of historic proceedings concerning the index child, or a sibling overseas, was unknown at the point that care proceedings were issued in England.

This raises the question of the 'trigger' for seeking and verifying background information on a child. CFAB social workers were asked about requests for background information from overseas, as CFAB can request this information from its partners in several countries (including non-Contracting States to the HC96).

> It is when family members or parents imply that there is something back home … that rings a bell … because not many of them would actually disclose that "social services were on to me in my country". But also, the kind of parenting issue that we're dealing with. If the parents are having, say substance misuse [issues], it is obviously looking to be quite long standing. (CFAB SW1)

CFAB SW2 thought that CFAB tended to get requests for record checks either where child protection concerns were being investigated, when parenting was being assessed or for kinship assessments within care proceedings. The point at which this background information is sought might be determined by the 'trigger' for investigating these issues.

In three cases, co-operation requests by local authorities via the Central Authority under BIIa revealed 'new' information, such as a history of child protection interventions or concerns by overseas state authorities. These cases might fall into Category 3 (Planned Relocation cases) – the families relocated and there were quiescent child protection concerns or historic (but relevant) proceedings.

Case 9. A BIIa Article 55 request by a local authority revealed that the mother's two elder children had been the subject of child protection interventions in an EU state, and that the mother had effectively abandoned those children to the care of their maternal and paternal grandparents respectively. This information was of particular concern to the children's Guardian as the local authority's care plan was for the child to remain in the care of his mother under a care order. Despite the Guardian's concerns, the case did conclude with a care order, with the child remaining in his mother's care. However, subsequently, the mother left the country with the child and moved between several EU states with a new partner, at one stage leaving the child with the maternal grandmother, in the same way as she had his elder half-siblings.

Case 88. The parents had come to the UK from an EU State to seek work. The child was born in the UK. Care proceedings were issued after a serious criminal incident in the home. The mother informed the local authority that the child had an elder half-sibling who was living with her paternal family and would soon be joining the mother in the UK. An BIIa Art 55 request to the EU State revealed that this information was false. The child's half sibling had in fact been the subject of child protection proceedings and had ultimately been adopted outside of the family.

Case 94. The mother had lived with the children in an EU State before moving to England as a family. The local authority initially conducted an assessment as the child was suspected to be at risk of significant harm (CA 89 s 47) and there followed a pre-proceedings plan for supporting the family. However, care proceedings were eventually issued. Throughout this time the mother had refused to provide information about the children's father or her life in the other country, including her previous addresses. In the care proceedings, a BIIa Art 55 request was made, but the request for information was ultimately progressed through CFAB, not the Central Authority. It was established that social services in the other country had been involved with the family for a long time. The children's father was also identified through the request. The case concluded with a supervision order and the children remaining in the care of their mother.

In a qualitative interview, LA Lawyer 6 reflected on a missed opportunity to gather information from overseas, which might have prevented a child from suffering neglect by remaining in the care of his parents. The case she described might fall into Category 2 – an 'Unknown Flight' case – the family were evading a child protection intervention in their home country, and the relevant authorities did not know where they had travelled to.

> The parents appeared here pregnant, and we never quite understood why they came over … it since transpired that they had children in (their home country) and they were fleeing social services … which is disappointing that we had missed a lot of opportunities in early assessment to liaise with (the parent's home country) as we would have found out the true extent of their concerns and things could have been done. It is a case we've chalked up to experience … if we engaged … at a much earlier stage – in section 47 (CA 89 s 47) – the child wouldn't have stayed in parental care for as long as he did. (L6)

BIIa/HC96 provide a formalised route for the exchange of relevant child protection information, and in all the cases discussed above, there was an awareness of the importance of providing and obtaining relevant background information to ensure a child is properly protected. In all the cases discussed, records existed, and were readily disclosed by competent authorities.[17]

However, another issue to consider (particularly in relation to cases where a child had a connection to a non-Contracting State) is the significant global variation in child protection systems, and how this relates to the availability of records concerning children. There was a perception amongst CFAB social workers that the availability of records may be patchier in non-Contracting States, although there were some where it would be possible to obtain background checks, including South Africa, Vietnam, the USA and Canada. In some states, background information about a child was held by public bodies but obtaining it is a more convoluted process. CFAB SW2 referred to Zimbabwe where state agencies may hold child protection information, but there are no digitised records, and someone would have to go to the location of the paper files and request the information. In Nigeria, CFAB SW3 described a significant variation in social services between states, however, CFAB had developed a practice of notifying state child protection agencies there where a child was placed with kin following care proceedings in England (see chapter 8). There was also a perception that some states find requests for background information on a child disproportionate or require a parent's consent to the disclosure of this information due to national rules on data protection.

> I think the procedures overseas might be different in that we would have to be very clear about why checks are being requested … even in the US … and I think already the UK

[17] The exchange of information under BIIa discussed in this Study took place during care proceedings. It would seem that the existence of proceedings was required to engage the co-operation provisions of BIIa (the regulation applied to 'civil matters whatever the nature of the court or tribunal' (Article 1) – although states may have taken a different interpretation of this provision. The HC96 is not so prescriptive and it may be that request for co-operation can be dealt with between Central Authorities where local authorities are taking or contemplating 'protective measures' in relation to a child (Article 1). However, conclusions cannot be drawn from this study about mechanisms for the exchange of child protection information outside of care proceedings.

> requires a lot of information from the other countries that are often seen as being a little bit too much. (CFAB SW1)

There were no cases in the sample, or discussed in interview, where child protection information had been shared or sought from a non-Contracting State e.g., through CFAB. This may reflect the characteristics of the children in the sample analysed but may also reflect assumptions about the availability of child protection records in non-Contracting States. It may also raise the question of the extent to which the existence of an infrastructure, in the form of Central Authorities designated by PIL, *invites* or supports the proactive exchange of child protection information between states – and, conversely, whether the absence of these legal frameworks impacts on the extent to which child protection information is exchanged or requested in relation to non-Contracting States.

As mentioned at the outset of this chapter, one of the recommendations of the Victoria Climbié Inquiry was for directors of social services to ensure that social workers were aware of how to access information concerning vulnerable children which may be held in other countries.[18] This recommendation arose because Victoria had travelled from the Ivory Coast to France in the care of her aunt, Kouao. Whilst in France, Victoria's school had become concerned enough about her worrying presentation at school – and frequent absences – to issue a 'Child At Risk Emergency Notification'. A social worker became involved. However, Kouao brought Victoria to England (in what might be considered a 'Category 2 Unknown Flight' relocation as it did not appear that the French authorities were aware that she was moving). Kouao reported to the English local authority that she had three elder children in France who she had left there. It is apparent from the Inquiry that Kouao's account of her reasons for coming to England, and that she had left elder children in France, operated as a 'trigger' for the local authority to seek to verify this information from the French authorities.[19] There were discussions at Strategy Meetings about the need to check what information was held about Victoria and Kouao in France, and Kouao's elder children. However, this was never undertaken. Had these checks been performed, it would have been apparent that Victoria's aunt had given false information about her life there, and the local authority would have learned of the concerns about Victoria by the French authorities. The review considered that the failure to undertake these checks may have been due to a lack of awareness about *how* to get this information from overseas. The review also highlighted that even where the child's country of origin is 'without a developed welfare system, the child may well have passed through a country with such a system before reaching the UK'.[20] It may be that greater awareness of the role of Central Authorities, as a means to gather information from overseas, has gone some way

[18] WH Laming, The Victoria Climbié Inquiry: Report of an Inquiry by Lord Laming (HMSO, 2003) 6.619.

[19] *Ibid* 4.164, 4.185, 6.431, 6.615.

[20] *Ibid* 6.619.

to implement this recommendation in practice – the existence of a channel may mean that 'triggers' to seek out information from overseas can be actioned – and this may in turn mean that local authorities seek out this information in more cases. That said, it is difficult, without further data, to draw conclusions about the extent to which the existence of Central Authorities designated by PIL influences seeking information from overseas, or the practices surrounding the exchange of child protection information with non-Contracting States, and the extent to which assumptions about the availability of records may impact on children with connections to such states. As is discussed in chapter 8, there are examples of relevant information being shared with authorities in non-Contracting States to ensure a child's safety after placement.

Overall, the data demonstrated recourse to co-operation through the Central Authorities as a means for the exchange of relevant child protection information between different countries. The success of this function in ensuring a child's protection depended on the type of case. Where state authorities knew that a child had travelled overseas and knew the country the child had travelled to (Category 1 'Known Flight' cases), there were examples of proactive and pre-emptive sharing of information through Central Authorities. This was not possible, however, where state authorities did not know where a child had been taken to (Category 2 Unknown Flight cases) or that a relocation had occurred (Category 3 Planned Relocation cases). As such, where a child was present in England, and their life or connections to another state were unclear, professionals (usually social workers) were reliant upon a history as reported by the parents, unless and until a request was made for background information from overseas. The trigger for requesting this information varied between cases.

Exchanging Child Protection Information: Comparison with Domestic Cases

When thinking about the experience of children with international connections, compared to those with domestic connections, parallels can be drawn in relation to the provision and exchange of background information.

In the domestic equivalent of a 'known flight' Category 1 case, a child on a child protection plan may move from one local authority in England to another. In these circumstances, statutory guidance requires local authorities to share information 'due to the risk that knowledge pertinent to keeping a child safe could be lost'.[21] Where there is a higher level of intervention through a care order, and a child is removed from their placement, a court can make a recovery order, which

[21] Department for Education, 'Working Together to Safeguard Children: A Guide to Inter-Agency Working to Safeguard and Promote the Welfare of Children, July 2018' (HM Government, 2020) 19.

authorises police to enter and search premises and remove a child in order to secure their return.[22]

If a child is moved to an unknown location (the domestic equivalent of a Category 2 'Unknown Flight' Case), there are wider powers and available guidance to locate the child. Enquiries might be made by the local authority as part of an ongoing investigation pursuant to CA89 s 47 (where a local authority has reasonable cause to suspect a child is at risk of significant harm).[23] If the child is 'looked after' and goes missing from their placement (which may be a placement with a parent), there is statutory guidance for Local Authorities and a 'Runaway and Missing from Care Protocol'.[24] Although this guidance is primarily directed towards children who go missing from local authority care, there exists a procedure for coordinating action between local authorities and policy at a national level. There are also statutory powers when a child is removed from care to an unknown location: a recovery order can require any person who has information about a child's whereabouts to disclose it to the police or the court.[25] These powers can be extended through wardship proceedings, where the court can make a location order or collection order which requires information about a child's whereabouts to be disclosed to the tipstaff, or a child to be removed.[26]

The same power to take proactive steps to locate children in other countries and take steps to ensure they are safe does not necessarily exist in cross-border cases – a local authority might have an 'inkling' that a child has travelled to Australia against a background of child protection concerns in England, and might transmit a tracing request under 96 HC Art 31 (c) to establish if this is the case.[27] But where there are no clues as to where a child has travelled to, it may be difficult for child protection authorities in a child's home state to take any action.

However, if a child moves within England against a background of previous child protection concerns (the equivalent of a Category 3 'Planned Relocation') it would be incumbent upon the social worker to seek out relevant information. The pen pictures of the cases illustrate that international cases can present the same challenges as domestic ones; parents may not give a truthful history of prior involvement with children's services or may seek to conceal prior involvement through giving incorrect information about names, dates of birth or previous addresses.[28]

[22] CA 89 s 50. The removal of a child from care is also a criminal offence CA 89 s 49.

[23] *Ibid* 18–20.

[24] DfE, 'Statutory Guidance on Children who Run Away or go Missing from Home or Care' (2014) DFE-00009-2014.

[25] CA 89 s 50 (3) (c).

[26] For an example, see *London Borough of Ealing v Connors*, [2013] EWHC 3493 (Fam).

[27] P Lagarde, 'Explanatory Report on the 1996 Hague Child Protection Convention', HCCH 1996 [150] suggests that states could use Article 31 (c) to trace a child, and then once they are located, communicate the relevant child protection information about the child pursuant to Article 36.

[28] For an example in a domestic context see *Re B (A Child) (Care Proceedings: Threshold Criteria)* [2013] UKSC 33; [2013] 1 WLR 1911.

Summary Conclusions: Co-Operation to Exchange Child Protection Information

- Cross-border cases present the same issues as domestic cases – parents may give an untruthful account of their background or connections to another country. However, there does not seem to be the same focus in international cases on information sharing as there is in domestic cases.
- The co-operation via Central Authorities was used to exchange relevant child protection information between different countries. The effectiveness of the provisions was determined to an extent by the nature of a child or their family's cross-border movement, and whether the information could be proactively provided by the overseas state, or whether this information had to be sought out by the professional in the receiving state. There is therefore likely to be a significant variation in the practice of obtaining relevant child protection information from overseas.
- Where there were care proceedings, there did not seem to be a developed practice requesting or exchanging information between English authorities and non-Contracting States, which might reflect assumptions about the availability of records in such states or indicate that the availability of an infrastructure in the form of Central Authorities invites professionals to seek out / provide this information.
- Overall, there were examples of positive practice in the sample of cases analysed, whereby relevant child protection information was exchanged using the co-operation provisions of BIIa and the HC96. Going forward, it would be highly desirable for more states to become Contracting Parties to the HC96 to facilitate this process at a global level.
- It may be that the existence of institutions in the form of Central Authorities, and a prescribed route for the exchange of this information, helps professionals to provide this information, and seek it out, when they encounter families with links to other countries. For social workers supporting children with links to other Contracting States, requests under HC96 Art 34 may assist with obtaining background information on families. Children who travel to other Contracting States against a background of child protection concerns may be traced using HC96 Article 31 (c), and child protection concerns may be communicated to authorities in both Contracting and non-Contracting States using HC96 Art 36. Systematic use of these provisions would go some way to ensure that a child can continue to be protected by state-based systems even where they move across borders.

7

Findings on Overseas Assessments in Care Proceedings

This chapter considers issues around the assessment of prospective carers for a child overseas in care proceedings, a practice which may engage the co-operation provisions of international or regionally agreed PIL frameworks concerning children. Overseas assessments were considered or conducted in a large proportion of cases in the sample of cases analysed. In 91 cases, the child had a parent or potential kinship carer overseas who required assessment, and in 21 cases the child was placed overseas at the conclusion of proceedings. Overseas assessments were also a significant preoccupation for interviewees, who often spoke at length of the challenges they had experienced in relation to obtaining such assessments.

Overseas Assessments: Domestic Context

If a local authority is looking after a child, they must arrange for that child to live with their parent (unless this is inconsistent with the child's welfare or not reasonably practicable).[1] If a looked after child cannot live with their parent, a local authority must identify the 'most appropriate' placement, with first preference being given to individuals who are relatives, friends or otherwise connected to the child (i.e. referred to as kin in this chapter).[2] In determining a parent or kinship carer's suitability to look after a child, there are statutory criteria for assessments.

For parenting assessments, the Care Planning, Placement and Case Review (England) Regulations 2010 set out in detail the matters that must be included in a parenting assessment. These include the parent's ability to meet the child's needs, protect them from harm, promote their upbringing and provide a stable environment, as well as matters relating to their relationships, family composition, health, and family history.[3]

[1] CA 89 s 22C (2)-(4).
[2] CA 89 s 22C (6), (7).
[3] Care Planning, Placement and Case Review (England) Regulations 2010 SI 2010/959 Reg 17 Sch 3. A child may be placed with their parent before an assessment is completed subject to the criteria in Reg 19.

The process for assessing kinship carers for looked after children is also highly regulated.[4] As discussed in chapter 4, there has been a concern to ensure that special guardianship placements are appropriately assessed and supported, in recognition of the fact that a child who has suffered abuse or maltreatment will require a high level of care, and a stable, appropriately supported placement.[5] Particularly, special guardianship assessments must address the matters contained in the Schedule to the SGO Regulations.[6] A court may not make a SGO unless it has received a report – of enabling a direct assessment of a prospective carer, as well as an evaluation of their home and living conditions, by a professional who may have closer knowledge of their culture and language and community.[7] One method of achieving a local assessment of kin is via the Central Authority designated by the HC96 (or, pre-Brexit, BIIa).

It would appear, however, that the co-operation provisions of HC96, which in turn inspired the provisions of BIIa, did not specifically contemplate their use for obtaining overseas assessments. Both instruments contain a general provision that Central Authorities will co-operate to achieve the purposes of BIIa/96.[8] The co-operation provisions in BIIa refer to the collection and exchange of 'information' (as distinguished from assessment which might be classified as 'evidence').[9] The HC96 has a series of co-operation provisions for children in various situations,

[4] The proportion of kinship care arrangements which have been subject to an assessment by local authority children's service may represent a small fraction of kinship care arrangements generally. Most children living in kinship care in the UK are living in 'informal arrangements' and are not looked after children (S Nandy et al, 'Spotlight on Kinship Care Using Census Microdata to Examine the Extent and Nature of Kinship Care in the UK at the turn of the Twentieth century' (2001) *University of Bristol*, 118).

[5] S Bowyer et al, Impact of the Family Justice Reforms on Front-line Practice Phase Two: Special Guardianship Orders (Department for Education, 2015).

[6] CA 89 s 14A (8); Special Guardianship Regulations 2005, SI 2005/1109, Schedule, as amended by the Special Guardianship (Amendment) Regulations 2016, SI 2016/111.

[7] Department for Education, Working with Foreign Authorities: Child Protection Cases and Care Orders. Departmental Advice for Local Authorities, Social Workers, Service Managers and Children's Services Lawyers (DFE-00523-2014, July 2014); Cross Border Child Safeguarding Working Group, International Kinship Care Guide (November 2020); Family Justice Council Public Law Working Group, 'Recommendations to Achieve Best Practice in the Child Protection and Family Justice Systems: Special Guardianship Orders' (FJC, 2020) [34].

[8] BIIa Art 55, HC96 Art 30 (1).

[9] As noted in *Leicester City Council v S* [2014] EWHC 1575 (Fam) and J Munby, 'President's Guidance of 10 November 2014: The International Child Abduction and Contact Unit' (2014). This guidance noted that some EU Member States may require that kinship assessments be conducted using the EU Taking of Evidence Regulation (Council Regulation (EC) No 1206/2001 of 28 May 2001 on cooperation between the courts of the Member States in the taking of evidence in civil or commercial matters). In *Re A and B (Children: Brussels II Revised: Article 15)* [2014] EWFC 40, Pauffley J decided to request a transfer of jurisdiction to Czech Republic in part to facilitate assessments in that country. She noted that a request for assessment under the EU Taking of Evidence Regulation was likely to be 'cumbersome', 'incomplete' and 'outside the direct control of (the) Court' [42]. There was one case in the Sample where an assessment of a Paternal Grandmother in Germany was sought, and the German Central Authority said that the request had to be made through the Taking of Evidence Regulation. In the event the child remained in the care of the mother and the assessment was not pursued (Case 9). In the context of cases engaging the HC96, the relevant instrument for the taking of evidence would be the Hague Convention of 18 March 1970 on the Taking of Evidence Abroad in Civil or Commercial Matters.

but none fit easily into the commissioning of overseas kinship assessments.[10] HC96 Art 34 (1) provides that 'competent authorities under the Convention, if the situation of the child so requires, may request any authority of another Contracting State which has information relevant to the protection of the child to communicate such information'. As discussed in this previous chapter, this provision might be used to request relevant background information but may also be used to request a report or assessment as to a prospective carer's suitability to care for a child who is the subject of proceedings.[11]

Both instruments (BIIa Art 56 and HC96 Art 33) require that consent be sought from overseas competent authorities prior to placing a child there. In the case of the HC96, the receiving Contracting State must arrive at their own assessment of whether the placement is in the child's best interests.[12] The types of placement which fall into these provisions are not entirely clear, and research on their application in BIIa cases has established that many states interpret the provisions as requiring their consent where a child is placed in kinship care (for a further discussion of these provisions, see chapter 8).[13] However, the consent procedure in the co-operation provisions of BIIa/ HC96 is distinct from the process of commissioning of overseas assessments, as this is an evidence gathering process in the country where the child lives, to enable a competent authority to decide whether an overseas placement would be in a child's best interests.

Rather than seek an assessment through the Central Authority, a local authority can use CFAB to obtain a local assessment. This method can be used in both BIIa/HC96 states and non-Contracting States (depending on the availability and capacity of a partner in the relevant state). The picture is further complicated by the fact that CFAB's partner in some states is the Central Authority. Thus, in one case in the sample analysed which involved Lithuania, a local authority made a request for a kin assessment through CFAB, but CFAB's partner, the Lithuanian Central Authority, responded to the request via the English Central Authority (ICACU).

[10] The Brussels II ter Regulation might be said to reflect the use of BIIa to facilitate cross-border kinship placements. Brussels II ter Art 82 contains explicit reference to the cross-border placement of children with (non-parent) relatives (albeit in the context of consent to place children rather than assessments to see if such placements are viable).

[11] BII ter Art 80 (1) (b) contemplates that information might be requested on 'the situation of a parent, a relative or other person who may be suitable to care for the child, if the situation of the child so requires' – which would conceivably encompass an assessment of a parent or prospective kinship carer's ability to care permanently for a child. This provision may have developed in response to a demand for cross-border assessments of prospective carers.

[12] HC96 Art 33 (2). This provision is distinct from BIIa Art 55 also as it requires consent to be sought in all cases where there is a contemplated placement of child in a 'foster family or institutional care, or the provision of care by *kafala* or an analogous institution'. By contrast under BIIa Art 55, consent is only required 'where public authority intervention in that Member State is required for domestic cases of child placement (BIIa Art 55 (1). Brussels II ter amends this provision to provide that consent is required for all cases where a child is placed in another Member State with a non-parent (though states can designate that consent is not required for placements with certain categories of relative) – see Brussels II ter art 82 (1) and (2).

[13] L Carpaneto, 'Cross-Border Placement of Children in the European Union' (2016) European Parliament, Committee on Legal Affairs.

In the sample of cases analysed, there were 38 cases where CFAB was asked to conduct or obtain an assessment of a parent or potential kinship carer in a BII/HC96 state and seven cases where a request was made for assessment via the Central Authority. In these seven cases, there was an express reference to an assessment of a parent or family member being sought through the Central Authority. This reference was usually found in recitals or orders within case management directions. It is possible that the number of requests was higher, as a court order is not required to facilitate co-operation requests.[14]

There was also some crossover where assessments were requested through both CFAB and the Central Authority. Generally, it was common for duplicate requests for co-operation to be made to the Central Authority and to CFAB for the same thing – this occurred in n=15/52 cases (noting that in two of these cases, requests were made to the Central Authority for co-operation in relation to a non-Contracting State: see below). There are, therefore, convoluted and converging methods for obtaining local assessments, and confusion associated with the overlapping competence of CFAB and the Central Authority in certain Contracting States.

In respect of overseas kinship assessments, the absence of a single formalised route to obtaining these assessments stands in contrast to permanence by way of intercountry adoption under the HCA 1993. Under this instrument, the sending and receiving Contracting States follow a prescribed route for assessments, and assessments themselves must address the matters set out in the Convention.[15] There is also clarity in each Contracting State as to the identity of an assessing body, and their competence to conduct the assessments, which must be undertaken by Central Authorities, public bodies or 'accredited bodies'.[16] Whilst the content and quality of intercountry adoption assessments may vary, they must at least comply with an internationally prescribed minimum standard.[17] In other words, all Contracting States to the HCA 1993 have a shared expectation of the content of intercountry adoption assessments. The HCA 1993 also ensures the recognition of adoption orders made pursuant to the Convention in the country where the child will be living, an issue which may be challenging for international kinship placements, particularly where children are placed under SGOs overseas – see chapter 8 for more on this.[18]

[14] Furthermore, the number of requests for assessment from the Central Authority is likely to be lower within this sample which emanates from CFAB cases, given that one of CFAB's core functions is to assess family members overseas.

[15] Hague Convention of 29 May 1993 on Protection of Children and Co-operation in Respect of Intercountry Adoption Art 15, 16.

[16] HCA 1993 Art 11, 12, 13.

[17] For example, the bodies that conduct international adoption assessments in England and Wales may vary, as can the focus on the international aspect of the assessment (K Hoffman, 'Beyond a two-tier service? Preparation and assessment in intercountry adoption in the UK' (2013) 37 *Adoption and Fostering* 157).

[18] HCA 1993 Art 1 (c).

In contrast to the procedure for securing permanence by way of intercountry adoption under HCA 1993, an assessment of a prospective special guardian overseas is expected to comply with the same domestic regulations as an assessment of a prospective special guardian in England and Wales.[19] As will be demonstrated in this chapter, trying to fit a cross-border assessment into a domestic legal framework can present significant challenges.

Overseas Assessment: Which Method?

In addition to the lack of a formalised central route for commissioning overseas assessment, those requesting assessments may also adopt different practices, influenced by a variety of factors. For example, there is no charge to obtain an assessment through a Central Authority, but CFAB charges for assessments by overseas partners. In a qualitative interview, LA Lawyer 7 had made a request for assessment in a HC96 Contracting State though the Central Authority, feeling it was preferable as 'obviously you are then linked in if you need to get any orders.' However, there had been a delay because the overseas Central Authority could not identify anyone to do the assessment.

> (P)art of me is thinking if we had paid the money, we would probably have had the assessment by now. Obviously, it is scarce resources and if we can, we get it done by going through a different route. (L7)

The discretion and divergence in the practice of obtaining overseas assessments creates a significant area of complexity, and some confusion. For example, in the sample analysed there were three erroneous co-operation requests directed to the Central Authority for assessment where the parent or relative lived in a non-Contracting State. This may indicate that courts and / or lawyers were concerned to 'comply' with guidance on the use of Central Authorities without verifying the applicability of BIIa/96 HC or the existence of a competent Central Authority in the state in question.

Interviewees were aware that there was no uniform approach to overseas assessments, either within England or in receiving states:

> We have a very diverse population but … different judges and different barristers follow different procedures for international assessments, and different people are

[19] The disparity in approach to assessment and placement planning for special guardianship as compared to (domestic) adoption has been noted by participants in J Harwin et al, 'The Contribution of Supervision Orders and Special Guardianship to Children's Lives and Family Justice' (2019) *Centre for Child & Family Justice Research, Lancaster University*, 115, 117, 146. Furthermore, it is often difficult to facilitate kinship placements in the USA or Canada for children who do not have citizenship or a right to remain in these countries, and such placements may need to proceed by way of intercountry adoption under the HCA 1993 – the only reason for a different legal framework in such cases being immigration controls. See *Re S and T (Children)* [2015] EWHC 1753 (Fam) for an example.

> called upon to do international assessments … so I think there's no continuity … each case is always done in a slightly different way. (SW4)

> I think it would be helpful if it was more transparent, if local authorities could know in advance what was going to happen for each country … it wouldn't require amending treaties or anything, it would require Central Authorities to agree with each other that they would provide this information. (IAC)

CFAB SW1 perceived that some local authorities might favour CFAB as a means for commissioning overseas assessments, as the professionals who conducted them were often social workers.[20] She considered that the social work orientation of CFAB's work may therefore be better suited to care proceedings than the more legalistic route using Central Authorities, which are not necessarily staffed by social workers:

> The issue with the UK is that there are certain requirements … it is intensely social work … sometimes local authorities might prefer coming to CFAB for that reason, because they don't have to explain, and everything is understood as they put referral in. CFAB SW1

Assessments of parents or kin living in non-Contracting States cannot take place through Central Authorities. The approach to assessment in these cases depends on the state in question. CFAB has partners or independent social workers in some states, who can provide assessments. Embassies may also be able to assist:

> Sometimes, oddly, it is the countries which are not Hague 1996 or Brussels where there appears to be no route through it, actually the embassy is very helpful, and you get a better and quicker result. (IAC)

In some states, however, there are no options for assessment. In one case Paternal Grandparents lived in Afghanistan, but there was no means of assessing them, and FCO Advice warned against travelling to the relevant area. However, the children in this case were placed in alternative kinship placements elsewhere.

> If it is a country where for example they don't really have children's services … or a country that is war torn … it is much more difficult … Congo has had a civil war and we are told there is a family member there. There aren't social services operating there. And CFAB … may not operate in that country … it may be ultimately that we are not able to (do the assessment). L5

[20] That is not to say that the assessment of prospective kinship carers has always been a mainstay of children's social workers. Prior to the establishment of Cafcass, for example, a child's wishes and feelings in wardship proceedings might be undertaken by civil servants employed by the Official Solicitor's office who did not have social work training (N Lowe and R White, *Wards of Court* (Butterworths, 1979), 183–184).

Deciding whether to Conduct an Overseas Kinship Assessment

There is not usually a debate as to whether or not a parent should be assessed to care for their child in care proceedings in light of a local authority's duties to place a child with their parents where possible.[21] However, the assessment of kinship carers is a more complex issue. Participants in qualitative interviews noticed a greater tendency to assess kinship carers overseas in the light of *Re B* and *Re B-S*, particularly where adoption was a potential outcome to proceedings. Of the 67 cases where the index child had a potential kinship carer to be assessed overseas, there was an express reference in 45 cases (68%) to the local authority considering adoption as a potential plan for the child.[22]

> Where adoption is the care plan, I am noticing that these care proceedings are becoming very, very lengthy. These are the ones that are going well over the 26 weeks because the courts are making sure that the local authority is exploring every possible opportunity within the extended family to be able to evidence that nothing else will do, adoption is the last resort. And this is then meaning this involves doing assessment abroad. (SW4)
>
> I suspect that we are looking more to family. We must explore every option … I suppose the knock-on effect is necessarily that some of those kinship placements may be abroad … as opposed to saying, "oh that's too difficult" we need to be open to that. (L7)
>
> I was being sent by the judge to keep going (overseas) to do these assessments. They were positive and basically the judge had said "I don't want any stone left unturned". Because there was some case law in respect of exploring every option before adoption, and that is obviously our job and our duty. (SW2 and SW3)
>
> Just in general I find that when adoption is the care plan, we all are assessing people … I think the courts are really aware that if they failed to do that it is grounds for appeal. (SW4)

Balanced against this trend towards more overseas kinship assessment, there were examples of local authorities seeking to be discharged from orders to assess kin overseas, on the basis that such assessments would be disproportionate, both in terms of their cost and the delay assessment would cause to the proceedings.

The costs of an overseas assessment through CFAB are a particular concern for local authorities, especially (as raised by Lawyer 6 below) where assessments are brief or otherwise lacking.

> I had one done in (a non-Contracting State). It looked like it had been scribbled down on a scrap of paper. In that case it was actually a positive assessment, and we would have

[21] CA 89 s 22C.

[22] In n=27 there was no reference to the possibility for adoption for the child, in n=5 cases it was unclear from the papers whether adoption was being considered by the local authority.

> had to do further assessment … but the dad had actually been positively assessed over here … it was part of our contingency planning. It is irritating when it's a CFAB assessment because … only the local authority pays for that … you'll pay thousands of pounds and get a scrappy piece of paper. (L6)

In the sample analysed, there were examples of decisions being made whether to proceed with an overseas kinship assessment. Where a parent was overseas and potentially available to care for the child, a local authority has an obligation to place a looked after child with a parent (unless this would be inconsistent with their welfare or would not be reasonably practicable).[23]

Case 15. The index child's maternal grandmother lived in South Africa. The local authority conducted a viability assessment on the telephone but argued that it was not proportionate to proceed to a full assessment as the child's father had been positively assessed. A child arrangements order was ultimately made in his favour.

Case 18. The local authority did not want to do an assessment of the paternal grandparents in America because it seemed that the father would be a viable carer for the child. The Guardian insisted that the assessment should be conducted, but ultimately it wasn't possible to identify someone to do this.

Delay was also a factor as overseas assessments may take longer than domestic ones. There are no timescales under BIIa/HC96 for the provision of information requested via Central Authorities. National reports have indicated that there can be delays (including delays between Central Authorities and the authorities charged with gathering information).[24] Similarly, assessments commissioned through other local methods (including through CFAB) will not necessarily take place within the statutory timescales for care proceedings. Although the cases analysed for this sample were subject to a 26-week time limit (albeit one that could be extended where necessary to resolve proceedings justly), the average length of proceedings where an overseas assessment (either of kin or a parent) was sought was 43.6 weeks. To place this in context, the average length of care proceedings nationally between 2015 and 2018 was 29 weeks.[25]

Sometimes a local authority conducted an initial viability assessment of an overseas kinship carer which was negative, meaning that they did not seek a full assessment. Viability assessments, also known as 'screening' assessments or 'initial family and friends care assessments', are usually conducted by a local authority

[23] CA 89 s 22C (3), (4).
[24] V Lazić et al, *Regulation Brussels IIbis Guide for Application* (Asser Institute, 2018) 286–289.
[25] 'Annual Summaries' (Cafcass) https://www.cafcass.gov.uk/about-cafcass/our-data/annual-summaries/.

social worker in a relatively short timeframe.[26] It was possible to identify from the papers that viability assessments were conducted in at least 76% (n=51/67) of cases where a child had a potential kinship carer overseas. The most common method for viability assessments was telephone (n=39 cases) and Skype was used in n=2 cases. The recommendations of a viability assessment would often inform the decision over whether or not there should be a full kinship assessment overseas, however, there were some cases where a court refused to follow a local authority's recommendation and directed a full assessment notwithstanding a negative viability assessment. This finding has parallels with Hunt's study on the perspectives of specialist social workers practising in kinship care, where some participants felt that courts directed full assessments in the face of negative viability assessments more frequently in the light of *Re B* and *Re B-S*.[27]

Case 34. A maternal aunt in a HC96 Contracting State was put forward for assessment three months into proceedings. The local authority was slow to conduct an initial viability assessment of her, but it was positive. However, the local authority then sought to argue that a full assessment should not be conducted as this would lead to a delay in securing permanence for the child. The Judge and the Guardian disagreed with their approach and an SGO assessment was conducted through CFAB. It was very comprehensive, and recommended the children be placed with her. An SGO was made in her favour, and the children moved to her care in the HC96 State. The likely alternative for the child in this case would have been their placement for adoption; the child was very young when proceedings were issued, there were no other positive assessments of family in the UK and the local authority had applied for a placement order.

Case 81. The child was cared for by individuals who were not her parents. She was three years old when proceedings were issued and could not speak or understand English. There were no family members in the UK who could look after her and she was placed in a foster placement which was not a cultural match. The local authority had conducted a viability assessment of Maternal Grandparents who lived in an East Asian country, which was negative. However, the Guardian spoke to the grandparents

[26] Family Rights Group, Initial Family and Friends Care Assessment: A Good Practice Guide (FRG, 2017) 1.1.

[27] J Hunt, 'Practising in Kinship Care: The Perspectives of Specialist Social Workers' (2021) *Kinship, Cardiff University* 39.

through a translator and was able to persuade the court that there should be a full assessment. This was commissioned through CFAB and was positive, and the child was ultimately placed with her grandparents in their home country.

Case 107. At the end of the case the index child was placed in a West African country with the maternal grandparents, under an SGO. However, the grandparents had not been actively considered as potential carers earlier in the proceedings due to a negative viability assessment conducted by telephone and email by the local authority social worker. The social worker later conceded to the court that it had not been conducted with the rigour that would be afforded to potential kinship carers living in the UK. The judge ordered a full assessment, which took place via CFAB. This assessment was comprehensive and enabled the court to place the child with her grandparents at the end of the case. The alternative outcome for the child would have been a placement in long-term foster care in England.

In contrast to substantive kinship assessments, initial viability assessments are not subject to statutory regulation (it has been argued that they should be).[28] There have been concerns about the quality of initial viability assessments, and good practice guidance has been produced in response.[29] There may also be a need for specialist practitioners with experience of assessing kin to have some input into viability assessments.[30] Cases 34, 81 and 107 illustrate the importance for a child of a *decision* about whether to conduct an overseas assessment, and the significance of viability assessments in cross-border cases. It was notable, at least in cases 81 and 107, that the Guardian and the court respectively were not prepared to accept the negative viability assessment of a prospective overseas carer conducted by the local authority. In these cases, the decision to conduct a full assessment of an overseas kinship carer gave courts the option of exploring a family placement, as opposed to adoption or long-term foster care.

It may be that overseas kinship assessments are conducted more frequently than was previously the case, in the light of a general change in approach to

[28] S Bowyer et al, 'Impact of the Family Justice Reforms on Front-line Practice Phase Two: Special Guardianship Orders' (Department for Education, 2015) 35.

[29] Family Rights Group, *Initial Family and Friends Care Assessment: A Good Practice Guide* (FRG, 2017).

[30] J Hunt, 'Practising in Kinship Care: The Perspectives of Specialist Social Workers' (2021) *Kinship, Cardiff University*, 43.

kinship assessments and placements versus adoption.[31] There is, however, a point of tension in this practice. Overseas kinship assessments which take place through CFAB or by the instruction of an independent social worker will probably represent a significant financial cost to a local authority. Overseas assessments also take longer than domestic assessments, potentially causing delay to care proceedings and the decision about a child's placement. That said, in some cases, making the decision to conduct an overseas assessment may provide a child with the opportunity to live with their family, rather than remaining in long-term foster care or being placed for adoption.

These issues may also present themselves in care proceedings where there are prospective kinship carers based in the UK – particularly those who emerge at a late stage in proceedings – as costs and delay may mean that assessment is disproportionate.[32] There were seven cases in the sample of cases analysed where a prospective kinship carer was identified at a late stage in the proceedings, including two where identification occurred just before the scheduled final hearing. However, given the costs and timescales involved with an overseas kinship assessment, the stakes are higher in a decision over whether or not to proceed with an overseas assessment.

Adequacy of Overseas Assessments

The perceived 'quality' of assessments conducted by professionals overseas was an issue in many of the cases in the Sample and was a central concern of participants in qualitative interviews. Issues about assessment quality arose in cases where there were assessments through the Central Authority and for assessments conducted through CFAB, in both BIIa/96 States and non-Contracting States. It was not therefore the case that one method for assessment (Central Authority or

[31] In the light of *Re B (A Child) (Care Proceedings: Threshold Criteria)* [2013] UKSC 33; [2013] 1 WLR 1911; *Re B-S (Children) (Adoption: Leave to Oppose)* [2013] EWCA Civ 1146; [2014] 1 WLR 563 and the introduction of the Public Law Outline (FPR 2010 PD 12A) – see Chapter 4.

[32] Participants in the study by J Harwin *et al* study of special guardianship and supervision orders identified that potential kinship carers were sometimes identified at a late stage in proceedings, and this had a knock-on effect on the 26-week time limit (J Harwin et al, 'The Contribution of Supervision Orders and Special Guardianship to Children's Lives and Family Justice' (2019) *Centre for Child & Family Justice Research, Lancaster University*, 111). Good practice guidance on special guardianship has therefore emphasised the importance of early identification of prospective carers by a local authority (Family Justice Council Public Law Working Group, 'Recommendations to Achieve Best Practice in the Child Protection and Family Justice Systems: Special Guardianship Orders' (FJC, 2020) [49]). However, the late identification of prospective carers can reflect the 'inherent difficulty in complex and divided families where court proceedings are required to secure children's protection' rather than a failing of good practice (J Masson et al, *Child Protection in Court: Outcomes for Children* (School of Law, University of Bristol and the Centre for Research on Children and Families, University of East Anglia, 2019) 228).

CFAB) yielded a better-quality assessment than another but rather that the sufficiency of an assessment varied between states, and between the local professionals conducting them. However, when examined in greater detail, criticisms about quality primarily related to situations where the assessments lacked the information required by domestic assessment regulations or did not conform to the expectations for kinship assessments by English-trained social workers.

> In 38% of valid cases (n=20) criticisms were raised of overseas assessments, either by the local authority, the Guardian or by multiple parties.
>
> In 33% of valid cases (n=21) where an overseas assessment was conducted, there was a 'top up' assessment by a variety of methods, including social workers travelling overseas and carers being invited to the UK for assessment.

The primary challenge therefore was fitting assessments conducted by professionals in other countries into the juridified social work practice of assessing parents and kin in England and Wales. In some cases, this may result in professionals being faced with placing a child overseas based on an assessment which does not contain the information for a child moving to a domestic placement:

> Ideally, we would want to have the standard we would apply normally. Because we want to get the best decision we can for the child who at the end of the day is the only one whose interests matter. But sometimes that may not be possible, and the court will have to make a decision based on the information that it has. (L5)

That is not to say that professionals found the use of Central Authorities for assessment to be a wholly negative experience but rather that assessments through this method were assessed in relative terms. For example, SW4 recalled being 'pleasantly surprised' by an assessment received through the Central Authority from the Czech Republic which had been 14 pages long, had dealt with many issues and included an analysis – in other words, it was an assessment which looked more like an English assessment than they might have expected.

CFAB Social Workers often found themselves in a dilemma where they could anticipate that an assessment by an overseas partner would be criticised in care proceedings, and sought to pre-empt these criticisms, whilst not losing the essence of a local assessment conducted by an overseas professional. There were substantive, cultural issues – for example, CFAB SW1 and SW2 spoke about the reality of child labour in some countries where prospective carers might be paying for another child's schooling in exchange for that child working in their home, and how this might be perceived in this country. There were also, however, issues about the content of overseas assessments in terms of their depth, analysis and focus:

> We have developed a network of independent social workers so we can mould, more or less, into the way we work. In our mentoring and supervision with them … we can put questions, comment and challenge in a way … as we know what challenges will be brought up in court. (CFAB SW1)

When CFAB's partner in another country was not an independent social worker but a state body, pressures to fit their assessments into the expectations of the English court gave rise to tensions. There was a concern that criticisms and requests for further information might undermine overseas professionals.

> Can we really ask those countries to provide more thorough assessments? Or do we have to respect what they think is sufficient? And there's a tension in that. And what is the answer? Well, the answer for the UK is to keep asking for more information until they say no, really. (CFAB SW4)
>
> For some countries … the tone that I get is that "we know what we're doing – we are happy to provide you more information – if you have questions you want to ask the assessing social worker can go out and ask those questions, but in terms of our procedures and how we do our things? We know what we're doing." (CFAB SW3)

CFAB SW1 perceived the dilemma of overseas, local assessments and domestic expectations in terms of a legalistic framing of social work practice.:

> Although social workers' positions have been elevated by professionalizing, when we are in the court arena, our opinion is not as valued. And then we face lots of scrutiny and challenge. Whereas I am hearing from social workers coming from Canada to the UK to practice as social workers, they are really shocked about how much they have to justify their decisions. In their country, where they make a decision that is that. We get that from Spanish social workers. They are quite surprised how much that legal side of it is involved in telling social services what to do … So, I think there's a difference there. And sometimes we do the assessments preparing for court, and the court challenges you, saying, "What about this? What about that? Have you thought about this?" And therefore, our assessments are so information packed, trying to leave no stone unturned. CFAB SW1

Several CFAB Social Workers felt that there were positive aspects in the way that overseas assessments were conducted in some countries – areas which might represent an opportunity for learning and collaboration between UK social workers and overseas professionals. CFAB SW2 spoke about a parenting assessment in Lebanon conducted by a psychologist.[33] All CFAB social workers mentioned the

[33] The use of experts such as psychologists, psychiatrists and independent social workers was more commonplace in care proceedings in England and Wales prior to the introduction of the Public Law Outline and the Children and Families Act 2014, which curtailed the use of experts except where this was 'necessary to assist the court to resolve proceedings justly' (Children and Families Act 2014 s 13). The former President of the Family Division Sir James Munby in 2013 said, in the run up to the introduction of the Public Law Outline, that he hoped the reforms would 're-position social workers

multidisciplinary approach taken in Latvia and Lithuania where an assessment would also encompass a parenting course for a prospective carer. CFAB SW3 spoke about the possibility of a more expansive way of working:

> Everybody has their own procedures and how they do things. … And I think there should be a middle ground, if possible, for countries to learn off each other and look at best practices. Understand the reasons (for different ways of working). (CFAB SW3)

As set out in the outset of this chapter, domestic guidance directed to local authorities has urged the use of cross-border co-operation, including via Central Authorities, to commission assessments of prospective carers overseas, and cautioned against UK based social workers travelling overseas to conduct assessments. This guidance was produced in case law which emphasised principles of comity, co-operation and a need to avoid ethnocentrism as well as avoid the 'sins of insularity' in the practice of care proceedings with an international element.[34]

Despite this guidance, overseas kinship assessments continue to be framed in terms of the domestic legal criteria for parenting and kinship assessments. As such it is not surprising that local assessments were frequently criticised for their 'quality' by national actors and within the cases in the Sample. Formal kinship care in England is highly regulated in comparison to many other jurisdictions.[35] It may be relatively focused on risk due to the legalistic, child protection orientation in England in comparison to other jurisdictions which tend towards the provision of services to support a child and their family, or a focus on a child's rights in the context of state child protection systems.[36] It is unlikely that an assessment by a professional in another jurisdiction will focus on the same issues as an assessment in England.[37] Furthermore, there are countries where kinship care is far more

as trusted professionals playing the central role in care proceedings which too often of late has been overshadowed by our unnecessary use of and reliance upon other experts' (J Munby, 'View from the President's Chambers (3): The process of reform: expert evidence' (2013)).

[34] *Re E (A Child) (Care Proceedings: European Dimension)* [2014] EWHC 6 (Fam); [2014] 1 WLR 2670 [20]; *Re N (Children) (Adoption: Jurisdiction)* [2015] EWCA Civ 1112; [2016] 2 WLR 713 [21].

[35] Munro and Gilligan identified a slower trajectory in the growth of formal kinship care arrangements between England, and the less regulated care system in Ireland, although this may not be solely attributable to the influence of regulation. Other factors such as cultural differences in the role of the family may also play a role for example (ER Munro and R Gilligan, 'The 'dance' of kinship care in England and Ireland: Navigating a course between regulation and relationships' (2013) 22 *Psychosocial Intervention* 185).

[36] N Gilbert, N Parton, M Skivenes, 'Changing Patterns of Response and Emerging Orientations' in N Gilbert, N Parton, M Skivenes (eds), *Child Protection Systems: International Trends and Orientations* (OUP, 2011).

[37] Early case law on transfers of jurisdiction from England and Wales to other EU Member States under BIIa Art 15 often identified that the ability to facilitate a local kinship assessment for a child was often a factor which would mean that the overseas court was 'better placed' to hear a case. For example, in *A and B (Children – Brussels II Revised – Art 15)* [2014] EWHC 3516 (Fam) Pauffley J ordered that a request be made to transfer jurisdiction in care proceedings to the Czech Republic because (inter

common than in the UK and an accepted part of everyday life, however, it tends to exist as a formalised response to child protection in high income countries.[38] The culture clash in the regulation of kinship care becomes apparent when (as discussed in chapter 8) there are attempts to mirror English orders placing children with kin in non-Contracting States where kinship care is not often subject to extensive legal regulation.

As outlined earlier in this chapter, and in detail in chapter 4, some commentators have considered that the assessment criteria for special guardianship requires strengthening, as poor quality assessments are still produced for domestic placements, and SGO assessments are out of step with adoption assessments.[39] However in recent good practice guidance, there has been no real attempt to examine how cross-border assessments can meet this high standard and, at the same time, be carried out in a 'legally compliant and culturally relevant' manner.[40]

This gives rise to a troubling dilemma. Inevitably, overseas assessments do not fit into a domestic frame. National actors involved with care proceedings seek to patch up assessments through various means, to fit assessments into a domestic frame (see below). The alternative is that a court decides about whether a placement is in a child's best interests based on a 'lesser' assessment which does not deal with all the matters contained in domestic regulations. This has the potential to create an inequality between children with overseas family connections and those who have family based in the UK. CFAB social workers identified that cross-border assessments necessarily require a distinct frame, as they present challenges and issues. The framing of overseas assessments in relative terms is problematic (and, in a sense, inevitable), but CFAB social workers suggested that there were opportunities to learn from the misalignment between overseas and domestic assessments to bring about cross-border assessments which were tailored to the issue of a child moving to live with kin in a different country.

alia) the child's extended family, who required assessment, were in that country and could be assessed by local professionals. The judge considered that 'international procedures for obtaining such assessment may fail to achieve their stated aim to the satisfaction of the Local Authority and the court.' [57] In other words, any overseas kinship assessment by a local professional was unlikely to meet domestic criteria.

[38] N Hallett, J Garstang and J Taylor, 'Kinship Care and Child Protection in High-Income Countries: A Scoping Review' (2021) *Trauma, Violence and Abuse* 1.

[39] J Harwin et al, 'The contribution of supervision orders and special guardianship to children's lives and family justice' (2010) *Centre for Child & Family Justice Research*, 115; S Bowyer et al, *Impact of the Family Justice Reforms on Front-line Practice Phase Two: Special Guardianship Orders* (Department for Education, 2015) 35; Family Justice Council Public Law Working Group, 'Recommendations to Achieve Best Practice in the Child Protection and Family Justice Systems: Special Guardianship Orders' (2020) FJC.

[40] Family Justice Council Public Law Working Group, 'Recommendations to Achieve Best Practice in the Child Protection and Family Justice Systems: Special Guardianship Orders' (FJC, 2020) [34].

Assessing a Prospective Kinship Carer's Relationship with the Child

A fundamental misalignment between overseas kinship assessments and domestic requirements concerns the assessment of a prospective kinship carer's relationship with the child. As discussed in chapter 4, recent best practice guidance on special guardianship, informed by empirical research, has stressed the importance of assessing a prospective carers relationship with a child and, if possible, placing a child with their prospective carer prior to making a final order.[41] However, it is inevitable that an overseas kinship carer will have a more distant relationship with a child, who is habitually resident in England, and assessing the capacity for that relationship to grow is challenging – even more so when an assessment is conducted at a distance. Again, this is a feature which sets overseas kinship assessments apart from domestic assessments and makes it difficult to fit such assessments into a domestic frame.

In one case, it was clear that there should have been an opportunity to observe the child in the home of her prospective carers, and how that would impact on the pre-existing dynamics in the family. There were several assessments in this case – both through the Central Authority and by a UK based ISW – but, despite this, the obvious problems with the placement were neither identified nor considered as barriers to the child's placement:

Case 48: Care proceedings were issued for a child with connections to a BIIa Member State. The child had been born in the UK and one of her parents originated from an EU State. She had a younger sibling who was also the subject of proceedings. The relevant overseas Central Authority identified a couple living in the European state as potential carers for all the children – they were distant relatives of the family, but the children had no pre-existing relationship with them. The couple underwent a series of assessments by different methods; a telephone viability assessment by the local authority (which was negative); a report through the Central Authority (which was positive). The couple also travelled to the UK and underwent an assessment by an English ISW (which recommended that the children be placed with them). Background record checks were obtained on the couple. Overall, the recommendation was that all of the children be placed with the couple under an SGO.

The index child moved to the care of her special guardians before her younger sibling, as there were practical matters which needed to be resolved

[41] *Ibid.*

in England before the younger sibling could relocate. Following the index child's move overseas and placement, it became apparent that there was information which had not been disclosed by the special guardians during the assessment process. The couple had many children, all of whom were living with them in very cramped accommodation, and in an environment which was ill suited for the index child. Almost all of their children had additional needs including physical disabilities and behavioural issues and so there were significant strains on the family. In light of this, the placement of the younger sibling with the couple did not proceed and she was placed for adoption. It was unclear from the papers what happened to the child who had been made the subject of an SGO.

A variety of methods were employed to assess the prospective carers in Case 48, but none of these were sufficient to identify the fundamental problems with the placement. Mistakes such as this happen in care proceedings. However, the harm that the child in Case 48 suffered is quite remarkable, as she moved to a country she had never lived in, to a family unit which was completely unknown to her, to a disastrous placement. Perhaps if the child had been assessed in the placement the difficulties with it would have been identified.[42] This would, however, have entailed a significant disruption to the child – moving overseas for the purposes of further assessment in their potential placement, only to have to move back when it became apparent that the placement was not in fact viable. It is also notable that the prospective carers in Case 48 had undergone a 'local' assessment by competent authorities, following a request for co-operation made via the Central Authority pursuant to the co-operation provisions of BIIa. What might be taken from Case 48 – drawing on the structure and intention of the HCA 1993 – is that there is a need for minimum standards in the context of cross-border parental and kinship assessments undertaken pursuant to the co-operation provisions of BIIa or the HC96, which entail, at the least, a home visit of the prospective carers to verify information that they provide. This recommendation is discussed further in Chapter 9.

Due to challenges associated with the perceived inadequacy of local assessments of kin living overseas, there were 'top up' assessments of kin by other means in 18 cases. There has been some reference in guidance and case law to a collaborative process for overseas kinship assessments, and whilst there were no examples of social workers in England and overseas working jointly to assess a prospective carer, there were examples of local assessments being used to inform assessments

[42] The other troubling aspect of Case 48 is the lack of clarity about what would happen to the child after the problems with the placement were identified. Would the local authority receive the child back into their care, or would the child go into state care in the EU country she had been placed in? It was not clear from the case files what had happened to her.

by English social workers.[43] The remainder of this chapter addresses the two key methods used to top up overseas assessments.

'Top-Up' Assessments by Social Workers Travelling Overseas: 'One of Our Own'

As guidance developed encouraging the use of the co-operation provisions of BIIa/HC96 to facilitate overseas kinship assessments, the practice of UK social workers travelling overseas to conduct assessments has been discouraged. The judgment in *Leicester City Council v S* in 2014 highlighted that it may not be lawful for a social worker to practice in another EU Member State.[44] DfE guidance has also cautioned against the practice and emphasised the importance of local assessment to provide the cultural, religious, ethnic and community context of the potential placement.[45]

From the data analysed for this study it seemed that this guidance had been interpreted very strictly by some actors in Local Authorities, effectively as a prohibition on the practice:

> I think I remember times when you would just send a social worker over. Even recently it has only just sunk in that we can't send people across. (L7)

Some states have also taken a strict approach, for example by preventing social workers based in the UK conducting initial viability / screening assessments by Skype or telephone.[46] LA Lawyer 6 had experienced this and had thus sought an initial viability assessment through the relevant embassy:

> There are other countries that don't allow us to do (initial assessments over the phone) because of the way their national law operates and the licensing of social work they won't allow people to do. You would have to be a social worker licensed within a country to complete that assessment. L6

In Case 11, the local authority was required by the court to make enquiries of the US Embassy to see if they were permitted to undertake an initial viability assessment of some paternal relatives. CFAB's partner in the USA then indicated that they would not undertake the full assessment if the local authority conducted viability assessments by Skype. These cases represented an extremely restrictive

[43] DfE Working with foreign authorities: child protection cases and care orders' July 2014; *Re K, T and U (Placement of Children with Kinship Carers Abroad)* [2019] EWFC 59 [74-75].

[44] *Leicester City Council v S* [2014] EWHC 1575 (Fam); [2014] CN 931.

[45] Department for Education, Working with Foreign Authorities: Child Protection Cases and Care Orders. Departmental Advice for Local Authorities, Social Workers, Service Managers and Children's Services Lawyers (DFE-00523-2014, July 2014).

[46] In *Re V-Z (Children)* [2016] EWCA Civ 475 [22] Black LJ criticised a local authority for undertaking a Skype (audio) initial assessment of a grandmother without the prior consent of the Slovak authorities who, she considered, would not have consented to this taking place.

approach to overseas kinship assessment, which seemed to interpret social workers making telephone / skype enquiries overseas as 'practising' in the relevant country.[47]

There were nonetheless instances of social workers travelling overseas to conduct assessments. In some cases, this route was pursued where information obtained through the Central Authority was insufficient and / or subject to a delay which was considered unacceptable. It was apparent from the case files that this step was not taken lightly – it was raised as an issue with the court, and there was active consideration of the legality and necessity of this approach.

Case 84. There were three assessments of maternal grandparents who lived in an EU State. Initially an assessment through CFAB resulted in a very brief (4 page) positive report. An ISW from the UK travelled to the EU State and provided a further (positive) assessment. Finally, there was an SGO assessment which was completed based on the existing assessments, and a further trip by the allocated social worker to the EU State. This was a finely balanced case and ultimately the children were not placed in the care of their grandparents but remained with their foster carers under SGOs.

Case 52. The local authority requested an assessment of a maternal grandmother in a European State through the Central Authority. After being informed that this might take up to four months, the local authority chose to send one of their social workers who was qualified in the relevant country, to conduct a full SGO assessment. However, the grandmother withdrew from the assessment process. The child was placed in long-term foster care at the end of the case.

Case 12. A request for assessment of a paternal grandmother in a European State was made by the local authority, to take place through the Central Authority. However, eight weeks after the request was made, there was no response. The local authority therefore sought permission from the court for their social worker to travel overseas to assess the grandmother. Shortly before the application was made, information received through the Central Authority suggested that the grandmother did not want to be considered

[47] Restrictions on travel associated with the Covid-19 Pandemic have meant that remote assessments have become more commonplace, including in international cases. There does not appear to have been an objection to this practice by other countries in the context of the pandemic. See Kinship Care Alliance, 'Delivering Good Practice Initial Assessments of Family and Friends Carers in the Context of Covid-19' (June 2020) Coram BAAF, Family Rights Group 6-7.

as a carer for the children. However, the local authority social worker had received contradictory information from the grandmother and travelled overseas to conduct the assessment. Ultimately it was established that the information from the Central Authority was correct – the grandparents were already acting as foster carers for another child and could not care for two more.

Case 43. A request to the Central Authority for assessment of paternal aunt in a European country gave rise to a court interview by a Guardian in that state. The local authority wanted a more detailed assessment and sent an ISW to conduct a full assessment. The court said that the local authority had to inform the relevant state authorities that they were conducting this assessment. The assessment was positive but ultimately the child was placed with her stepfather and siblings in the UK under a supervision order.

SW4 felt strongly about the advantages of a local authority social worker assessing a prospective carer overseas. In her local authority there were several social workers who had qualified overseas before practising in the UK and were able to conduct assessments in their home country.

> It is certainly my view that if you can get your own social workers to go out to those countries to do the assessments, they are of a far higher quality. I think the general view is if we can get one of our own out, we have more confidence in those assessments because they are done by our own and they know the child … What I have noted in the last two or three years is that when the assessments have been done by us … I think the child has moved. There is definitely a correlation. (SW4)

For SW4, compliance with standardised assessment procedures in England was of overwhelming importance. SW4 saw a link between the 'quality' of an assessment, and the likelihood of a child being placed overseas. This link was also apparent in one of the cases analysed.

Case 32. An assessment of maternal grandparents in a West African country was conducted via CFAB and was positive. However, the local authority said that the assessment was insufficient and did not address risk management in relation to the parents. There was a further SGO assessment, but this was negative due to an 'absence of information' from overseas. In the light of this, the local authority changed their care plan to adoption. The Guardian did not agree, and ultimately the children were placed in the West African country with the maternal grandparents under the SGO. However, what is notable about this case is that the perceived 'inadequacy' of an assessment was, for a local authority, potentially determinative of the viability of a placement.

Case 32, and the description given by SW4, illustrate the primacy of the domestic legal frame in assessing an overseas kinship carer. This data raises the possibility that a child might lose the opportunity to live with family overseas – not due to any issues with the carer, or because it would not be in the child's best interests, but because of issues with the assessment itself not meeting domestic regulatory requirements.

Family Members Travelling to the UK for 'Top-Up' Assessments

Another method used to develop overseas assessments was for prospective carers to travel to the UK for further assessment by the social worker, and to meet and spend time with the child. There were 13 cases in the Sample where parents or potential kinship carers either travelled – or were invited to travel – to the UK to undergo such an assessment.

In four of these cases, the prospective carers were unable to get a visa to visit the UK from countries including Turkey, Jamaica and Bangladesh. In one case a prospective kinship carer from a Caribbean country was living in Spain but unable to travel to the UK because of her uncertain immigration status. This hurdle was overcome by way of a virtual 'split' assessment in Case 82:

> **Case 82.** There was a partial assessment of a father in a South Asian country conducted via CFAB which focused mainly on the father's home conditions. The local authority 'topped up' the assessment by a video link with the father using an interpreter. They had hoped that he would be able to come to the UK for assessment, but he was unable to get a visa. Despite this, the methods used were sufficient to enable the index child to be placed overseas.

If a prospective carer can travel to the UK for assessment, in addition to undergoing a local assessment, then it is more likely that the court will have sufficient evidence which meets domestic requirements to decide about whether the child should go to live with that parent or relative. The viability of this method will depend upon many factors.

A significant factor for family members who live outside the EU and are not British is whether it will be possible for them to get a visitor's visa to come to the UK for assessment. In some cases, local authorities assisted parents or relatives by providing letters of support for the Home Office setting out the maintenance and accommodation they would be provided with during their stay. However, in one case, the relative had a poor immigration history in the UK and could not obtain a visitor's visa for assessment. There are also practical issues for the prospective carer – they may have work commitments or other caring responsibilities in their home country which mean they cannot come to the UK.

Although a top up assessment through this method might tick the boxes for a domestic kinship assessment, there is an element of artifice in this process. The assessing professional must imagine how the child would settle into a home environment in another country, as described by an overseas professional, based on a relationship between the prospective carer and the child observed over a couple of weeks.

In some cases, this is more straightforward than others. In Case 88 (discussed in Chapter 8), a visit by the paternal uncle and aunt to England to spend time with the child was very significant in adding to the overseas assessment through the Central Authority – it solidified their commitment to the child, the description of the bond they formed with her over a short space of time was vivid and powerful, and it was clear that they were in a position to do whatever was needed to make the child comfortable in her new home. In Case 42 (described above), the prospective carers were also positively assessed in England, in addition to undergoing an overseas assessment. However, whilst this ticked the boxes for a special guardianship assessment, there was something missing in the assessment process which failed to account for the struggle the child would experience as part of a new family unit with many competing demands on the carers.

'Testing' an Overseas Kinship Placement

The struggle to reconcile domestic guidance on kinship assessments with cross-border situations was discussed in chapter 4. Similarly, one of the difficulties experienced by participants in qualitative interviews was reconciling domestic guidance surrounding 'untested' kinship placements with cross-border situations where a prospective carer lived overseas. Qualitative interviews for this study were conducted at a time when guidance from Keehan J suggested that SGOs should not be made until a child has lived for an 'appreciable period' with their carer.[48] This guidance was considered by the Court of Appeal in *Re P-S*[49] and arose in circumstances where studies by Harwin *et al* and Masson *et al* identified that a third of children were not living with their special guardian at the time of making an SGO, and as such a significant proportion of special guardianship placements were 'untested'.[50]

[48] See *Re P-S (Children) (Care Proceedings: Special Guardianship Orders) (Association of Lawyers for Children Intervening)* [2018] EWCA Civ 1407; [2018] 4 WLR 99 [15].

[49] *Ibid* and see the discussion in Chapter 4.

[50] J Harwin et al, 'The Contribution of Supervision Orders and Special Guardianship to Children's Lives and Family Justice' (2019) Centre for Child & Family Justice Research, Lancaster University, 116; J Masson et al, *Child Protection in Court: Outcomes for Children* (School of Law, University of Bristol and the Centre for Research on Children and Families, University of East Anglia, 2019) 47.

The Family Justice Council's guidance on special guardianship has suggested a series of options for placing a child with kin on an interim basis, to enable a child to form a relationship with their kinship carer and for the strength and quality of that relationship to be assessed. None of the options laid out in the Family Justice Council guidance is well suited to placements overseas.[51] For example, if a child is to be placed overseas under an ICO, a prospective carer would need to be approved as a temporary foster carer for 16 weeks pursuant to the Care Planning Placement and Case Review (England) Regulations 2010 Reg 24, or approved by a fostering panel pursuant to Reg 22.[52] The local authority also has an obligation to comply with these Regulations in the same way as for domestic placements (for example, by arranging for the child to be regularly visited in their placement) so far as is reasonably practicable, and to set out in its care plan arrangements for the supervision of the placement.[53] Alternatively, a child could be placed overseas with a prospective carer under a CAO with a supervision order to the local authority. However, if the placement broke down, and the child needed to return to England, the local authority would not have parental responsibility for the child which may hinder their options to secure the child's safe return.[54] In summary, an interim placement overseas will either place the local authority in a position where it is difficult (or impossible) to exercise its statutory duties to ensure the child's safety, or alternatively will remove responsibility from the local authority and entrust interim care to the prospective carer. Both options have the potential to expose a child to harm.[55]

LA Lawyer 6 felt strongly that it was not appropriate to place children overseas under ICOs to 'test' placements, and that it was preferable to transfer jurisdiction under BIIa to an overseas state authority and permit that authority to monitor and implement the placement decision:

> How can a local authority exercise its statutory duties if a child is placed overseas under an interim care order? You can't. And if the child is being neglected in that country, how can we oversee it? We can't. We can't do the statutory visits once every four weeks … you must also think one of the implications of keeping (a child) on a care order is that

[51] Family Justice Council Public Law Working Group, 'Recommendations to Achieve Best Practice in the Child Protection and Family Justice Systems: Special Guardianship Orders' (FJC, 2020) Sub-Appendix B 66.

[52] SI 2010/959.

[53] SI 2010/959 Reg 12.

[54] In *K, T and U (Placement of Children with Kinship Carers Abroad)* [2019] EWFC 59 [101] Recorder Samuels QC expressed 'some concerns about how such a placement would work in the context of kinship carers based abroad', as the local authority would not be able to manage the placement, contact arrangements, and he considered that the local authority may face difficulties intervening in an overseas placement where it does not have parental responsibility for the children.

[55] There are reported cases of interim overseas kinship placements. In *London Borough of Islington v EV* [2010] EWHC 3240, a child was placed in Turkey under an ICO with his father. In *Re HA* [2019] 1 WLUK 291 a child was placed in Pakistan under an ICO on an interim basis for the purposes of further assessment. The court in this case rejected the argument that the appropriate legal structure for this placement was in wardship, due to the power to place a child overseas under an ICO under CA 89 Sch 1 Para 19.

> you're essentially saying, "Oh I want them to go but I'm not sure if I want them to stay." And you have to think about the uncertainty for the child … if you send the child over and then have to bring them back again … what about the damage that could do to the child, it is obscene. (L6)

SW2 and 3 experienced some of these challenges in a case where a child was placed under an ICO in a BIIa State:

> We don't get regular updates from the foster carer … we just have to trust that the foster carer (who is a family member) is doing everything right … that's why we want rid of the care order because this is not how we manage foster carers here in England. We can't do unannounced visits … so I don't feel they meet our fostering regulations. (SW2 and SW3)

SW1 also had a case where there was an interim placement with prospective carers, which caused a delay in securing the children's transition and permanent placement with their kinship carers:

> The plan is for them to go over the summer. Because of case precedent. You can't place and apply for an SGO now, there has to be that test period. We were going to use the summer holidays to get the children that time to settle, get them used to being in that completely new environment … that is no longer an option … (SW1)

LA Lawyer 7 had a case where a child was placed in a non-Contracting State with prospective carers under an Interim CAO, and the local authority did not therefore have parental responsibility for the child when he was placed overseas. As it would not be straightforward to recognise and enforce any return order made by the English court in the non-Contracting State, LA Lawyer 7 was asked whether she had considered what might happen if the child was not returned to the UK at the end of the interim placement. The local authority had been advised by a lawyer qualified in the relevant country that it might be very difficult to get the child back in these circumstances. However, LA Lawyer 7 said that the local authority had felt it could trust the prospective carers and they had a strong written agreement with them about the interim placement, which had been successful.[56]

The sample of cases analysed included no cases where an overseas interim placement was used to 'test' an overseas kinship placement. However, there were cases where prospective carers were invited to the UK and their relationship with the child was assessed in accommodation funded by the local authority. This may result in an assessment which is more likely to comply with special guardianship regulations. However, it is questionable whether this situation can be described as a child 'living with' their prospective carer for an appreciable period, as it takes place away from the home environment the child will experience if they are placed overseas.

[56] There are cases involving transnational adoption where courts have considered interim placements. See *M and T (Proposed Convention Adoption – Habitual Residence)* [2015] EWFC B239; *Kent County Council v PA-K and IA (a child)* [2013] EWHC 578 (Fam).

Compliance with this domestic guidance on 'testing' kinship placements is another area where domestic guidance does not adequately account for the challenges presented where kin live overseas. Despite this, qualitative interviews revealed that attempts were made to apply domestic guidance to cross-border situations. These attempts revealed new challenges for local authorities, legal complexities and potential risks for the children involved. Local authorities were caught between a 'hands on' or 'hands off' approach for interim overseas placements – to either continue to supervise placements overseas (so far as is possible) or, alternatively, to relinquish control to a child's relatives and trust that children would be safe in interim placements overseas. When thinking about the underlying intention of the guidance, to enable a child to form a relationship with a prospective carer and to facilitate the assessment of this relationship, it is far more difficult to achieve this objective by a child travelling to Pakistan or Australia than it is for a child to stay with relatives in England, or even within the same local authority. In addition to this, a child's experiences and understanding of an interim overseas kinship placement (particularly if they are travelling from a foster placement) are likely to be complex. In the case described by SW1 above, the children had travelled overseas to stay with their relatives in the summer holidays, to test the kinship placement. However, fitting the testing of an overseas kinship placement into a child's life will not always be easy, and may entail a disruption to education, a child's routine and contact with their parents. It may be the child's first experience of international travel or of visiting another country. If an interim overseas placement is not regularly monitored by a local professional, the question arises as to how a child's negative experiences might be identified and responded to if an urgent issue arises. Rigid adherence to the guidance on testing overseas kinship placements may therefore be counterproductive to assessing whether those placements will meet a child's best interests.

Summary Conclusions: Overseas Assessments

- Methods for securing assessments of parents and kin overseas varied considerably and were subject to legal / regulatory restrictions imposed by individual states e.g., preventing UK social workers from conducting assessments in the relevant state (including, sometimes, remote assessments by telephone or skype) or requiring assessments to be directed through particular routes which may not necessarily provide the best or swiftest method for assessment. It would be preferable if there was a greater awareness as to the regulatory requirements imposed by individual states as to the assessment of prospective carers of children, in light of the diversity of approaches in this area.
- National actors felt that there was a greater tendency to assess prospective kinship carers overseas especially when adoption was a potential outcome of proceedings. Local authorities sometimes argued that it was disproportionate

to assess kin living overseas, especially where there would be a significant cost or delay, or where there was a viable UK placement for the child. However, in some cases, a decision to conduct an overseas assessment provided a court with an option to place a child with family, rather than in long-term foster care or for adoption. There may be a need for judges and Guardians to scrutinise more carefully negative initial viability assessments undertaken where a prospective carer lives overseas, given that relatives overseas are less likely to have an awareness of the court process, the background concerns of the local authority or the child's situation, and there may be issues around language, understanding and cultural differences which mean that a summary viability assessment process may not easily identify viable potential carers overseas.

- There was an issue about the 'quality' of assessments conducted overseas, but this was an issue for all assessments conducted by 'local' practitioners, whether they were conducted through the Central Authority or CFAB, and whether they were in a BIIa /HC96 State or a non-Contracting State. The primary issue was that these assessments often did not correspond with domestic norms around social work assessment and legal regulations which set out what assessments should contain (particularly in relation to special guardianship assessments). The value of local assessments conducted by professionals in a country where a child may be living is clear, and it cannot be expected that a social worker in another country will assess a prospective carer in the same way as a social worker in England. However, local professionals are best placed to identify potential risks of a placement arising from prospective carers' backgrounds and home situations. There may therefore be scope for the introduction of minimum standards or criteria for assessments conducted by competent authorities following co-operation requests under the HC96. A similar structure can be seen under the HCA 1993 Art 15 which sets out the matters a receiving Contracting State must consider when assessing prospective adopters, including (but not limited to) their 'identity, eligibility and suitability to adopt, background, family and medical history, social environment'. This is expanded upon in Chapter 9.
- It was often necessary for 'top up' assessments to be conducted after local assessments to ensure compliance with domestic regulations. There was a perception that social workers should not generally travel overseas to conduct assessments, and this option was explored conscientiously and in consultation with overseas state authorities. Parents or kin were sometimes invited to the UK to undergo further assessment and spend time with the child, though this was not always possible particularly due to immigration restrictions, and especially where prospective carers lived in non-Contracting States. It would be consistent with a child's best interests if prospective carers were permitted to enter the UK on a visitor's visa for the purposes of a kinship or parental assessment, particularly as a successful assessment may result in a child being placed with that relative overseas.

- In light of the issues around the 'quality' of overseas assessments, there needs to be a change in the approach to cross-border family assessments, and a recognition that cross-border placements cannot be regulated by a domestic regime which was not devised with cross-border situations in mind. The recommendations in this regard are expanded upon in Chapter 9.
- Overall, whilst the focus of care proceedings is intended to be promoting children's welfare, when it comes to overseas assessments, there are significant legal and practical barriers which prevent a child's best interest from remaining a central focus. Without a more systematic approach, which sets in place child-focused practices and standards, difficulties will continue – some children will lose out on opportunities to be brought up by kin overseas and others will lack preparation for placements when they move to live overseas. A systematic approach to overseas assessment must be focused on the cross-border nature of the child / carer relationship and the transnational nature of the placement.

8

Findings 4: Overseas Kinship Placements

Introduction

This chapter considers the legal issues around placing children overseas in care proceedings, primarily in kinship care. In the life of a care case, this will usually occur at the conclusion of proceedings, and feeds into the practicalities of securing legal permanence for children with international connections (for further discussion of legal permanence in care proceedings, see chapter 4).

One way in which legal permanence is achieved for children to live with kin is by way of private law orders which give kin parental responsibility and confirm a child lives with them: a Special Guardianship Order (SGO); or a Child Arrangements Order (CAO). As discussed in chapter 2, a core function of BIIa/HC96 is to provide a regime for the mutual recognition of judgments, or (to use the language of HC96), 'measures of protection', between Member or Contracting States. Accordingly, where a child is placed with kin overseas under an SGO / CAO, PIL frameworks can operate to ensure that these orders are recognised and capable of enforcement in the country where the child will be living. This chapter discusses the operation of PIL in this context, as well as the way that the instruments are used or are engaged in planning for a child to live overseas, in the light of domestic guidance on kinship care.

Consent to Place a Child in a BIIa/HC96 State

The co-operation provisions in BIIa (Art 56) and the HC96 (Art 33) require that consent be obtained from competent authorities overseas prior to placing a child in 'foster care' with a 'foster family', in 'institutional care', or (in the case of HC96) 'the provision of care by *kafala* or an analogous institution'.[1] In the case of

[1] *Kafala* is a form of alternative care for children found in countries which adopt or are inspired by Islamic law, which preserves a child's biological family links, and is capable of revocation but provides for a child's needs when they cannot live or remain with their immediate family ('International Social Service Kafala or Analogous Institution; Casework, Technical Assistance and Advocacy' (HCCH)). The inclusion of *kafala* in the 1996 Hague Convention was informed by submissions by the Moroccan delegation to the Hague Special Commission (Lagarde Report (HCCH 1996) [23].

BIIa, the consent requirement only applied where 'public authority intervention is required for domestic cases of child placement' in the relevant state.[2] Where a public authority intervention was not required for the type of placement contemplated, there was merely a requirement to inform the relevant state about the placement – not to obtain their consent.[3] The HC96 does not make this distinction, and so it falls to the overseas state to determine whether the placement is one which requires their consent. There is also a requirement under the HC96 for the overseas Contracting State to arrive at its own assessment as to whether the placement is in a child's best interests, before providing its consent.[4]

A failure to obtain appropriate consent under BIIa Art 56 or HC96 Art 33 could lead to the order placing the child overseas not being recognised.[5] The Explanatory Report to the HC96 explains that this is the only non-recognition ground which can be invoked by the requested state. The rationale for this provision is to avoid states being faced with a *fait accompli* where children are placed without prior consultation.[6] Instead, it 'allows the authorities to determine in advance the conditions under which the child will stay in the receiving State, in particular in respect of immigration laws in force in that State, or even the sharing of the costs involved in carrying out the placement measure'.[7]

The requirement to engage in the consultation / consent procedure in cases where a child will move to a form of state care – including placements where children are deprived of their liberty in secure units – is clear.[8] However, the application of the provisions to cross-border kinship placements which might classically be understood as private law arrangements is less clear.[9] There is also contradictory domestic guidance on this issue. Guidance from the DfE on the operation of the HC96 says that consent will not be required for 'private law' overseas placements, including SGOs, as these do not constitute placements by the local authority.[10] However, guidance from the former President of the Family Division stresses that it is for the receiving state to consider whether any contemplated overseas kinship placement is one which requires consent pursuant to BIIa Art 56/HC96 Art 33. A study on this issue commissioned by the European Parliament in the context of BIIa Art 56 identified as an inconsistent approach

[2] BIIa Art 56 (1).

[3] BIIa Art 56 (4).

[4] HC96 Art 33 (2).

[5] BIIa Art 23 (f), HC96 Art 23 (f).

[6] P Lagarde 'Explanatory Report' (1996) HCCH [127]. The consent procedure under HC96 Art 33 is also described as a 'mandatory procedure' (ibid).

[7] *Ibid.*

[8] (C-92/12 PPU) *Health Service Executive v S.C. and A.C.* ECLI:EU:C:2012:255; [2012] 2 FLR 1040.

[9] See L Carpaneto, 'Cross-Border Placement of Children in the European Union' (2016) *European Parliament, Committee on Legal Affairs.*

[10] Department for Education, 'Cross-Border Child Protection Cases: The 1996 Hague Convention. Departmental Advice for Local Authorities, Social Workers, Service Managers and Children's Services Lawyers, October 2012' (DfE, 2012) 14.

between EU Member States to the consent procedure – with some requiring that they provide consent to all kinship placements, others for certain relatives, and others not deeming family placements to require BIIa Art 56 consent.[11] A number of Contracting States also require that their consent be sought to kinship placements pursuant to HC96 Art 33.[12] More recently, domestic guidance through case law has suggested that consent will be required for special guardianship placements with non-relatives.[13] The Brussels II ter Regulation has also attempted to introduce some clarity to the consent / consultation procedure for intra-EU kinship placements – Member States may decide that their consent is not required for placements within their own territory with certain categories of close relatives in addition to parents, and that they can provide this information to the European Commission.[14]

Whilst the rationale for the consent procedure under BIIa/HC96 is to facilitate cross-border placements, the extent to which this juridified procedure provides practical assistance for children may vary. For example, CFAB SW3 and SW4 spoke vividly about a case where a child had been placed in a BIIa state with grandparents. In the case, it was important that the overseas child protection authorities were aware of the placement because the child needed help and support in her transition from foster care in England, to the care of her grandparents. There was also a plan for post-placement support to be implemented by the overseas child protection authorities. The local authority made a co-operation request through the Central Authority pursuant to BIIa Art 56 and provided relevant documents via this route, including court orders and plans for the child. However, the child then moved at very short notice; the overseas authorities were not aware of the child's imminent arrival and had not received any of the documents the local authority had sent via Central Authority. CFAB SW3 and SW4 reflected on the case:

> I do question whether there is some confusion with the local authority solicitor sending off documents to the Central Authority … and they think that's done and everything is being dealt with … but where is the correspondence back to confirm? (CFAB SW2)

[11] See L Carpaneto, 'Cross-Border Placement of Children in the European Union' (2016) European Parliament, Committee on Legal Affairs.

[12] For example, 'Special Commission on the Practical Operation of the 1980 and 1996 Hague Conventions 10-17 October 2017: Conclusions and recommendations Adopted by the Special Commission' (2017) *HCCH* [42]; Germany – Bundesamt für Justiz, 'International Parent and Child Matters Information from the Federal Office of Justice on the return of abducted children, on cross-border conflicts relating to access and custody, and the cross-border placement of children' (July 2020) 42; S Dominelli, 'Cross-Border Placement of Children within the European Judicial Space: First Thoughts on the Recast Brussels IIa Regulation in Light of the German Experience' (2016) *SSRN Electronic Journal* https://ssrn.com/abstract=2939488.

[13] *Re S (No 3) (Care Proceedings) (Article 56 Placement in the Republic of Ireland)* [2019] EWFC 36 [57]; *Re K, T and U (Placement of Children with Kinship Carers Abroad)* [2019] EWFC 59 [108].

[14] Brussels II ter Art 83; Art 103. Brussels II ter also provides for a consultation procedure under Art 83 (3) for cross-border kinship placements.

> Maybe it is like a check box thing … like it is enough that the Local authority notify the Central Authority – and if the Central Authority confirm receipt – then that's it (CFAB SW3)
>
> But it is like Eileen Munro said in her review of social work … if it's a tick box exercise you are not actually focussing on what you're trying to do. You've just ticked a box by sending it to the Central Authority and not thinking about it holistically. (CFAB SW4)

CFABSW3 and SW4 drew a contrast with a case CFABSW3 had worked on involving a placement of a child in Nigeria. This was a placement in a non-Contracting State, and as such the local authority were not required to seek the consent of the Nigerian state authorities and there was no Central Authority to facilitate communication. However, there was extensive planning for the child's placement in Nigeria. CFAB's partner conducted a pre-placement assessment, identified local support services and health services, conducted post-placement visits and made a referral to children's services in Nigeria, so that they were aware of the child's placement.

The Nigerian case described by CFAB can be seen as an example of effective cross-border social work practice where a child's overseas placement was planned in collaboration with local services where the child would be living. By contrast, communication with children's services in the EU case took place in a legalised sphere, which was ultimately less effective for the child. Carpaneto distinguishes cases in the context of BIIa Art 56 'where solution of care envisaged comes from the State of origin' as raising particular problems, compared to 'pure' cross-border placement cases where the requesting state chooses to make use of a particular type of placement in the requested state.[15] It appears that the consultation / consent procedure contained in BIIa Art 56 / HC96 Art 33 may not be an effective means of implementing post-placement support and monitoring kinship placements in relation to children who have previously been in care, or at least is not a substitute for direct communication and agreement between social work professionals in different countries.

There was only one case in the sample of cases analysed where it was possible to identify a reference to a BIIa Art 56 request. This was in the context of a case where there was a transfer of jurisdiction under BIIa Art 15 (Case 2) which was discussed in chapter 5. As set out in the discussion of the case, there was a lack of clarity at the point of the BIIa Art 15 transfer as to the placement the child would be moving to (a placement with grandparents, or a placement in foster care). In the light of DfE guidance on the operation of the HC96 as referenced above, it may be expected that the consent procedure was not widely referenced in the Sample, although this may change as the HC96 becomes the primary PIL instrument for care proceedings with an international dimension.

[15] L Carpaneto, 'Cross-Border Placement of Children in the European Union' (2016) *European Parliament, Committee on Legal Affairs* [4.3.1].

Securing Legal Permanence Overseas: Recognition and Enforcement under BIIa/HC96 and Mirror Orders

There were 10 cases where the child was placed with kin overseas at the end of proceedings following a substantive welfare decision, as opposed to a jurisdictional decision (see Chapter 5). These included n=4 in a BIIa State, n=1 in a HC96 State and n=5 in a non-Contracting State. BIIa and the HC96 contain provisions for the mutual recognition of orders in matters of parental responsibility. Thus, an order placing a child with kin in a BIIa/HC96 State should be recognised by 'operation of law' / 'without any special procedure being required.'[16] In theory, these provisions should enable a court order made in England to be recognised in any other BIIa Member State or HC96 Contracting State without the need to issue any proceedings overseas.

As discussed in chapter 2, both HC96 and BIIa instruments permit an application to be made for recognition of an order made in another Member or Contracting State.[17] This can provide certainty that an order will be recognised – and under the HC96 it is possible to seek 'advance recognition' whereby an overseas competent authority is asked to decide on the issue of recognition before a child actually moves.[18] There were no cases in the sample where advance recognition was used to facilitate an overseas kinship placement and it would appear that HC96 Art 24 is rarely used to achieve advance recognition generally. The recent questionnaire response on the operation of the HC96 prepared by the English Central Authority and Judiciary, in advance of the 2023 HCCH Special Commission, recorded little experience of incoming HC96 Art 24 advance recognition requests, and there is (to the author's knowledge) no reported case law where advance recognition has been used in this context.[19] However, the provision may be well suited to situations where a child is moving to another Contracting State at the end of proceedings under an English order, and there is a need to ensure that the measure will be recognised in the country where the child will be living. That said, it is notable that the HC96 Art 24 process does not require a 'simple and rapid' procedure (in contrast to a declaration of enforceability under HC96 Article 26 (2)) and the process will be determined by national law in the requested state.[20] Furthermore, as identified by Lowe and Nicholls, the advance recognition procedure in HC96 Art 24 can only be invoked by an 'interested person' and as

[16] HC96 Art 23 (1); BIIa Art 21 (1).

[17] HC96 Art 24; Brussels IIa Art 21 (3).

[18] 96 HC Art 24.

[19] Questionnaire concerning the Practical Operation of the 1996 Child Protection Convention (England and Wales) (2023) available at https://assets.hcch.net/docs/bade4c6b-d949-4f54-895a-d5698079c15b.pdf.

[20] N Lowe and M Nicholls, *The 1996 Hague Convention on the Protection of Children* (LexisNexis, 2012) 5.8.

such local authorities may not be permitted to apply for advance recognition.[21] This is returned to in Chapter 9.

There are also grounds for non-recognition of orders under both BIIa/HC96, both of which are contained in Article 23 of each instrument. It is possible for recognition and enforcement to be challenged and refused by an overseas court if any of the grounds for non-recognition are made out. Grounds for non-recognition are discussed further in chapter 2.

In the sample of cases analysed, there were cases where active consideration was given to how the order would be recognised in the BIIa country where the child was living. In two of the four cases where a child was placed in a BIIa state, it was apparent from the papers that a BIIa Article 39 (Annex II) Certificate was attached to the order. The certificates in BIIa are intended to assist with recognition of orders by confirming their validity and the circumstances in which they were made:

Case 88. A CAO was made in favour of a Paternal Uncle and Aunt who lived in an Eastern European state. The order recited that the parents were not to have any contact with the child. The court attached the appropriate certificate required by BIIa Article 39 (Annex II) to the order.

Case 20. The local authority in this case went a step further and provided a small sum of money to enable a Paternal Grandmother to apply for recognition of an BIIa Article 21 (3). The final order set out some specific features of the SGO to assist with recognition e.g., that it gave the paternal grandmother parental responsibility for the child, and the way that this impacted upon the parental responsibility of the mother and father. The order was also specific as to the arrangements for contact.

The need to consider the recognition of English orders to secure overseas kinship placements under BIIa arose in some cases where a parent left England during care proceedings and returned to their home country. In eight cases in the sample, parents returned to home during care proceedings. Where a child would be placed in that country with kin, national actors were sometimes concerned that parents would disrupt overseas kinship placements:

Case 20. The local authority had been considering placing a child with a maternal grandmother in an Eastern European state. The mother returned to that state during the course of proceedings and moved very close to where the maternal grandmother was living. This triggered the local

[21] *Ibid* 5.11.

authority to propose a SGO rather than a CAO as the legal framework for the placement.

Court orders in these cases could be used as an attempt to control what happened once a child lived overseas. In practice, there is not much a local authority or court can do in England to control the future of a child overseas. At the conclusion of any care proceedings which result in a private law order placing a child with family, there is always the possibility of orders being varied or discharged by applications by the parents or carers. However, in such situations, the English court would have access to evidence from the previous proceedings and any findings made. This may not be the case for overseas placements. In particular, as confirmed by the HC96 Art 15 (3), where a child moves from one Contracting State to another, and a measure of protection was taken in relation to that child in the Contracting State of their former habitual residence, the 'conditions of application' of that measure are determined by the law of the child's new habitual residence.[22] The Practical Handbook envisages that there may be practical difficulties with applying measures taken in another Contracting State, which mean that those measures must be altered or new measures taken.[23] In any event, once a child acquires a habitual residence in another BIIa/HC96 state, after proceedings have concluded, that state's courts or authorities will be competent to make welfare decisions about a child.[24]

Case 86: There had been previous care proceedings concerning the children which had resulted in the placement of two children with their grandmother in a European State under a CAO. It had been decided by the English court that the children could not safely live with their mother or father in England. After the proceedings had concluded, the father had successfully obtained an order from the overseas court for the placement of the children with him and he returned to the UK. There followed a second set of care proceedings in England because of neglect by the father.

SGOs are often used in England and Wales as a way of securing legal permanence for children living with kinship carers. However, in several cases in the sample, the court and the parties identified that there could be difficulties in ensuring that an SGO was recognised in another state, as it provides a specific

[22] Hague Conference on Private International Law, Practical Handbook on the Operation of the 1996 Hague Child Protection Convention (The Hague, 2014) 9.3-9.8.
[23] *Ibid* 9.7.
[24] BIIa Art 8, HC96 Art 5.

set of rights and responsibilities to a carer. The structure of an SGO, and its impact on the parental responsibility of a child's parents, may be unfamiliar in other jurisdictions.[25] In Case 48 this issue was explored through a co-operation request through the Central Authority, and the EU State in question confirmed that an SGO would be recognised under BIIa Article 21. In other cases, including cases where a child was placed in a non-Contracting State, the final order set out expressly what an SGO means in terms of the carer's parental responsibility to assist with the recognition of the order overseas.

Case 88. The Paternal Uncle and Aunt were very clear they wished to care for the child permanently and expressed a wish to adopt her. However, the assessment of them conducted via CFAB contained several gaps, and the Guardian felt it was brief. For this reason, the local authority proposed the child be placed with her uncle and aunt under a CAO rather than an SGO.

Case 30. A CAO was made in relation to maternal relatives who lived in a HC96 Contracting State. Their assessment conducted via CFAB was deemed insufficient, and more akin to an initial viability assessment. The prospective carers were unable to travel to the UK for further assessment for immigration reasons. The children were living in a placement which was not a cultural match, and the Guardian was concerned about the impact of this on the children. Advice was obtained on the recognition of English orders in the relevant state, and in the light of this advice, and the adequacy of the assessment, the children were placed with their maternal relatives under a CAO.

CFAB's study into cross-border placements also found differences (with no obvious explanation) in the orders used to place children overseas at the conclusion of care proceedings.[26] This disparity in approach to legal permanence for overseas kinship placements has several dimensions. Taking a broad view, from a child's point of view there may be little difference between a CAO and an SGO when the legal system in the country they are living in does not necessarily have a distinct legal status akin to special guardianship. However, the disparity may also be seen to give rise to an inequality of treatment between children placed with kin overseas and children placed with kin in England; with the former facing

[25] E.g., 'Cross Border Child Safeguarding Working Group, International Kinship Care Guide: A Good Practice Guide for Professionals Placing Children from Local Authority Care with Family Members Abroad' (November 2020), 24.

[26] 'Cross Border Child Safeguarding: Challenges, Effective Social Work Practice and Outcomes for Children' (2018) *CFAB* 6.2.4.

placement under 'lesser orders' and losing out on the option of special guardianship because it is too difficult to ensure that such orders are recognised overseas or to obtain an assessment rigorous enough to comply with the SGO Regulations (see chapter 7).[27] In particular, it is notable that Masson *et al*'s study of care proceedings reform (which primarily concerned 'domestic' cases) identified that CAOs were far more frequently used to place children with parents rather than kinship carers, and where CAOs were used for kinship placements, there were usually clear reasons for doing so which were connected with the child's welfare needs.[28]

The disparity in the use of orders also engages with the 'irrational and unjustifiable' regime for support for kinship carers which is based on a child's legal status.[29] If a CAO is made at the end of proceedings placing a child with a non-parent relative, the local authority has discretion over whether to provide financial support for the benefit of the child.[30] By contrast, a local authority has an obligation to assess a prospective special guardian's need for support services (which can include financial support), and an ongoing responsibility to provide any services considered necessary after the SGO is made, provided that the child was looked after immediately before the making of the SGO.[31] That said, CFAB's research has established an inconsistent approach to post-placement support for overseas placements, irrespective of the form of order used, and a misconception that local authorities had no obligation to support such placements once a child had left the jurisdiction.[32] To an extent this was also reflected in this Sample – in six of the 10 cases where a child was placed overseas with kin, no proposals for post-placement support for the child were apparent from the papers.

What might be taken from this discussion is that children placed overseas may have an inconsistent experience of legal permanence. The type of order made to place a child overseas may not be dictated by what is in the individual child's best interests but rather by what is possible by reference to the domestic criteria for kinship assessments, or what is likely to be recognised in the country where the child will be living. What is positive is that there was an awareness from courts and local authorities of the operation of BIIa/HC96 to recognise SGO/CAOs in

[27] See also K, T and U (Placement of Children with Kinship Carers Abroad) [2019] EWFC 59.

[28] J Masson et al, *Child Protection in Court: Outcomes for Children* (School of Law, University of Bristol and the Centre for Research on Children and Families, University of East Anglia, 2019) 150.

[29] *Ibid* 247.

[30] CA 89 Schedule 1 Para 15.

[31] In *K, T and U (Placement of Children with Kinship Carers Abroad)* [2019] EWFC 59, Recorder Samuels QC considered that in the absence of specific guidance on support for overseas special guardianship placements, a local authority's obligations to assess and provide special guardianship support services in relation to a child who is looked after immediately prior to the making of an SGO are the same as for 'out of area' placements in a different local authority – the local authority in which the child was looked after retains a responsibility for support for three years from the making of an SGO (except for financial support where a decision to provide it was made prior to the date of the SGO) (Special Guardianship Regulations Reg 5; CA 89 s 14F).

[32] 'Cross Border Child Safeguarding: Challenges, Effective Social Work Practice and Outcomes for Children' (2018) *CFAB*, 6.2.4.

other countries. Without this awareness, a kinship carer might have been left with an English order confirming their care of the child, without any additional steps being taken to assist them in ensuring that their parental responsibility and custody for the child is recognised in their home country. Going forward, as the HC96 becomes an instrument which is more widely used, following the loss of BIIa after the end of the Brexit transition period, Article 24 of this instrument may begin to be more widely used to facilitate recognition of SGOs and CAOs in other Contracting States. If a party seeks 'advance recognition' under HC96 Art 24, this may provide an additional level of certainty that an SGO (for example) will be recognised in the country where the child will be living and mitigate concerns that courts might have about placements being disrupted or challenged by parents in their countries of origin.

Securing legal permanence for children to live with kin in non-Contracting States was achieved by way of mirror orders – a more involved process which was informed by expert evidence from foreign lawyers or advice from the relevant consulate. In all five cases where a child was placed in a non-Contracting State, expert evidence was obtained in relation to this issue (compared to 0/5 BIIa/HC96 cases). An application for a mirror order would be made in the relevant country, usually by the carers after the child moved, although on occasion it was possible for carers to apply for a mirror order / recognition before the child physically moved overseas.

LA Lawyer 6 had a case where advice from a foreign qualified lawyer informed the structure of a final order.

> (we had advice on) what (the relative) would need to do to get an order to secure the child's care and explained that there is a presumption … up until a certain age of maternal care. So, she suggested it was [made] very clear on the face of our order the reasons why he couldn't live with his mother … he went and got an order before we finalised the (care proceedings). (L6)

Obtaining a mirror order requires proceedings to be issued in the state where the child will be living. The IAC highlighted that this could be problematic in some cases:

> they will start proceedings for an equivalent order in another country and we will say 'you won't necessarily get the same outcome'. People talk merrily about mirror orders but there will be an investigation on the merits and what if that country comes to a completely different view on what is to happen to the child? People don't see that as a risk, but I do. (IAC)

The comments from the IAC are illustrated by a reported case involving a mirror order in Bangladesh.[33] Care proceedings were issued in relation to a child who had suffered burns, inflicted by either his mother or father, who had held him against a heater. The English court had determined that it was in the child's best

[33] *Re J (Care Proceedings: Placement in Bangladesh)* [2020] EWHC 490 (Fam) (5 March 2020).

interests to live with his aunt in Bangladesh, and informed by expert evidence, a Compromise Decree had been submitted to the court in Bangladesh confirming these arrangements. However (without being fully aware of the background to the case), the court in Bangladesh had made a contact order of its own motion for the child to have contact with his parents twice per week. This was said to be an order made 'in accordance with cultural norms' in Bangladesh; but according to the English court, this would have exposed the child to a risk of physical and emotional harm.[34]

One social worker at CFAB also questioned the value of mirror orders in navigating cultural expectations around contact:

> When there have been kinship assessments for maternal grandparents it comes up when we are talking about contact. The way they are looking at it, culturally that parent still has a right to see the children and what gives them something to use to fight back? They may say we can give the commitments, but how do we enforce that commitment to ensure that, you know, contact is supervised, or when they can take the child away? (CFAB SW3).

CFAB SW3's comments were apparent in one case where a child was placed in a non-Contracting State, and the local authority was concerned that the child's parents would return to that country and attempt to have unsupervised contact with the child or resume their care. The child's grandparents were required to give undertakings that they would not allow the child to have unsupervised contact with their parents which were included in the order. However, the country in which the child was placed was one where kinship care was a common informal cultural practice for children who could not be cared for by their parent but was not usually regulated or supported by the state.

Thus, it can be seen that the approach to legal permanence where children are placed in non-Contracting States is framed by reference to the way that kinship care is regulated in England. Mirror orders seek to reflect English SGOs or CAOs as closely as possible (even where SGOs or equivalent orders are not a part of the legal system where the child will be living). Less attention is given to the way that kinship care is regarded and regulated in the country where the child is expected to live permanently.

Similarly, BIIa/HC96 were used to secure the recognition of SGOs and CAOs placing children with overseas kinship carers in states which apply these instruments. Again, the starting point for these placements was the making of an English order, rather than a consideration of the way that kinship care was regulated in that country. In both BIIa / HC96 states and non-Contracting States, there was an inconsistent approach to the use of SGOs versus CAOs. This inconsistency was due to legal considerations (e.g. the extent to which it was possible to obtain an assessment compliant with the SGO regulations – see Chapter 7 – or issues surrounding the recognition of SGOs overseas) rather than welfare considerations

[34] *Ibid* [19] [25].

which indicated that a CAO would be preferable to an SGO.[35] Generally, national actors were sometimes concerned that parents might disrupt placement plans for children to live with kin overseas. There is, however, a limit to the extent that an English court can control an overseas kinship placement once a child moves overseas, and the English court loses jurisdiction to make welfare decisions about a child.

Conclusion

- Routes to securing legal permanence for children to live overseas were primarily framed in domestic terms – there was, for example, a desire to translate SGOs into other jurisdictions which may not be familiar with this form of order. Attempts to 'test' overseas kinship placements also evidenced attempts to apply domestic guidance to cross-border cases, a practice which can cause additional challenges and legal and jurisdictional complexities, as well as expose a child to potential risks which are difficult to manage in practice.
- When contrasting the approach to overseas kinship placements to domestic kinship placements (RQ3), it might be said the approach is less individualised, and overlayed by assumptions and legal compliance. This can be seen in the approach to placement 'testing' – attempting to fit an overseas placement into domestic guidance when this is not necessarily in a child's best interests.
- The Art 56 / Art 33 consultation procedure is a legalised process but one which is insufficient to ensure tailored or individualised post-placement support for a child.

Overall, the standpoint for overseas kinship placements is domestic rather than transnational. There is a desire to secure the recognition of private law orders placing children with kin overseas, rather than focussing on the approach to the regulation of kinship care in the country where the child will be living. Options for legal permanence may be limited or restricted by the cross-border nature of proceedings. However, there are options within the provisions of the HC96 (which were not explored in the cases analysed in this study) which can be considered in the context of care proceedings which may avoid some of the difficulties associated with trying to 'fit' the domestic regulation of kinship care placements into cross-border situations. This may include the application of the Applicable Law provisions of the HC96 to enable courts to take into account foreign law or terminology when considering a potential placement in another Contracting or non-Contracting state.[36] This is discussed further in Chapter 9.

[35] Cf J Masson et al, *Child Protection in Court: Outcomes for Children* (School of Law, University of Bristol and the Centre for Research on Children and Families, University of East Anglia, 2019) 150.

[36] See the discussion of the Applicable Law provisions, particularly HC96 Art 15 (2).

9

Conclusions and Recommendations

The events, as described in chapter 1, which prompted the empirical study reported/ discussed in this book, took place at a time when the UK was an EU Member State and BIIa applied to care proceedings with an EU dimension. As a result of Brexit, BIIa no longer applies to care proceedings, and has been replaced by the HC96 as the primary internationally agreed PIL framework governing the transnational aspects of these proceedings.[1] Given the historic lack of integration of EU PIL into the practice of care proceedings described in chapter 1, it is now even more important to consider the operation of care proceedings with an international dimension, and the ways that the HC96 can be used to support practice in these cases. This chapter summarises the main findings of the empirical study and makes recommendations as to future practice.

Through a broad, bottom-up analysis of the operation of care proceedings with an international dimension, the study identified four principal areas where internationally / regionally agreed PIL frameworks operate in the processing of care cases, set out in chapters 5–8. These are: 1) the operation of jurisdictional rules; 2) cross-border co-operation in relation to the exchange of child protection information; 3) overseas assessments; and 4) overseas placements, which may engage the mutual recognition provisions of the instruments discussed.

Practice in these areas has been shaped by a national wave of juridification through case law and guidance as discussed in chapter 1, relating primarily to the role of BIIa. This wave was triggered by cases where state actors from other EU States (particularly overseas embassies and Central Authorities) influenced the reframing of care cases by reference to BIIa.[2] The cases involved challenges to

[1] European Union (Withdrawal) Act 2018 s 1, s 1A; European Union (Withdrawal Agreement) Act 2020 s 39. Care proceedings issued before 11pm on 31 December 2020, but concluding after this date, may still engage with BIIa. For example, the recognition and enforcement of any orders made in proceedings issued before the end of the implementation period (but concluding after this date) is governed by BIIa (Agreement on the withdrawal of the United Kingdom of Great Britain and Northern Ireland from the European Union and the European Atomic Energy Community 2019 OJ C/384I Art 67(2)(b)).

[2] E.g. *Re B (Children)* [2012] EWCA Civ 1940; *Re T (A Child) (Care Proceedings: Request to Assume Jurisdiction)* [2013] EWCA Civ 895; [2014] Fam 130; *Re T (A Child) (Care Proceedings: Request to Assume Jurisdiction)* [2013] EWHC 521 (Fam) [2013] 2 WLR 1263; *Re MP (Fact-finding Hearing: Care Proceedings: Art15)* [2013] EWHC 2063 (Fam); [2014] 1 FLR 702; *Re E (A Child) (Care Proceedings: European Dimension)* [2014] EWHC 6 (Fam); [2014] 1 WLR 2670; *Re CK (Children) (Care Proceedings: Habitual Residence: Article 15)* [2015] EWHC 2666 (Fam); *Merton London Borough Council v B*

the legitimacy of courts' and local authorities' interventions where children had connections to other countries or were foreign nationals; criticism of the practice of non-consensual adoption in England and Wales; a strong emphasis on the need to use formal channels (i.e. Central Authorities) for cross-border co-operation; and comity in relation to state child protection practices in other EU states.[3] Within this wave of case law, a successful jurisdictional challenge (or an overseas placement which was supported by a formalised process of cross-border co-operation) would avoid the possibility of a foreign national child being placed for adoption in England and Wales at the end of care proceedings. The reframing process for care proceedings with an international dimension coincided with a general fall in adoption rates in England and Wales, and a corresponding rise in kinship placements, influenced by domestic procedural reforms and the 'disruptive judgments' of *Re B* and *Re B-S*.[4]

This study has found that the operation of internationally and regionally agreed PIL frameworks in care proceedings has been influenced by the reframing process described above but that the different dimensions of the instruments discussed operate in distinct ways in the cases themselves.

For example, as discussed in chapter 5, it was apparent in the cases analysed that there were strenuous attempts by parties, and by the court, to identify jurisdictional issues in proceedings, a practice which may have been influenced by the guidance and case law referenced above. However, there was a lack of proficiency in using and applying the jurisdictional provisions contained in BIIa/HC96. This meant that jurisdictional issues were sometimes litigated unnecessarily, in situations where the jurisdictional basis for proceedings was clear, or there was a mistaken belief that a court might lack jurisdiction because of a parent's residence overseas or a child's foreign nationality. There was also inconsistency in the procedural approach to identifying jurisdictional issues between local authorities and courts at the outset of proceedings.

There was, furthermore, a close connection between the exploration of jurisdictional issues and ideas about comity and cross-border co-operation, particularly by reference to a perceived need to notify foreign embassies of care proceedings – a practice drawn from a judicial interpretation of the Vienna Convention on Consular Relations 1967 Art 36 and 37, which has been

(Central Authority of the Republic of Latvia intervening) [2015] EWCA Civ 888; [2016] Fam. 123; *Medway Council v JB* [2015] EWHC 3064 (Fam); [2016] 2 FLR 1360.

[3] *Nottingham City Council v LM and others* [2014] EWCA Civ 152 [2014] WLR (D) 092 Ryder LJ [19]; *Re T (A Child) (Care Proceedings: Request to Assume Jurisdiction)* [2013] EWCA Civ 895; [2014] 2 WLR 1204. R Lamont, 'Care Proceedings with a European Dimension under Brussels IIa: Jurisdiction, Mutual Trust and the Best Interests of the Child' (2016) 28 *Child and Family Law Quarterly* 67.

[4] J Masson, 'Disruptive Judgments' (2017) 29 *Child and Family Law Quarterly* 401; *Re B (A Child) (Care Proceedings: Threshold Criteria)* [2013] UKSC 33; [2013] 1 WLR 191; *Re B-S (Children) (Adoption: Leave to Oppose)* [2013] EWCA Civ 1146; [2014] 1 WLR 563; J Masson et al, *Child Protection in Court: Outcomes for Children* (School of Law, University of Bristol and the Centre for Research on Children and Families, University of East Anglia, 2019) 140; J Harwin et al, 'A National Study of the Usage of Supervision Orders and Special Guardianship over Time (2007-2016)' (2015) *Nuffield Foundation* 4.

subsequently qualified through case law and guidance.[5] Local authorities were conscious that a failure to address jurisdictional issues assiduously through the involvement of foreign state bodies might lead to them being criticised at a later stage.

Chapter 2 of this book discussed the way that different jurisdictional decisions can impact on a child's welfare, with a particular focus on cases where children are removed overseas to avoid care proceedings. In the cases analysed in this book, contextualised by the perceptions of the local authority lawyers and social workers interviewed, it was clear that in some, jurisdictional decisions in care proceedings could bring about a child's move to a country where they have never previously lived, to live with people they had never met (or, as occurred in one case in the sample, to move into institutional care overseas). By contrast, when a child moves at the end of care proceedings to a kinship placement (for example) as a result of a welfare decision, there is a significant concern to ensure that the placement has been assessed by reference to domestic criteria, and (where possible) 'tested' (chapter 7). A finding that the court lacks jurisdiction on the basis of the child's habitual residence or a decision that a request should be made to transfer jurisdiction to another BIIa Member or HC96 Contracting State could bring about a particular outcome (such as the child's physical move overseas) without the court embarking on the same kind of detailed exploration of whether this might be in the child's best interests as would be expected if the court was being asked to consider an overseas family placement as an outcome at the end of care proceedings.[6]

Building on this finding, there were situations in some of the study cases considered in chapter 5 where options were available under BIIa, which could have been explored, to enable the child to remain in an interim placement in the UK pending a substantive welfare decision by an overseas court, rather than the child moving overseas immediately after a jurisdictional decision was made. Exploring these options may have meant that children did not have to be uprooted from an interim foster care placement (for example) until the competent jurisdiction had arrived at a substantive decision as to the placement which met the child's best interests.[7] These options are expanded upon by reference to the jurisdictional scheme in the HC96 in the Recommendations set out below.

[5] *Re E (A Child) (Care Proceedings: European Dimension)* [2014] EWHC 6 (Fam); [2014] 1 WLR 2670 and *Merton London Borough Council v B* [2015] EWCA Civ 888; [2016] Fam 123 [79] but as observed by Bodey J in *Re K (A Child)* [2017] EWHC 2017 (Fam) these provisions of the Vienna Convention have not been incorporated into domestic law through the Consular Relations Act 1968. Subsequent guidance has noted that it can in some cases place a child or their extended family at risk to notify the embassy of their presence in England, particularly if the child or their parents has fled the country due to state persecution and has sought asylum: Macdonald J, Moylan J, 'Family Courts Informing Consular Authorities of Proceedings' (18 April 2019) International Family Justice Office.

[6] Albeit that following the Supreme Court's decision in *Re N*, the short- and long-term impact of a transfer of jurisdiction is an important part of the court's assessment of whether it is in a child's best interests (*Re N (Children) (Adoption: Jurisdiction) (AIRE Centre and others intervening)* [2016] UKSC 15, [2017] AC 167).

[7] As illustrated by the approach taken in the case of *Re S (A Child) (Care Proceedings: Jurisdiction)* [2008] EWHC 3013 (Fam); [2009] 2 FLR 550; *Re S (No. 2) (Care Proceedings) (Article 15: Second*

Whilst jurisdictional issues were litigated in a distinct way which sought to draw upon the domestic guidance on care proceedings with an international element, overseas assessments of parents and kin were approached differently (chapter 7). It was clear that national actors were aware of the guidance emphasising the importance of local assessments, encouraging the use of Central Authorities designated by BIIa and the HC96 to support the assessment process, and discouraging the practice of UK based social workers travelling overseas.[8] However, there were significant conflicts and tensions associated with fitting local assessments into the domestic frame for care proceedings. These tensions existed whether or not local assessments were commissioned in a BIIa/HC96 state, or in a non-Contracting State.

On the surface these were procedural conflicts – an assessment by a professional overseas would be unlikely to cover the matters required for parental or kinship assessments by domestic regulations. There were concerted efforts by national actors to 'top up' local assessments by various means. However, there were broader issues engaged in these conflicts, particularly in relation to overseas kinship assessment. On the one hand, domestic care proceedings practice has seen an increase in kinship care placements, and, following on from this, an emphasis on rigour, compliance with regulations in assessing kin and caution in relation to 'untested' kinship placements.[9] On the other hand, overseas kinship assessments are unlikely to meet the standards set for formal kinship care arrangements, and most cross-border kinship placements will be untested as it is unlikely that the child has previously lived with the prospective kinship carer overseas.

The guidance available for courts and local authorities at the time of writing does not adequately account for the challenges of assessing cross-border kinship placements. Perhaps more importantly, however, the emphasis on compliance with regulations and guidance (including in relation to overseas assessments) constitutes a juridification of an area of social work practice. This process of juridification has the potential for a dysfunctional impact because an overemphasis on compliance with domestic criteria may overlook the individual issues, challenges and strengths associated with a cross-border kinship placement. These might include: a) the impact on a child of moving from one country, culture, community and language to another; b) the nature of the child's relationship with a prospective carer and how this has subsisted or waned across borders and time; c) how the child will fare in a new environment; and d) the infrastructure

Application for Second Transfer) [2019] EWFC 12; [2019] 1 WLR 5045; *Re S (No. 3) (Care Proceedings) (Article 56 Placement in the Republic of Ireland)* [2019] EWFC 36) where Irish court transferred jurisdiction to the UK, but the child remained in foster care in Ireland while the courts of England and Wales resolved the care proceedings.

[8] Department for Education, Working with Foreign Authorities: Child Protection Cases and Care Orders. Departmental Advice for Local Authorities, Social Workers, Service Managers and Children's Services Lawyers (DFE-00523-2014, July 2014); *Leicester City Council v S* [2014] EWHC 1575 (Fam); [2014] CN 931.

[9] See chapter 2.

or services in that country available to support the child's individual needs (including the child's needs associated with their experiences of neglect or abuse, which place additional demands on a kinship carer). This area of practice may be better served by a practical and collaborative approach to assessment led by social workers, which is attentive to the cross-border characteristics of an overseas placement, than attempting to fit evidence gathered from overseas into a domestic framework.

Drawing on this consideration, the operation of BIIa/HC96 in the field of cross-border co-operation through Central Authorities to exchange child protection information emerged as a distinct function of these instruments in care proceedings, and one which has not been the subject of extensive national guidance from the judiciary or the government (see chapter 6). This was primarily a social work driven area of practice arising where there was a concern that a child at risk had moved across national borders. It emerged from the ethical imperative either to secure the child's protection or to gather background information which could be used to inform the type of intervention or support the child needed. The success of the co-operation provisions of BIIa/HC96 in supporting this function was determined by the nature of a family's cross-border move. Where professionals know where a vulnerable child is travelling to ('Known Flight' cases) it is possible, proactively, to share information through Central Authorities. However, where a child is moved to an unknown country ('Unknown Flight' cases), or when authorities are not aware of a child's move because any child protection interventions were historic ('Planned Relocation' cases), it is incumbent upon professionals in the receiving country to identify the need for background information and to seek it out.

Broadly the same challenges around identifying the need to share or gather background information about a vulnerable child present themselves in domestic cases where a child or family moves between local authorities. However, there are clear duties and established practices for dealing with the movement of families between local authorities, which are not replicated in cross-border situations.[10] The absence of a formal route for the exchange of this relevant child protection information with non-Contracting States, coupled with a variation in child protection systems and record keeping, means that information is less likely to be readily exchanged where there is no Central Authority to support this process.

This study has highlighted situations where cross-border co-operation through the exchange of child protection information between Central Authorities played a vital role in keeping children safe. This has occurred primarily through creative practice where practitioners engage with the instruments, rather than through professionals following guidance. The Climbié inquiry (now over 20 years old)

[10] E.g. Department for Education, 'Working Together to Safeguard Children: A Guide to Inter-Agency Working to Safeguard and Promote the Welfare of Children, July 2018' (HM Government, 2020) 19. See discussion in Chapter 6.

highlighted the importance of local authorities learning how to obtain child protection information from overseas.[11] The approach taken in the cases analysed suggests that there is some awareness in local authorities on the use of Central Authorities to obtain this information but that there could be greater consistency in this practice, both in terms of the timing for seeking out information and the methods for requesting child protection information from non-Contracting States.

The operation of PIL instruments to secure legal permanence for children to live with kin overseas was the final core area of practice considered in this study (chapter 8). This was an area which has not been widely considered in national case law and guidance in a care proceeding context. Overall, the data analysed demonstrated an awareness of the operation of BIIa/HC96 to recognise orders placing children with family members in other Member or Contracting States at the end of care proceedings. However, the approach taken to placing children overseas reflected a desire to replicate the domestic form of legal permanence in another country, rather than considering the approach to permanence and the way that kinship care might be regulated (or unregulated) in the country where the child would be living. This was apparent where plans were made for the recognition of SGOs in other countries under BIIa/HC96 (with uncertainty about whether the distinct legal structure of an SGO would be recognised and understood in the country in question). It was also apparent in the approach to 'mirror orders' for placements in non-Contracting States. Overall, there was a desire by courts to mirror the English regulation of the kinship placement as closely as possible but without any real certainty as to whether the recognition or mirroring of the order would be successful in the legal and cultural context in which the child would be living. As was discussed in chapter 8, using the HC96 to its full potential may support the process of placing children with kin in Contracting States, in particular through the use of 'advance recognition' under HC96 Art 24, providing greater certainty as to the recognition of the order in question (albeit that this may further delay the child's placement overseas, compounding the significant delays in these cases, as discussed below). It may also be appropriate in cases where children are placed in either Contracting or non-Contracting states, for courts to consider the foreign law of the State where the child will be placed when devising an appropriate legal framework for that placement, pursuant to HC96 Art 15 (2). The use of HC96 Art 24 and Art 15 (2) was not apparent in any of the cases analysed, a matter returned to in the Recommendations set out below.

More generally, it was apparent from this study that care proceedings with an international dimension were complex and suffered from delay – two issues which have dominated discussions around the need for care proceedings reform

[11] WH Laming, The Victoria Climbié Inquiry: Report of an Inquiry by Lord Laming (HMSO, 2003) 6.619.

generally (as set out in chapter 4). For example, in the sample of cases analysed, 50% of cases were re-allocated to a higher level of judge (High Court or Circuit Judge level) during the proceedings. This may indicate that cases with an international dimension presented unforeseen complexities which emerged and evolved during the course of proceedings. Furthermore, the average length of proceedings was 42 weeks (compared to a national average of 29 weeks for the same period, 2015–2018).[12] Thirty per cent of cases lasted 51 weeks or more (one case lasted 93 weeks in total). Delay – whatever its cause – has a significant impact on the child, particularly if they are living in an interim placement during proceedings, and then are faced with moving (domestically or overseas) at the end of proceedings.[13] In 75 of the 100 cases analysed, proceedings started with an ICO which separated the child from their usual carer (most frequently into unrelated foster care). When proceedings take a year or more to resolve, a child may spend that time in an 'interim' placement(s), awaiting a decision as to where they will live. During this time children may be cared for by many different carers, living in different parts of the country, attending different schools, awaiting the court's decision about where they will live permanently.

The complexity of proceedings, and any knock-on impact that this might have on their duration, can be understood by an analysis of what is being asked of national actors involved in the cases. Guidance on practice in cross-border cases makes a series of edicts – 'do not overlook jurisdictional issues'; 'do consider transfer of jurisdiction where appropriate'; 'do not send UK social workers overseas to conduct assessments'; 'do use the Central Authority to co-operate with overseas authorities'; 'do involve embassies in care proceedings concerning foreign nationals'. These 'cross-border' edicts are suffused into the complex and multidisciplinary environment in care proceedings which already contains multiple 'domestic' requirements – minimising delay in proceedings, exploring placements with kin, ensuring kinship assessments are sufficiently rigorous and prioritising legal permanence. The integration of cross-border guidance into this environment is challenging, and national actors may be torn between complying with these 'cross-border edicts' and keeping a child's interests at the centre of the proceedings. One of the findings in chapter 7 in relation to overseas placements was that the approach to securing legal permanence for children to live overseas was less individualised than that expected in a domestic case. The focus was on compliance with procedures rather than the way that an individual child might be best served by a particular framework or outcome. The same finding is applied more broadly to many of the areas discussed in this– a micro focus on law and procedure has the potential to hinder an individualised approach to supporting children in

[12] 'Annual Summaries' (Cafcass) https://www.cafcass.gov.uk/about-cafcass/our-data/annual-summaries/.

[13] See also CA 89 s 1 (2) in relation to the impact of delay on a child's welfare.

cross-border care proceedings. As detailed by Maria Rosén *et al* in relation to the concept of passive legal framing, 'legal discourse can creep into our heads, live in our bodies, and form how we relate to and behave with each other.'[14]

However, practice in relation to cross-border co-operation to share child protection information between Central Authorities provides a glimpse of what might be possible when internationally agreed PIL instruments are viewed as *supportive or facilitative mechanisms*, rather than instruments which must be 'complied with'. This may also direct attention to any disparities in the approach taken between children with links to non-Contracting States and those with links to a state where there is an operative internationally or regionally agreed PIL framework. The child's situation remains at the heart of a case, but professionals are attentive to a child's international links and mindful of the multiple ways in which the HC96 might be engaged to support the operation of the case. This might be seen as a bottom-up approach, albeit one which is proficient and aware of what internationally / regionally agreed frameworks of PIL do and how they work.

This approach can also be seen as re-focusing on the initial aims of the HC96. As discussed in chapter 2, HC96 was an instrument which was developed and shaped by an individualised approach to children's rights, and with the protection of children involved in transnational situations at its core. This focus may have been obscured by BIIa – an instrument which did not embody a specific child protection imperative but was developed to support the functioning of the internal market. The development of case law and guidance on the operation of BIIa arose from a wider political context.[15]

In accordance with the child protection focus of HC96, some recommendations are made below as to how an individualised approach to cross-border cases could operate in practice. Some of these recommendations suggest a change in the dynamics of care proceedings with an international element. Dickens and Masson described the relationship between courts and child protection social work as 'tail wags dog'.[16] They suggest a recalibration of this relationship through collaborative ways of working, with 'judges and social work leaders sharing their different disciplinary knowledge and understandings, listening to each other without lecturing, recognising their respective contributions in non-blaming ways and agreeing on standards of practice'.[17] The same sort of recalibration could occur in the context of care proceedings with an international element; law does not necessarily control the process but law and social work co-exist as complementary but distinct disciplines which come together to secure outcomes for children which maintain, so far as possible, a child's international connections in a way which meets their best interests.

[14] M Rosén, E Arneback and A Bergh, 'A Conceptual Framework for Understanding Juridification of and in Education' [2020] *Journal of Education Policy* 1, 12.

[15] See chapter 2.

[16] J Dickens and J Masson, 'The Courts and Child Protection Social Work in England: Tail Wags Dog?' (2014) 46 *British Journal of Social Work* 355.

[17] *Ibid* 367.

Recommendations

The HC96 is now the primary international PIL instrument which governs care proceedings with an international dimension in England and Wales. Therefore, it may be appropriate to cast aside the previous national guidance on care proceedings with an international element, and focus on the way that the HC96 can operate in care proceedings to support children's best interests. The HC96 – like all the Conventions produced by the HCCH – is a living instrument, and its practical operation can adapt to national developments.[18] Drawing on this observation, as well as the diversity of ways in which the work of the HCCH can improve national practices in implementing its Conventions, there is potential for the development of a specific stream of work which focuses on good practice for the operation of the HC96 in relation to public law child protection measures and placements in kinship care. The production of an addendum practice guide using practical examples which illustrate the operation of the HC96 in a public law context would support this process. The following recommendations about the operation of the HC96 are made to support this.

Co-Operation

1. In a public law context, where child protection measures are taken or contemplated in relation to a child who has previously lived in another HC96 Contracting State, or who has family members in another Contracting State, HC96 Art 34 (1) should be used to request background information about a child or their family which may be held by the competent authorities in that Contracting State, except where this would place the child or their family at risk (HC96 Art 37). Background information of this nature will assist in identifying any prior involvement with child protection authorities, or previous court proceedings in relation to the child or their siblings. Access to this information can ensure that competent authorities are equipped with the relevant background information necessary to make a decision which protects a child and promotes their best interests.
2. In order to ensure that children remain protected by competent child protection authorities after crossing national borders, HC96 Art 36 should be used to pass information about child protection concerns, or prior child protection interventions, to competent authorities in both Contracting and non-Contracting States (except where this would place the child or their family at risk – HC96 Art 37). HC96 Art 36 may be used, for example, when vulnerable children move across borders as part of a planned relocation, or where their relocation is unplanned or occurs in an effort to evade the

[18] Ignacio Goicoechea and Brody Warren, 'National Organs and Central Authorities under HCCH Conventions' in Paul Beaumont and Jayne Holliday (eds), *A Guide to Global Private International Law* (Hart, 2022) 108.

scrutiny of child protection authorities in a particular state. As highlighted in the Practical Handbook and Explanatory Report to the HC96, where there is uncertainty as to a child's whereabouts in another Contracting State, HC96 Art 31 (c) may be used in conjunction with HC96 Art 36 to secure the co-operation of the authorities in the requested Contracting State to locate the child, as well as ensuring that authority is aware of the relevant child protection background.[19]

3. When engaging in cross-border co-operation generally (both pursuant to the HC96 Chapter V, or directly with state authorities in non-Contracting States) it is important to recall that some children, or their families, may be placed at risk or endangered by this process. This may arise particularly where a child or their parents have sought asylum from another country, or where there are issues around persecution in the country of origin. In each case it is necessary the individual child's circumstances and whether this form of co-operation is in the child's best interests or may pose a risk to any family members overseas should be considered.[20]
4. Where the HC96 is used to facilitate a child's placement, by a competent authority, with a parent or kinship carer in a different Contracting State, the co-operation provisions in Chapter V of the Convention can be used to support this process. In particular:
    a. HC96 Art 34 (1) may be used to gather information about a child, or their family members, from another Contracting State. This may encompass both:
        i. background information held by competent authorities in the Contracting State (see above at (1)), and
        ii. evidence, in the form of an assessment, of a parent or potential kinship carer.
    b. Where the information sought pursuant to Article 34 (1) is an assessment of a parent or potential kinship carer, such assessments should be sufficient to enable the requesting state to make an informed decision about the prospective carer's capacity to care for the child, in light of the child's particular characteristics, previous experiences and care. In this context, competent authorities should put in place minimum standards and criteria for assessments completed following an Article 34 (1) request. These may draw upon the criteria for assessing of prospective adopters under the HCA 1993 Art 15, and address the prospective

[19] P Lagarde, 'Explanatory Report on the 1996 Hague Child Protection Convention', HCCH 1996 [150]; Hague Conference on Private International Law, *Practical Handbook on the Operation of the 1996 Hague Child Protection Convention* (The Hague, 2014) 122–123.

[20] See HC96 Art 37; Macdonald J, Moylan J, 'Family Courts Informing Consular Authorities of Proceedings' (18 April 2019) International Family Justice Office; Department for Education, 'Care of Unaccompanied Migrant Children and Child Victims of Modern Slavery: Statutory Guidance for Local Authorities' (DfE, 2017) 58.

carer's identity, eligibility and suitability to care for the child permanently, background, family and medical history, social environment, reasons for wishing to care for the child and ability (or capacity) to provide that care.

c. The Seventh Special Commission (2017) confirmed that the consultation mechanism in HC96 Art 33 may be engaged in circumstances where children are placed with relatives.[21] Contracting States are encouraged to publish their national Article 33 procedure, addressing:
   i. Whether placement with a relative falls within the scope of HC96 Article 33 under national law, and, if so, whether there are any categories of close relative in relation to whom the procedure does not apply.[22]
   ii. Whether there are any specific requirements in terms of the content of a 'report on the child (and) reasons for the proposed placement or provision of care' which are necessary for the Article 33 request to be considered.
   iii. Timescales for responding to Article 33 requests (noting that EU Member States must respond to equivalent requests under BII ter within 3 months).[23]

d. More generally, Contracting States must ensure that Article 33 requests are dealt with swiftly, and that the Art 33 procedure operates to facilitate a child's placement in a supported and planned manner and does not represent a bureaucratic impediment to the child's placement with a family member.

Recognition and Enforcement

5. The recognition and enforcement provisions of HC96 Art 23–28 may be used to ensure that an order placing child with a kinship carer in another Contracting State is recognised in the country where the child will be living. The co-operation provisions may support this process, for example:
   a. HC96 Art 30 – Central Authorities 'may provide information as to the laws of, and services available in, their States relating to the protection of children.' A request may be made for information as to the national procedures for recognition and enforcement under HC96 Chapter IV.

[21] 'Special Commission on the Practical Operation of the 1980 and 1996 Hague Conventions (10-17 October 2017): Conclusions and recommendations Adopted by the Special Commission' (2017) HCCH [42].

[22] Cf Brussels II ter Art 83, 103. See discussion in chapter 8.

[23] Brussels II ter Art 82 (6) provides that a decision to consent to a placement will be provided within three months of receipt of the request.

b. HC96 Article 35 (1) – a request may be made for assistance in the implementation of measures of protection taken under the Convention.

6. In particular, HC96 Art 24 may be used to achieve 'advance recognition' of orders placing children with parents or kin in other Contracting States and provide certainty that an order will be recognised in the country where the child will be living. Contracting States are encouraged to adopt a simple and rapid procedure for requests for advance recognition under HC96 Art 24 (notwithstanding that there is no express requirement to do so in the HC96).
7. It would be beneficial, in this context, if Contracting States could consider their national procedures for dealing with advance recognition requests and provide information as to how these requests can be made, and the timescales for dealing with them, in a way which can be accessed and understood by parties to proceedings in other jurisdictions. This will assist competent authorities in factoring in requests for advance recognition into the court timetable for proceedings.

Jurisdiction

8. In cases where there is a plan to place a child with a parent or kinship carer in a different Contracting State, it may be appropriate for jurisdiction to be transferred to that Contracting State using the provisions in Articles 8 or 9 of the HC96 so that the legal and practical framework for that placement can be resolved by the authorities in the country where the child will be living. This may be appropriate in cases where there is certainty about a child's placement with a parent or kinship carer, but the legal framework, or arrangements for post-placement support by local state-based services, needs to be resolved by the authorities in the requested Contracting State. This may not be appropriate where there is a risk of further litigation in the requested Contracting State which may undermine the plan formulated and judged to be in the child's best interests by the competent authorities of the requesting Contracting States.
9. It should also be recalled that transfer of jurisdiction under Art 8 or Art 9 does not necessarily need to coincide with a child's physical move to the requested Contracting State. In cases where a child has been placed in interim foster care, for example, it may be appropriate for the authorities of the requesting Contracting State to continue to exercise jurisdiction on the basis of a child's presence under Articles 11 and 12 of the HC96, until there is certainty as to the child's placement in the requested state, its legal framework and arrangements for post-placement support. At this point arrangements can be made for the child's transition into their final placement in the requested Contracting State.

Applicable Law

10. Different Contracting and non-Contracting states will have different approaches to the regulation of kinship care arrangements. In some states, it is not customary for such arrangements to be regulated by the courts or through national legislation. HC96 Article 15 (2) permits courts / authorities to consider or apply foreign law where this is in a child's best interests. This provision can be used when considering the legal framework which will govern a child's placement with kin in another Contracting (or non-Contracting) State to ensure that any measure taken is consistent with the law of that State, both in terms of the terminology used and the substantive effect of the measure taken.

National Recommendations

At a national level, the following recommendations are made in light of the findings in this thesis. These should be read in conjunction with the recommendations above on the operation of the HC96.

1. Guidance from the Department for Education on the operation of the 1996 Hague Convention for local authorities should be updated in the following key respects:
   a) to account for the diversity of ways that the HC96 may be engaged to support the operation of care proceedings with an international dimension (as set out above).
   b) to update the explanation given as to the meaning of habitual residence to account for the significant developments in the interpretation of the concept which have occurred over the last ten years, and to refer to the discussion of habitual residence contained in the Practical Handbook to the HC96.[24]
   c) to reflect that a number of Contracting States require compliance with the Art 33 procedure for placements with relatives, as was confirmed in the 2017 Special Commission.[25] The current (date) guidance also states that the Art 33 procedure is not engaged for placements under SGOs as these are 'private law orders'.[26]

[24] See discussion in chapter 2.

[25] 'Special Commission on the Practical Operation of the 1980 and 1996 Hague Conventions (10-17 October 2017): Conclusions and recommendations Adopted by the Special Commission' (2017) HCCH [42].

[26] Department for Education, 'Cross-Border Child Protection Cases: The 1996 Hague Convention. Departmental Advice for Local Authorities, Social Workers, Service Managers and Children's Services Lawyers, October 2012' (DfE, 2012) 14.

2. Social workers and local authority lawyers must receive training on how to access information about vulnerable children which may be held in other countries. This was a recommendation made in the Climbié Inquiry over twenty years ago.[27] Such information should also be included on local authority electronic systems used by child protection social workers. This study has found an inconsistent approach to accessing such information. It has also identified cases where earlier disclosure of overseas child protection information may have altered the professional approach taken to protecting a child in the UK. Social workers should know how to make requests for background information under HC96 Art 34 (1) via Central Authorities, and this should be integrated into the training social workers receive on multi-agency working and information gathering in a child protection context (noting that in some jurisdictions, it may be necessary for parents to consent to the disclosure of this information). Social workers and local authority lawyers should also receive additional training which ensures that they are able to identify situations (which are likely to be relatively uncommon) where liaising with overseas state authorities may run contrary to a child's best interests.

   Social workers and local authority lawyers should also be aware of how to request background information from non-Contracting States e.g., via embassies or through CFAB, noting that there will be a significant diversity globally in the availability of records and the ability to access them but that it should not be assumed that records do not exist if the child has connections to a non-Contracting State.
3. There is a need for a greater emphasis on establishing the nature and extent of a child's international connections before or no later than the outset of care proceedings through evidence of matters such as where they have lived previously, their kinship connections overseas, their nationality, how long they have been present in England and their immigration status. This will be a factual, evidence gathering, process to be included in a social worker's initial statement of evidence. However, this evidence will foreground the consideration of international issues, and support the following (vital) processes:
   i. The early identification of jurisdictional issues in care proceedings (through attention to a child's connections to England or other countries).
   ii. The identification of potential carers overseas, and early consideration of their assessment.
   iii. The identification of immigration issues at an early stage, so that these can be resolved. This may mean regularising the immigration status of

[27] WH Laming, *The Victoria Climbié Inquiry: Report of an Inquiry by Lord Laming* (HMSO, 2003) 6.619.

a looked after child in England but also identifying a child's right to live overseas with parent or kin, which may be contingent upon their nationality or dual nationality.

4. There is also a need for additional training, and awareness raising, as to the operation of the provisions of the HC96 in the context of care proceedings. Training for the judiciary can be provided by the judicial college. Training and awareness raising for local authorities nationally may be co-ordinated through Local Family Justice Boards. However, training in this context should not be limited to legal actors – it is essential that social workers and Guardians also have a good understanding of the provisions of the HC96 and their relevance to their professional practice. Social work practice in care proceedings with an international element can play an important part in supporting courts to arrive at decisions in cross-border cases. For example:
   i) As set out above, a social worker's initial statement of evidence can address many of the factual issues which will be relevant to a habitual residence determination (e.g. duration and reasons for the child's presence in the UK, the extent of the child's integration into a social and family environment, the child's nationality and other international connections (discussed further below), the intention of the child's parents, the child's transnational and national family connections).
   ii) Social workers and Guardians can also consider in their welfare analyses the impact of a jurisdictional decision on a child's welfare interests, including:
      a. whether it would be in a child's best interests for jurisdiction to be transferred to another Contracting State.
      b. the welfare impact on a child of moving across borders as a result of a jurisdictional decision, and how any negative impact might be lessened (e.g. through remaining in an interim foster placement pending a fuller welfare decision overseas as to their final placement).
5. When developing and applying existing guidance on kinship care placements, and special guardianship, there is a need to recognise international kinship care as a distinct form of care. It is impossible to fit cross-border placements of this nature into the domestic regulatory regime for kinship care in England and Wales. In fact, an intense focus on compliance with (for example) the special guardianship regulations for a cross-border kinship placement may overlook the unique challenges and benefits for a child moving to live with kin overseas. Similarly, a focus on the domestic approach to regulating kinship care placements may overlook important aspects of the approach to kinship care in the country where the child is expected to spend their childhood.

6. When assessing prospective carers for a child overseas, co-operation through Central Authorities designated by the HC96 is one means of exploring this option. The creation of minimum criteria for the assessment of prospective carers pursuant to HC96 Art 34 (1), as recommended above, may provide a more consistent form of evidence in this context. However, the appropriate method for assessing a prospective carer overseas will depend upon the needs of the individual child, their relationship with the prospective carer and the depth and scope of any local assessment. This may mean in some cases that there is a co-operative approach with social workers collaborating across borders, in other cases an assessment through the Central Authority or via CFAB. In cases where a carer might be able to travel to the UK to spend further time with the child it would be desirable if the Home Office could facilitate visitor visas for prospective carers to come to the UK for this limited purpose. Overall, the focus in these situations should not be on compliance with domestic criteria but instead should be attentive to the specific cross-border nature of the proposed placement and obtaining the best evidence possible to enable the court to decide whether it is in the child's best interests to move overseas to live with kin. The judiciary will play a vital role in facilitating this process.
7. The legal framework for a child's placement with kin (or a parent) overseas should be informed by the approach to the regulation of the arrangement in the country where the child will be living. Expert evidence from the relevant country may support this process, but it may also be informed by social work evidence as to the cultural and community context for the placement. As set out above, HC96 Art 15 (2) provides that a court may 'exceptionally take into consideration or apply the law of another State with which the situation has a substantial connection'. The application of this provision in situations where an overseas kinship placement is contemplated may help to ensure that the legal framework for the placement is effectively implemented and understood in the country where the child will be living. Advance recognition (HC96 Art 24) may assist in providing certainty that an English order placing a child with kin in a Contracting State will be recognised prior to the child relocating. The consequence of applying these provisions may mean that an SGO is not an appropriate order to place a child with a kinship carer in a particular country. This should not, however, mean that the child or their kinship carer loses out on post-placement support services they would be entitled to if an SGO were made, simply because of issues around the recognition of an SGO in the country where the child will be living. Post placement support must be determined by the child's needs rather than the legal status of their placement.[28]

[28] DfE, *Family and Friends Care: Statutory Guidance for Local Authorities* (2010) 2.12.

8. HC96 Art 39 permits Contracting States to enter into agreements with each other to 'improve the application of (Chapter V – Co-Operation) in their mutual relations'. Such agreements must be deposited with the HCCH. It may be appropriate for the UK to consider entering into agreements with other Contracting States (particularly Ireland) to support the processing of child protection cases pursuant to HC96 Art 39. Such agreements may deal with timescales and procedures for overseas assessment and arrangements for the recognition of orders placing children in either Contracting State.

Appendix

Sample Description

A core source of data for this study was a sample of 100 care cases which were heard before the English courts between January 2015 and January 2018. Documents from the cases were used for purposes of a quantitative study, and a qualitative case file analysis. This Appendix sets out a description of the sample of 100 cases to provide context for the findings in this study at Chapters 5–8.

The Index Child – Age and Gender as Recorded

The Sample contained 62% female and 38% male index children. Using the Department of Education's age grouping criteria, 87% of the Sample (n=87) concerned children aged 9 or under. Some 26% (n=26) of index children were infants under the age of one. The age range of children in the Sample was similar to the study of Masson *et al* of care proceedings over a similar period; 58% of children were under the age of five (*cf* 56.2% and 52.1% in the two samples of Masson *et al*).[1] Due to Cafcass requiring that the child's date of birth not be recorded (only their month and year of birth), it was not possible to aggregate data on the number of newborn babies in the Sample in line with Broadhurst's age grouping criteria for children 'born into care' (e.g. under seven days of age, 1-3 weeks, 4-12 weeks etc).[2] However, due to the small sample size it is possible to identify that there were seven cases concerning babies, either newborn where proceedings were issued at birth, or under three months of age due to babies being placed with their parents in parent / mother and baby foster placements under CA 89 s20 before proceedings were issued. Unusually, in one case the index child

[1] J Masson et al, *Child Protection in Court: Outcomes for Children* (School of Law, University of Bristol and the Centre for Research on Children and Families, University of East Anglia, 2019) 81.

[2] K Broadhurst et al, 'Born into Care: Newborns in Care Proceedings in England' (2018) *The Nuffield Family Justice Observatory: Nuffield Foundation* 16.

was 16 years of age, however, there were also proceedings concerning her younger sibling who had been born in the UK.

Table 1 Index Child's Age at Issue

	Index Child's Age at Issue		
	Frequency	**Percent**	**Cumulative Percent**
Under 1	26	26.0	26.0
1–4 years of age	32	32.0	58.0
5–9 years of age	29	29.0	87.0
10–15 years of age	12	12.0	99.0
16+ years	1	1.0	100.0
Total	100	100.0	

Mothers and Fathers

The mean age of the mother was 32.6 and the father 37.3. There were five deceased parents (n=3 fathers and n=2 mothers).

Many cases within the Sample concerned children who had mothers and fathers who lived overseas (14% of mothers and 27% of fathers). Of those, some overseas parents were unidentified, meaning that they could not be found during the currency of the proceedings, and accordingly did not receive notice of the proceedings (or participate). More fathers were unidentified or identified later in the proceedings than mothers. There was only one mother who could not be identified.

Some 16 fathers were unidentified, or their identity needed to be confirmed, at the outset of proceedings. Five of these 'missing' fathers were found during proceedings. However, 11 fathers remained unidentified throughout the proceedings, of whom eight were overseas and three were based in the UK. Although due to the small sample size it is difficult to draw comparisons with other studies; in Masson et al. (2019), a similar proportion of fathers (10%) were unidentified during the proceedings.[3] The inability to identify parents in care proceedings will necessarily have implications for exploring a child's placement with their family during those proceedings, but also for future life-story work with a child who will need to understand how they came to be looked after

[3] J Masson et al, *Child Protection in Court: Outcomes for Children*' (School of Law, University of Bristol and the Centre for Research on Children and Families, University of East Anglia, 2019), 83.

by a local authority, and separated from their main carer. Where a parent is unidentified and living overseas, finding them may be even more difficult than it is where a parent is unidentified but believed to be present in the UK. The discussion in Chapter 6 about exchanging child protection information across borders is relevant to this issue – in particular that a parent present in the UK may seek to withhold information about the other parent (who lives overseas) from a local authority. As illustrated by Case 94, discussed in Chapter 6, it may be possible to identify overseas parents through a process of cross-border co-operation.

Table 2 Birth Mother's Identity Known?

Birth Mother's Identity Known?			
	Frequency	**Percent**	**Cumulative Percent**
Unidentified overseas mother	1	1.0	1.0
Mother in UK-identity known	84	84.0	85.0
Identified overseas Mother	13	13.0	98.0
Mother is deceased	2	2.0	100.0
Total	100	100.0	

Table 3 Birth Father's Identity Known?

Birth Father's Identity Known?			
	Frequency	**Percent**	**Cumulative Percent**
Unidentified overseas father	8	8.0	8.0
Unidentified father in UK	3	3.0	11.0
Father's identity known	62	62.0	73.0
Father's identity emerged / confirmed in proceedings	5	5.0	78.0
Identified overseas Father	19	19.0	97.0
Father deceased	3	3.0	100.0
Total	100	100.0	

On the basis of the document filed at the issue of proceedings, more than a quarter of fathers (28%) did not have parental responsibility for the index child at the point of issue.

Table 4 Father's Parental Responsibility

Birth Father has Parental Responsibility at issue?					
		Frequency	**Percent**	**Valid Percent**	**Cumulative Percent**
Valid	No	28	28	34.1	34.1
	Yes, from UK	40	40	48.8	82.9
	Yes, from overseas	14	14	17.1	100
	Total	82	82	100	
Missing	Birth father deceased	3	3		
	Don't Know – Not Recorded	15	15		
	Total	18	18		
Total		100	100		

Family Composition

In most cases (44%), the index child was living with their mother as a lone parent at the point that proceedings were issued, followed by both parents (27%). In just 4% of cases the father was the sole carer. Similar proportions were found in the samples taken by Masson *et al* (42% of children lived with their mother as a lone parent, 19% with both parents and 4% with their father as a lone parent).[4] In nine cases the child was cared for by someone other than their mother and father (either alone, or with a partner or other family member). This included carers outside of their family. This was often a feature in cases where a child had come to the UK without their parents.

Table 5 Child's Usual Carer

Index Child's Usual Carer			
	Frequency	**Percent**	**Cumulative Percent**
Mother	44	44.0	44.0
Father	4	4.0	48.0
Both	27	27.0	75.0
Mother and Partner	11	11.0	86.0
Father and Partner	4	4.0	90.0

(continued)

[4] J Masson et al, *Child Protection in Court: Outcomes for Children* (School of Law, University of Bristol and the Centre for Research on Children and Families, University of East Anglia, 2019) 84.

Table 5 ***(Continued)***

Index Child's Usual Carer			
	Frequency	**Percent**	**Cumulative Percent**
Maternal Family Member/s	2	2.0	92.0
Paternal Family Member/s	3	3.0	95.0
Other	3	3.0	98.0
Mother and Maternal Grandmother	1	1.0	99.0
Mother's Partner	1	1.0	100.0
Total	100	100.0	

Siblings

The discussion of sibling relationships in this section is necessarily 'frozen' in time – children may have acquired more siblings after the end of care proceedings. Some 78% of children in the Sample had one or more siblings, including half-siblings. Some 21% were 'only children' (cf 29% Masson *et al* 2019).[5] Siblings were recorded as reflected in the case file papers, namely full siblings, half siblings and step siblings. It should be noted that way of recording sibling relationships may not reflect the nature and extent of those relationships from the perspective of the index child.

Table 6 Index Child's Siblings

Index Child's Number of Siblings			
	Frequency	**Percent**	**Cumulative Percent**
No Siblings	21	21	21
One Sibling	33	33	54
Two Siblings	26	26	80
Three Siblings	6	6	86
Four Siblings	9	9	95
Five or more siblings	4	4	99
Don't Know / Unclear	1	1	100
Total	100	100	

Of those children who had siblings, more than a quarter (28%) had siblings who lived overseas according to court papers. However, information about overseas

[5] *Ibid* 83.

siblings was sometimes lacking, particularly the local authority's documents filed at issue. Siblings who live elsewhere, particularly paternal half-siblings, can be difficult to identify.[6] This difficulty is likely to be compounded where siblings live overseas unless work has been done at a pre-proceedings stage to identify overseas siblings and find out more about their relationship with the subject child and their circumstances.

Table 7 Siblings Overseas

Number of Siblings who live overseas					
		Frequency	**Percent**	**Valid Percent**	**Cumulative Percent**
Valid	One	12	12.0	15.4	15.4
	Two	7	7.0	9.0	24.4
	Three	1	1.0	1.3	25.6
	Four	2	2.0	2.6	28.2
	None, all in UK	56	56.0	71.8	100.0
	Total	78	78.0	100.0	
Missing	Child has no siblings	21	21.0		
	Unclear where sibling lives	1	1.0		
	Total	22	22.0		
Total		100	100.0		

In 65% of cases where the index child had a sibling, one or more of their siblings were also the subject of those proceedings. The relatively high proportion of siblings who were not also the subject of proceedings (35%) may be explained by the large number of siblings resident overseas.

Table 8 Siblings in the Same Proceedings

Number of the index child's siblings who are the subject of the same proceedings at issue				
	Frequency	**Percent**	**Valid Percent**	**Cumulative Percent**
One	26	26	32.9	32.9
Two	19	19	24.1	57
Three	4	4	5.1	62
Four	1	1	1.3	63.3

(continued)

[6] D Monk and J Macvarish, *Siblings, Contact and the Law: An Overlooked Relationship* (London: Birkbeck, 2018) 33.

Table 8 *(Continued)*

Number of the index child's siblings who are the subject of the same proceedings at issue				
	Frequency	**Percent**	**Valid Percent**	**Cumulative Percent**
Five	1	1	1.3	64.6
None	28	28	35.4	100
Total	79	79	100	
Index Child has no Siblings	21	21		
Total	100	100		

A number of studies have examined recurrent care proceedings where parents experience public law intervention in relation to successive children or sibling groups.[7] The family structures of mothers and fathers in recurrent care proceedings differ – mothers often with new partners or as lone parents, and fathers as part of a recurrent family or couple.[8] Recurrent parents were also evident within this Sample, although empirically these families will be harder to identify where public law interventions took place overseas, and such families are absent from studies on this topic based on Cafcass data. In 22% of cases where a child had a sibling, the sibling had been involved in previous public law proceedings.

Table 9 Siblings in Previous Public Law Proceedings

Number of Siblings in previous public law proceedings					
		Frequency	**Percent**	**Valid Percent**	**Cumulative Percent**
Valid	One	9	9	11.5	11.5
	Two	4	4	5.1	16.7
	Three	2	2	2.6	19.2
	Four	2	2	2.6	21.8
	None	61	61	78.2	100
	Total	78	78	100	

(continued)

[7] K Broadhurst et al, 'Connecting Events in Time to Identify a Hidden Population: Birth Mothers and Their Children in Recurrent Care Proceedings in England' (2015) 45 *The British Journal of Social Work*, 2241; K Broadhurst et al, 'Vulnerable Birth Mothers and Recurrent Care Proceedings: Final Summary Report' (2017) Nuffield Foundation; S Bedson et al, 'Linked lives: Gender, family relations and recurrent care proceedings in England' (2019) 105 *Children and Youth Services Review*, 104392; G Philip et al, "I had no hope, I had no help at all": insights from a first study of fathers and recurrent care proceedings' (2020) 10 *Societies*, 8.

[8] Bedson (ibid).

Table 9 *(Continued)*

Number of Siblings in previous public law proceedings					
		Frequency	**Percent**	**Valid Percent**	**Cumulative Percent**
Missing	Not Applicable	21	21		
	Don't Know / Not Recorded	1	1		
	Total	22	22		
Total		100	100		

At the conclusion of the proceedings, in 24% of cases, the index child lived in a different country from their sibling(s). This figure does not account for those cases where siblings were already separated across borders. Rather, it is intended to illustrate a particular issue which may arise in cross-border cases, as contrasted to cases where a child has no international connections. Mapping the sibling relationships, and how those might continue (or be developed) across borders, requires particular thought and planning, and the co-operation of carers overseas, who may have had little or no previous contact with the care system in England.

Table 10 Siblings separated across borders at the end of the case

Siblings separated across borders at end of case?					
		Frequency	**Percent**	**Valid Percent**	**Cumulative Percent**
Valid	No	56	56.0	75.7	75.7
	Yes	18	18.0	24.3	100.0
	Total	74	74.0	100.0	
Missing	No other subject children	26	26.0		
Total		100	100.0		

Family Residence

The concept of 'residence' was used to collect data which reflected the strength of a family's connections to the UK. Categories mirrored those used by Masson *et al.*[9] In 70% of cases, the index child was born in the UK. Overall, in 92% of cases, the index child had a strong connection to the UK, either by being born here, or by living here for over six months before proceedings were issued.

[9] J Masson et al, *Care Profiling Study* (Ministry of Justice, 2008).

Table 11 Index Child's Residence

Index Child's Residence				
	Frequency	**Percent**	**Valid Percent**	**Cumulative Percent**
UK Born	70	70	70	70
Immigrant long-term resident	22	22	22	92
Recent Immigrant (less than 6 months)	7	7	7	99
Trafficked / Suspected Trafficking	1	1	1	100
Total	100	100	100	

In contrast to the residence of the index child, most mothers and fathers in the Sample were not born in the UK. The greatest proportion were long-term residents in the UK who had migrated from another country (52% of mothers and 26% of fathers). On the whole the Sample reflected children and parents with relatively strong links to the UK, with children having stronger connections than their parents. However, it is important that this category is not overstated, as there were also a sizeable proportion of parents (and children, as outlined above) whose links to the UK were less strong, and who did not have a legal right to remain in the UK. This issue is discussed further below by reference to the nationality and immigration status of the families involved in the cases.

Table 12 Birth Mother's Residence

Birth Mother's Residence				
	Frequency	**Percent**	**Valid Percent**	**Cumulative Percent**
UK Born	27	27	27.3	27.3
Immigrant long-term resident	52	52	52.5	79.8
Recent Immigrant (less than six months)	5	5	5.1	84.8
Unclear – Frequent Cross Border Movements	1	1	1	85.9
Resident Overseas	14	14	14.1	100
Total	99	99	100	
Don't Know / Not Recorded	1	1		
Total	100	100		

Table 13 Birth Father's Residence

Birth Father's Residence					
		Frequency	**Percent**	**Valid Percent**	**Cumulative Percent**
Valid	UK Born	12	12.0	13.5	13.5
	Immigrant long-term resident	46	46.0	51.7	65.2
	Recent Immigrant (less than six months)	3	3.0	3.4	68.5
	Visiting UK from outside the EU	1	1.0	1.1	69.7
	Born Overseas, Over stayer	1	1.0	1.1	70.8
	Unclear – Frequent Cross Border Movements	1	1.0	1.1	71.9
	Resident Overseas	25	25.0	28.1	100.0
	Total	89	89.0	100.0	
Missing	Birth Father Deceased	3	3.0		
	Don't Know / Not Recorded	8	8.0		
	Total	11	11.0		
Total		100	100.0		

Ethnicity

Ethnicity was recorded using the same categories as are used by the Department for Education. Ethnicity was well recorded in the Sample generally, in contrast to nationality and immigration status. Some 45% of the children in the Sample were described as white – 'White other' being the largest category (30%) which included a high proportion of children from Eastern Europe. The children involved in the Sample were ethnically diverse, and 20% were of mixed heritage.

Table 14 Index Child's Ethnicity

Index Child's Ethnicity				
	Frequency	Percent	Valid Percent	Cumulative Percent
White British	15	15.0	15.0	15.0
White Other	30	30.0	30.0	45.0
Black African	14	14.0	14.0	59.0
Black Caribbean	2	2.0	2.0	61.0
Black Other	5	5.0	5.0	66.0
Indian	1	1.0	1.0	67.0
Pakistani	2	2.0	2.0	69.0
Bangladeshi	3	3.0	3.0	72.0
Asian Other	3	3.0	3.0	75.0
Mixed White and Black Caribbean	5	5.0	5.0	80.0
Mixed White and Black African	3	3.0	3.0	83.0
Mixed White and Asian	1	1.0	1.0	84.0
Mixed Other	11	11.0	11.0	95.0
Chinese	2	2.0	2.0	97.0
Roma	1	1.0	1.0	98.0
Arab	2	2.0	2.0	100.0
Total	100	100.0	100.0	

Most mothers and fathers of index children were white, reflecting a large eastern European representation in the Sample. There were also many black African parents, which may reflect the fact that CFAB's partners in non-BIIa/HC96 Hague Convention Contracting States are often based in African countries.

Table 15 Birth Mother's Ethnicity

Birth Mother's Ethnicity					
		Frequency	Percent	Valid Percent	Cumulative Percent
Valid	White British	26	26.0	26.8	26.8
	White Other	33	33.0	34.0	60.8
	Black African	16	16.0	16.5	77.3
	Black Caribbean	2	2.0	2.1	79.4
	Indian	3	3.0	3.1	82.5
	Pakistani	2	2.0	2.1	84.5

(continued)

Table 15 *(Continued)*

Birth Mother's Ethnicity					
		Frequency	**Percent**	**Valid Percent**	**Cumulative Percent**
	Bangladeshi	3	3.0	3.1	87.6
	Asian Other	3	3.0	3.1	90.7
	Mixed White and Black African	2	2.0	2.1	92.8
	Chinese	2	2.0	2.1	94.8
	Roma	2	2.0	2.1	96.9
	Arab	3	3.0	3.1	100.0
	Total	97	97.0	100.0	
Missing	Mother Deceased / Not Identified	3	3.0		
Total		100	100.0		

Table 16 Birth Father's Ethnicity

Birth Father's Ethnicity					
		Frequency	**Percent**	**Valid Percent**	**Cumulative Percent**
Valid	White British	13	13.0	14.6	14.6
	White Other	30	30.0	33.7	48.3
	Black African	18	18.0	20.2	68.5
	Black Caribbean	6	6.0	6.7	75.3
	Black Other	1	1.0	1.1	76.4
	Indian	1	1.0	1.1	77.5
	Pakistani	4	4.0	4.5	82.0
	Bangladeshi	2	2.0	2.2	84.3
	Asian Other	3	3.0	3.4	87.6
	Mixed White and Black Caribbean	1	1.0	1.1	88.8
	Mixed Other	1	1.0	1.1	89.9
	Chinese	2	2.0	2.2	92.1
	Roma	1	1.0	1.1	93.3
	Arab	5	5.0	5.6	98.9
	Other	1	1.0	1.1	100.0
	Total	89	89.0	100.0	

(continued)

Table 16 *(Continued)*

Birth Father's Ethnicity					
		Frequency	Percent	Valid Percent	Cumulative Percent
Missing	Father Unidentified	11	11.0		
Total		100	100.0		

Family Nationality

Data on the nationality of the child and their parents/ carers was collected. As discussed in Chapter 2, the development of case law and guidance on care proceedings with an international element has seen a renewed focus on nationality, despite the centrality of habitual residence with the legal frameworks regulating these cases. As such it is helpful to consider the extent to which the Sample contained families with foreign nationality and, following on from this, the ways that nationality arose as an issue in practice.

However, in 75% of cases, the child's nationality was not recorded in the documents filed by the local authority at the issue of proceedings. The application form for a Care or Supervision Order (C110A) does not specifically require the child's nationality to be recorded (although it does have space to particularise any international element to a case). The local authority Social Work Evidence Template (SWET) produced by the ADCS, Cafcass and endorsed by the former President of the Family Division Sir James Munby also does not specifically direct attention to the recording of a child's nationality. Confusingly, the template does have a space for the nationality of family members to be recorded, and so the nationality of parents was recorded when this part of the document was completed. The fact that the index child's nationality was not regularly recorded at the outset of proceedings meant that nationality arose as an issue more organically; it was often clarified during the course of proceedings, especially if an issue or problem arose which required the actors in the case to give direct consideration to nationality The consequence of this, however, was sometimes delay, or sometimes going down paths which led to dead ends, as illustrated by the penpictures below.

Table 17 Child's nationality recorded in documents at issue?

Child's nationality recorded in documents at issue?					
		Frequency	Percent	Valid Percent	Cumulative Percent
Valid	No	75	75.0	75.8	75.8
	Yes	24	24.0	24.2	100.0
	Total	99	99.0	100.0	

(continued)

Table 17 *(Continued)*

Child's nationality recorded in documents at issue?					
		Frequency	**Percent**	**Valid Percent**	**Cumulative Percent**
Missing	Unclear (insufficient documents)	1	1.0		
Total		100	100.0		

Table 18 Child's nationality recorded by end of case?

Child's nationality recorded by end of the case					
		Frequency	**Percent**	**Valid Percent**	**Cumulative Percent**
Valid	No	27	27	28.1	28.1
	Yes	69	69	71.9	100
	Total	96	96	100	
Missing	Unclear	4	4		
Total		100	100		

Case 2

The court requested that an EU Member State court assume jurisdiction in relation to a six-month old baby who had been placed in foster care after her birth under an interim care order. After the request for transfer of jurisdiction under BIIa was accepted by the overseas courts, the proceedings in England concluded. However, the move of the baby overseas was significantly delayed by the local authority attempting (unsuccessfully) to apply for a British passport for the baby when she was not a British national, before eventually ascertaining that they should instead be applying for the relevant foreign passport or travel document. During this period of unnecessary delay in this baby's short life, she remained in foster care and was unable to move to the care of her paternal family overseas. Had consideration been given to her nationality at the outset of proceedings, this delay could have been avoided.

Case 48

These care proceedings were protracted, lasting over two years in total. There was a plan for the child to be placed with kinship carers in an EU State with an older sibling who had moved earlier in the proceeding. Despite this, there was a delay in facilitating the placement of the child overseas because his nationality and immigration status were only established at the point at which he was due to move to the overseas placement. It had been assumed by the local authority that the child was entitled to a British passport, but it transpired that the parents did not have indefinite leave to remain, nor had they lived in the UK for five years. Accordingly, it was necessary to obtain an emergency travel document for the child to travel overseas on the basis that their kinship carer would apply for the relevant overseas passport once he was there. In the event, the placement did not proceed, and the child was placed for adoption in England.

So as to provide a fuller picture of the nationalities involved in the Sample, where possible, the index child's nationality was deduced from the information in the case files. The recording of parents' nationality was far more consistent due to it usually being recorded in the initial SWET and accordingly where both parents were, for example, British nationals, the index child's nationality was deduced as being on the basis of British citizenship, and so on. This process of deduction is not likely to be completely accurate – not least because parents' nationalities may not be recorded accurately. However, it is notable that on any view, around a quarter of cases concerned children who were British nationals (23%–25%).

Table 19 Index Child's Nationality as Recorded and Deduced

		Index Child's Nationality as Recorded	**Index Child's Nationality as deduced by PI**
		Percent	**Percent**
Valid	British	19	22
	Dual British / EU	4	3
	EU	17	26
	Outside of EU	12	19
	Dual British / Outside of EU	13	22
	Dual EU / Outside of EU	4	7
	Total	69	99
Missing	Not Recorded	31	1
Total		100	100

Nationality and immigration status can sometimes be determinative of a child's ability to live with kin overseas – where a child cannot obtain a visa to live permanently in the relevant country, it may be only possible to for them to secure immigration status there through intercountry adoption. Nationality and immigration status can also determine the type of assessment required (i.e., a kinship assessment or adoption assessment). Within the Sample this was apparent in cases involving Australia and the USA.

Case 44

The court discharged a direction for a full assessment of a relative who lived in Australia. The children were British nationals and were not entitled to Australian nationality. Information received by the local authority suggested that the only way that the children might be placed in Australia is via an 'Orphan Relative Visa' which is available where a child's parents cannot care for a child because they are 'deceased, permanently incapacitated or of unknown whereabouts'. The sponsor of this visa must meet certain criteria including by way of their relationship to the child and their right to remain in Australia. The relative in question was not a sufficiently close relation to sponsor an Orphan Relative Visa for the children. The alternative option was to pursue an adoption assessment and apply for an adoption visa. However, the local authority chose not to pursue this route on the basis that any visa application for the child would be unlikely to succeed. Their view appeared to be based on the misplaced belief that the case did not 'fit' within the Hague Convention on Intercountry adoption as there were potential adopters available in the UK. This case concluded with care and placement orders.

By contrast in Case 79, the local authority identified a paternal relative in the USA who wished to be assessed to care of the child, who was a national of a West African country. The local authority were made aware that they would need to pursue a placement by way of intercountry adoption if this was to proceed, in light of the child's nationality. However, the relative did not wish to adopt the child (and was only prepared to offer care by way of a kinship placement). Ultimately the child was placed with family in the country of his nationality.

It should be noted that ascertaining a child's nationality is not always straightforward. A child may have multiple nationalities, by birth, decent or naturalisation, depending upon the laws of the state in question. The existence of a passport evidences a child's citizenship, but there will be cases concerning children who have never had passports (see Cases 2 and 48 described above), or who do not have passports for every country of which they are citizens.

In this vein, where consideration was given to nationality, it was recorded incorrectly in many cases, or its recording evidenced misunderstandings about what nationality constitutes. In four separate cases, family members' nationalities were recorded as 'African' on forms, including within a placement order application (Cases 40, 67, 85, 105). One father was recorded as being Belarusian when he was in fact a Latvian national (Case 88). Another father's nationality was recorded as 'Czech Roma' (Case 14). These examples might be said to illustrate a failure of standardisation to deal with this particular area of practice. If nationality as a concept is not fully understood and explored, having a box on a form for nationality will not make up for that deficit.

In light of this poor recording of nationality, it was difficult to ascertain the extent to which local authorities engaged in the practice of notifying a consulate or embassy of a child's nationality in care proceedings concerning foreign nationals. As discussed in Chapter 3, through case law, particularly *Re E (A Child) (Care Proceedings; European Dimension)* and *Merton London Borough Council v B*, Munby P had suggested that courts and / or local authorities should notify embassies of care proceedings concerning foreign national children.[10] This guidance developed in response to complaints by overseas state authorities of a violation of the Vienna Convention on Consular Relations 1967 by local authorities by not informing them of proceedings. On the basis of deduced (rather than recorded) nationality, it seemed that there were 63 cases involving a child with a foreign nationality. Of those, it appeared that the relevant embassy had not been notified of proceedings in 22 cases (35%). Where embassies were notified, this usually occurred after the first CMH.

Table 20 Stage at Which Embassy Notified of Proceedings

Stage at which Embassy Notified of Proceedings		
Before Issue	Count	11
	% within Case where overseas consular authorities should have been notified?	17.50%
Before first CMH	Count	2
	% within Case where overseas consular authorities should have been notified?	3.20%
After first CMH	Count	16
	% within Case where overseas consular authorities should have been notified?	25.40%
Before IRH	Count	10
	% within Case where overseas consular authorities should have been notified?	15.90%
Before Final Hearing	Count	2
	% within Case where overseas consular authorities should have been notified?	3.20%
Not Notified	Count	22
	% within Case where overseas consular authorities should have been notified?	34.90%
Total Count		63

[10] *Re E (A Child) (Care Proceedings: European Dimension)* [2014] EWHC 6 (Fam); [2014] 1 WLR 2670, *Merton London Borough Council v B* [2015] EWCA Civ 888; [2016] Fam 123 [79].

The nationality of parents was well recorded on the SWET, as discussed above. Data was collected on the basis of the nationality as recorded at issue; in some cases where the SWET was absent, nationality was deduced where it was obvious. Most cases involved mothers and fathers who were British or EU nationals. The recording of nationality in relation to fathers was patchier due to there being less information on fathers in the Sample generally and recording sometimes suggesting confusion about what nationality is (see above).

Table 21 Birth Mother's Nationality

Birth Mother's Nationality					
		Frequency	**Percent**	**Valid Percent**	**Cumulative Percent**
Valid	British	29	29.0	30.2	30.2
	EU	33	33.0	34.4	64.6
	Outside of EU	30	30.0	31.3	95.8
	Dual British / Outside of EU	3	3.0	3.1	99.0
	Dual EU / Outside of EU	1	1.0	1.0	100.0
	Total	96	96.0	100.0	
Missing	Don't Know / Not Recorded	4	4.0		
Total		100	100.0		

Table 22 Birth Father's Nationality

Birth Father's Nationality					
		Frequency	**Percent**	**Valid Percent**	**Cumulative Percent**
Valid	British	17	17.0	20.5	20.5
	EU	26	26.0	31.3	51.8
	Outside of EU	34	34.0	41.0	92.8
	Dual British / Outside of EU	4	4.0	4.8	97.6
	Dual EU / Outside of EU	2	2.0	2.4	100.0
	Total	83	83.0	100.0	

(continued)

Table 22 ***(Continued)***

Birth Father's Nationality					
		Frequency	**Percent**	**Valid Percent**	**Cumulative Percent**
Missing	Not Applicable – No Birth Father	4	4.0		
	Don't Know / Not Recorded	13	13.0		
	Total	17	17.0		
Total		100	100.0		

Family Immigration Status

The recording of a child's immigration status was also relatively poor, although it was apparent that there were a number of cases where request was made to the Home Office for clarification as to any applications made by the parties or on behalf of the children. The results of these requests were almost always absent from the files provided, and it was unclear therefore the extent to which these requests assisted with clarifying immigration status. There was no standardised 'prompt' for recording immigration status as there was for family members' nationalities, and accordingly it is perhaps unsurprising that in 46% of cases, immigration status was not recorded. Of course, a child's immigration status will not be an issue in many, even the majority of, cases, and as such it may feel pointless to record it – arguably the last thing that is required is another box to fill in. However, as with nationality, immigration status is an integral part of securing legal permanence for a child. If a child cannot live permanently in a particular country, they have not been given a permanent placement at the conclusion of court proceedings.

Based on a comparison between immigration status as recorded, and as deduced, between 5 and 10% of children in the Sample had no immigration status in the UK. These children have an additional vulnerability, and these cases will have an additional complexity. Specialist immigration advice was often required to establish how a child could live permanently with a particular kinship carer, or indeed how their status could be regularised were they to remain in local authority care.

Table 23 Index Child's Immigration Status as Recorded

Index Child's Immigration Status as Recorded					
		Frequency	**Percent**	**Valid Percent**	**Cumulative Percent**
Valid	British Citizen	36	36.0	66.7	66.7
	ILR / Permanent Residence	1	1.0	1.9	68.5
	EEA National / Dependent of EEA National	11	11.0	20.4	88.9
	Visitor	1	1.0	1.9	90.7
	No immigration status	5	5.0	9.3	100.0
	Total	54	54.0	100.0	
Missing	Don't Know / Not Recorded	46	46.0		
Total		100	100.0		

Table 24 Index Child's Immigration Status as Deduced

Index Child's Immigration Status as Deduced				
	Frequency	**Percent**	**Valid Percent**	**Cumulative Percent**
British Citizen	46	46.0	46.0	46.0
ILR / Permanent Residence	1	1.0	1.0	47.0
EEA National / Dependent of EEA National	33	33.0	33.0	80.0
Visitor	1	1.0	1.0	81.0
No immigration status	10	10.0	10.0	91.0
Don't Know / Not Recorded / Insufficient information.	9	9.0	9.0	100.0
Total	100	100.0	100.0	

On case in particular exemplifies the complexities that may arise in relation to immigration status and nationality in care proceedings with an international element.

Case 7

Three children had come from a West African Country to the UK to live with their father and stepmother. One of the children alleged physical abuse against their stepmother and all of the children were accommodated in foster care. Once there, the children informed their foster carers that the person thought to be their father was not their father, and that they were not in fact siblings. They had entered the UK on genuine documents containing entirely false information, including in relation to their dates of birth. Their mother was reportedly deceased, and their real father could not be traced. These proceedings concluded with a care order with a care plan for long-term foster care. There were insufficient documents in this case file to ascertain what enquiries were made to clarify the children's nationalities, identities and relationships with each other and their parents, but the facts of the case demonstrate that ascertaining nationality and immigration status will not always be straightforward, and it will not necessarily be enough to rely on information given by carers.

As with the immigration status of the index child, the immigration status of parents was not always recorded, and was deduced where possible. However, it was possible to identify where parents either had no immigration status in the UK or had a pending application for asylum or leave to remain (mothers, n=11, fathers n=17).

Table 25 Birth Mother's Immigration Status (Deduced)

Birth Mother's Immigration Status (Deduced)					
		Frequency	Percent	Valid Percent	Cumulative Percent
Valid	British Citizen	32	32.0	34.8	34.8
	ILR / Permanent Residency	6	6.0	6.5	41.3
	EEA National / Dependent of EEA National	30	30.0	32.6	73.9
	Seeking Asylum	1	1.0	1.1	75.0
	Overstayer	1	1.0	1.1	76.1
	Visitor	1	1.0	1.1	77.2
	Application Pending	2	2.0	2.2	79.3
	Permanently Resident Overseas	13	13.0	14.1	93.5

(continued)

Table 25 *(Continued)*

Birth Mother's Immigration Status (Deduced)					
		Frequency	**Percent**	**Valid Percent**	**Cumulative Percent**
	Spousal Visa	1	1.0	1.1	94.6
	No Immigration Status	5	5.0	5.4	100.0
	Total	92	92.0	100.0	
Missing	Don't Know / Not Recorded / Insufficient information	8	8.0		
Total		100	100.0		

Table 26 Birth Father's Immigration Status (Deduced)

Birth Father's Immigration Status (Deduced)					
		Frequency	**Percent**	**Valid Percent**	**Cumulative Percent**
Valid	British Citizen	20	20.0	26.0	26.0
	ILR / Permanent Residency	1	1.0	1.3	27.3
	EEA National / Dependent of EEA National	21	21.0	27.3	54.5
	Overstayer	2	2.0	2.6	57.1
	Application Pending	7	7.0	9.1	66.2
	Permanently Resident Overseas	21	21.0	27.3	93.5
	Spousal Visa	2	2.0	2.6	96.1
	Student Visa	1	1.0	1.3	97.4
	No immigration status	2	2.0	2.6	100.0
	Total	77	77.0	100.0	
Missing	Not Applicable – No Birth Father Recorded	4	4.0		
	Don't Know / Not Recorded / Insufficient information	19	19.0		
	Total	23	23.0		
Total		100	100.0		

The sample analysed for this study concerned cases which pre-dated the UK's departure from the EU, on 31 January 2020. As such, the children involved in the cases in the sample who were EU Citizens (including UK Citizens) would have enjoyed a right to Freedom of Movement within the EU. This is relevant to this study in two key respects. Firstly, post-Brexit, EU nationals living in the UK were able to apply to the EU Settlement Scheme for Settled Status (if they could evidence five years' continual residence in the UK) or pre-settled status (for less than five years' residence). It is therefore important to ascertain whether EU families have regularised their immigration status in this way. The Migration Observatory identified that children of EU Citizens were a group at risk of unsettled status through the EU Settlement Scheme.[11] Furthermore, pre-settled status under the scheme lasts only for five years – following which a further application must be made for settled status. Secondly, the loss of EU freedom of movement may impact on the placement of British children with kin in EU Member States. It may require the exploration of the immigration status that the child will be entitled to in the country in question. The starting point for the exploration of these issues is the identification at an early stage in care proceedings (and ideally before proceedings are commenced) of the nationality and immigration status of the child and their parents.

[11] M Sumption and M Fernández-Reino, 'Unsettled Status – 2020: Which EU Citizens are at Risk of Failing to Secure their Rights after Brexit?" *Migration Observatory*, 24 September 2020 https://migrationobservatory.ox.ac.uk/resources/reports/unsettled-status-2020/.

BIBLIOGRAPHY

'Annex to the EU Strategy on the Rights of the Child: EU Aquis and Policy Documents on the Rights of the A71 (2021) European Commission

'European Judicial Network in Civil and Commercial Matters: Report of Activities since the 7th Meeting of the Central Authorities in June 2013 (Dublin) United Kingdom'

'GDPR Details for Researchers' (University of Bristol) <http://www.bristol.ac.uk/secretary/data-protection/gdpr/gdpr-details-for-researchers/> accessed 17 January 2022

'International Social Service Kafala or Analogous Institution; Casework, Technical Assistance and Advocacy' (HCCH)

'Outbound Permanence Service' (IAC) https://www.icacentre.org.uk/professionals/outbound-permanence-service/ accessed 17 January 2022

'Annual Summaries' (Cafcass) https://www.cafcass.gov.uk/about-cafcass/our-data/annual-summaries/ accessed 17 March 2022

'Cross Border Child Safeguarding: Challenges, Effective Social Work Practice and Outcomes for Children' (2018) CFAB

'Revealed: The Networks Helping Families Flee Social Services' (Channel 4 News, 20 July 2012) https://www.channel4.com/news/revealed-the-networks-helping-families-flee-social-services accessed 7 March 2022

'Special Commission on the Practical Operation of the 1980 and 1996 Hague Conventions (10–17 October 2017: Conclusions and recommendations Adopted by the Special Commission' (2017) HCCH

The Implementation and Operation of the 1993 Hague Intercountry Adoption Convention: Guide to Good Practice. Guide No. 1 under the Hague Convention of 29 May, 1993 on Protection of Children and Co-Operation in Respect of Intercountry Adoption. (HCCH, Family Law 2008)

Questionnaire concerning the Practical Operation of the 1996 Child Protection Convention (England and Wales) (2023) available at https://assets.hcch.net/docs/bade4c6b-d949-4f54-895a-d5698079c15b.pdf

Hague Conference on Private International Law, Practical Handbook on the Operation of the 1996 Hague Child Protection Convention (The Hague, 2014) available at https://www.hcch.net/en/publications-and-studies/details4/?pid=6096&dtid=3

Bainham A, 'Private and Public Children Law: An Underexplored Relationship' (2013) 25 *Child and Family Law Quarterly* 138

Balasundaram N, 'British Families Flee to Ireland to Escape Threat of Social Services' (Irish Post, 19 August 2015) https://www.irishpost.com/news/british-families-flee-to-ireland-to-escape-threat-of-social-services-63574> accessed 7 March 2022

Banakar R, 'On Socio-Legal Design' (2019) SSRN Electronic Journal https://www.ssrn.com/abstract=3463028 accessed 9 November 2020

Beaumont P, Walker L, Holliday J, 'Conflicts of EU courts on child abduction: the reality of Article 11(6)–(8) Brussels IIa proceedings across the EU' (2016) 12 *Journal of Private International Law* 211

Beaumont P and Holliday J, 'Recent Developments on the Meaning of "Habitual Residence" in Alleged Child Abduction Cases' in Mirela Župan (ed), *Private International Law in the Jurisprudence of European Courts – Family at Focus* (University of Osijek, Croatia 2015)

Beaumont P and Danov M, 'Introduction: Research Aims and Methodology' in Beaumont and others (eds), *Cross-Border Litigation in Europe* (Hart Publishing, 2017)

Beaumont P and Trimmings K, 'Court of Justice of the European Union's Case Law on Family Law Matters under Brussels IIa and Maintenance' in Paul Beaumont, Mihail Danov, Katarina Trimming and Burcu Yüksel (eds), *Cross Border Litigation in Europe* (Hart, 2017)

Beaumont P and Holliday J, 'Conclusion: Mapping of the Strength of Global Private International Law' in Paul Beaumont and Jayne Holliday (eds), *A Guide to Global Private International Law* (Hart, 2022)

Bedson S et al, 'Linked lives: Gender, family relations and recurrent care proceedings in England' (2019) 105 *Children and Youth Services Review* 104392

Benford R and Snow D, 'Framing Processes and Social Movements: An Overview and Assessment' (2000) 26 *Annual Review of Sociology* 611

Berrick J et al, 'Care Order Templates as Institutional Scripts in Child Protection: A Cross-System Analysis' (2018) 84 *Children and Youth Services Review* 40

Biesta G, 'Pragmatism and the philosophical foundations of mixed methods research', in Abbas Tashakkori and Charles Teddlie (eds), *SAGE Handbook of Mixed Methods in Social & Behavioural Research* (2nd ed. SAGE Publications, 2010)

Blaikie N, 'A Critique of the use of Triangulation in Social Research' (1991) 25 *Quality and Quantity* 115

Blichner L and Molander A, 'Mapping Juridification' (2008) 14 *European Law Journal* 36

Boddy J et al, 'Beyond Contact? Policy approaches to work with families of looked after children in four European countries' (2014) 28 *Children & Society* 152

Boddy J, 'Understanding Permanence for Looked after Children: A Review of Research for the Care Inquiry' (2013) The Care Inquiry

Boele-Woelki K (ed), *Perspectives for the Unification and Harmonisation of Family Law in Europe* (Intersentia, 2003)

Booker C, 'Slovaks Protest at Britain's "Illegal Child Snatching" (The Telegraph, 22 September 2012) https://www.telegraph.co.uk/comment/9559657/Slovaks-protest-at-Britains-illegal-child-snatching.html accessed 3 March 2022

Booker C, 'Slovaks Protest at Britain's "Illegal Child Snatching" *The Telegraph* (22 September 2012) https://www.telegraph.co.uk/comment/9559657/Slovaks-protest-at-Britains-illegal-child-snatching.html accessed 20 April 2022

Borrás A, 'Explanatory Report on the Convention, drawn up based on Article K.3 of the Treaty on European Union, on Jurisdiction and the Recognition and Enforcement of Judgments in Matrimonial Matters' [1998] OJ C221/04

Borzova O, 'Social services in Europe: Legislation and Practice of the Removal of Children from Their Families in Council of Europe Member States' (Council of Europe, 2015)

Bowcott O, 'Latvia Complains to UK Parliament over Forced Adoptions' (the Guardian, 9 March 2015) https://www.theguardian.com/uk-news/2015/mar/09/latvia-complains-to-uk-parliament-over-forced-adoptions accessed 3 March 2022

Bowcott O, 'Latvia Complains to UK Parliament over Forced Adoptions' the Guardian (9 March 2015) https://www.theguardian.com/uk-news/2015/mar/09/latvia-complains-to-uk-parliament-over-forced-adoptions accessed 3 March 2022

Bowyer S et al, *Special Guardianship: Qualitative Case File Analysis Research Report* (Department for Education, 2015)

Bowyer S et al, *Impact of the Family Justice Reforms on Front-line Practice Phase Two: Special Guardianship Orders* (Department for Education, 2015)

Brannick T and Coghlan D, 'In Defense of Being "Native": The Case for Insider Academic Research' (2017) 10 *Organisational Research Methods* 59

Braun V and Clarke V, 'Using Thematic Analysis in Psychology' (2006) 3 *Qualitative Research in Psychology* 77

Breen C et al, 'Family Life for Children in State Care, An Analysis of the European Court of Human Rights' Reasoning on Adoption Without Consent' (2020) 1 *International Journal of Children's Rights* 1

Broadhurst K et al, 'Performing "Initial Assessment": Identifying the Latent Conditions for Error at the Front-Door of Local Authority Children's Services' (2010) 40 *British Journal of Social Work* 352

Broadhurst K et al, 'Connecting Events in Time to Identify a Hidden Population: Birth Mothers and Their Children in Recurrent Care Proceedings in England' (2015) 45 *The British Journal of Social Work*, 2241

Broadhurst, K et al, 'Born into Care: Newborns in Care Proceedings in England' (2018) The Nuffield Family Justice Observatory: Nuffield Foundation, London

Broadhurst K et al, 'Vulnerable Birth Mothers and Recurrent Care Proceedings: Final Summary Report' (2017) Nuffield Foundation

Broberg N and Ludolph L, 'Migration and Redistributive Spending: Evidence from Local Authorities in England' (2 December 2021) Robert Schuman Centre for Advanced Studies Working Paper RSC Working Paper 2021/86 https://papers.ssrn.com/sol3/papers.cfm?abstract_id=3972303 accessed 28 April 2022

Brophy J, Jhutti-Johal J and Owen C, *Significant Harm: Child Protection in a Multicultural Setting* (Lord Chancellor's Department, 2003)

Bruch C, 'The Central Authority's Role under the Hague Child Abduction Convention: A Friend in Deed' (1994) 28 *Family Law Quarterly* 35

Bundesamt für Justiz, 'International Parent and Child Matters Information from the Federal Office of Justice on the return of abducted children, on cross-border conflicts relating to access and custody, and the cross-border placement of children' (July 2020)

Byford D, 'Serious Case Review Overview Report: Megan' (Gloucestershire Safeguarding Children Board 2020)

Carpaneto L, 'Cross-Border Placement of Children in the European Union' (2016) European Parliament, Committee on Legal Affairs

Chua L and Engel D, 'Legal Consciousness Reconsidered' (2019) 15 *Annual Review of Law and Social Science* 335

Cleaver H and Rose W, Safeguarding children living with foster carers, adopters and special guardians: learning from case reviews 2007–2019 (Coram/Baaf 2020)

Cooper D, 'Local Government Legal Consciousness in the Shadow of Juridification' (1995) 22 *Journal of Law and Society* 506

Collins L and Harris J (gen eds), *Dicey, Morris and Collins, The Conflict of Laws* (16th edn, Sweet & Maxwell, 2022)

Cotterrell R, 'Why must legal ideas be interpreted sociologically?' (1998) 25 *Journal of Law and Society* 171

Cowan D, Halliday S and Hunter C, 'Adjudicating the Implementation of Homelessness Law: The Promise of Socio-Legal Studies' (2006) 21 *Housing Studies* 381

De Baere G and Gutman K, 'The impact of the European Union and the European Court of Justice on European family law' in Jens M. Scherpe (ed), *European Family Law Vol 1* (Elgar, 2016)

Della Porta D and Keating M, *Approaches and Methodologies in the Social Sciences* (Cambridge University Press, 2012)

Denzin N, 'Triangulation 2.0' (2012) 6 *Journal of Mixed Methods Research*

Department for Children, Schools and Families, *The Children Act 1989 Guidance and Regulations Volume 1, Court Orders* (2008, TSO)

Department for Education and Home Office, *Safeguarding Children who may have been Trafficked* (HM Government, 2011)

Department for Education, 'Cross-Border Child Protection Cases: The 1996 Hague Convention. Departmental Advice for Local Authorities, Social Workers, Service Managers and Children's Services Lawyers, October 2012' (DfE, 2012)

Department for Education, 'Advice on Placement of Looked After Children across Member States of the European Union. For Local Authority Children's Services, July 2013' (DfE, 2013)

Department for Education, 'Working with Foreign Authorities: Child Protection Cases and Care Orders. Departmental Advice for Local Authorities, Social Workers, Service Managers and Children's Services Lawyers, July 2014' (DfE, 2014)

Department for Education, 'Special Guardianship Review: Report on Findings Government Consultation Response, 2015' (DfE, 2015)

Department for Education, 'The Children Act 1989 Guidance and Regulations. Volume 2: Care Planning, Placement and Case Review, July 2021' (DfE, 2015). Department for Education, 'Special Guardianship Guidance: Statutory Guidance for Local Authorities on the Special Guardianship Regulations 2005 (as amended by the Special Guardianship (Amendment) Regulations 2016), January 2017' (HM Government, 2016)

Department for Education, 'Care of Unaccompanied Migrant Children and Child Victims of Modern: Statutory Guidance for Local Authorities' Slavery (DfE, 2017)

Department for Education, 'Information sharing: Advice for practitioners providing safeguarding services to children, young people, parents and carers, July 2018' (2018, HM Government)

Department for Education, 'Working Together to Safeguard Children: A Guide to Inter-Agency Working to Safeguard and Promote the Welfare of Children, July 2018' (HM Government, 2020)

Department of Health, Adoption: A New Approach (White Paper, Cm 5017, 2009)

Dezalay Y and Madsen MR, 'The Force of Law and Lawyers: Pierre Bourdieu and the Reflexive Sociology of Law' (2012) 8 *Annual Review of Law and Social Science* 433

Dickens J and Masson J, 'The Courts and Child Protection Social Work in England: Tail Wags Dog?' (2014) 46 *British Journal of Social Work* 355

Dickens J, 'Welfare, Law and Managerialism: Inter-Discursivity and Inter-Professional Practice in Child Care Social Work' (2008) 8 *Journal of Social Work* 45

Dickens J, Beckett C and Bailey S, 'Justice, Speed and Thoroughness in Child Protection Court Proceedings: Messages from England' (2014) 46 *Children and Youth Services Review* 103

Dominelli S, 'Cross-Border Placement of Children within the European Judicial Space: First Thoughts on the Recast Brussels IIa Regulation in Light of the German Experience' (2016) SSRN Electronic Journal https://ssrn.com/abstract=2939488 accessed 18 March 2022

Doughty J et al, 'Transparency through publication of family court judgments: An evaluation of the responses to, and effects of, judicial guidance on publishing family court judgments involving children and young people' (2017) Cardiff University

Dyer A, 'The Internationalization of Family Law' (1997) 30 *University of California, Davis*, 625

Eekelaar J, 'The Role of the Best Interests Principle in Decisions Affecting Children and Decisions about Children' (2015) 23 *The International Journal of Children's Rights* 3

Estin A, 'Where (in the World) do Children Belong?' (2011) 25 *Brigham Young University Journal of Public Law* 217

Estin A, 'Transjudicial Child Welfare: Local Governments and International Law' (2013) 22 *Transnational Law & Contemporary Problems* 595

Ewick P and Silbey S, *The Common Place of Law: Stories from Everyday Life* (University of Chicago Press, 1998)

Family Justice Council Public Law Working Group, 'Recommendations to Achieve Best Practice in the Child Protection and Family Justice Systems: Special Guardianship Orders' (FJC, 2020)

Family Justice Review Panel, 'Family Justice Review: Final Report' (Ministry of Justice and Welsh Government, 2011)

Family Rights Group, *Initial Family and Friends Care Assessment: A Good Practice Guide* (FRG, 2017)

Feeley MM, 'Three Voices of Socio-Legal Studies' (2001) 35 *Israel Law Review* 175, 187

Felstiner W, Abel R and Sarat A, 'The Emergence and Transformation of Disputes: Naming, Blaming, Claiming ...' (1980) *Law and Society Review* 631

Fenton-Glynn C, 'Re N – Conflict and Confluence of Adoption Law in Europe' (2015) 45 *Family Law* 1433

Fenton-Glynn C, 'Adoption without Consent' (Policy Department for Citizens' Rights and Constitutional Affairs, European Parliament 2015)

Fenton-Glynn C, 'Adoption without Consent: Update 2016' (Policy Department for Citizens' Rights and Constitutional Affairs, European Parliament 2016)

Ferguson H, 'How Children Become Invisible in Child Protection Work: Findings from Research into Day-to-Day Social Work Practice' (2017) 47 *The British Journal of Social Work*

Fiorini A, 'The Protection of the Best Interests of Migrant Children – Private International Law Perspectives' (May 1, 2016). To appear in G Biagioni and F Ippolito (eds), *Migrant Children in the XXI Century. Selected Issues of Public and Private International Law*, Series "La ricerca del diritto" (2016 Editoriale Scientific) 25. Available at SSRN: https://ssrn.com/abstract=2862361 accessed 7 March 2022

Flick U, 'Mantras and Myths: The Disenchantment of Mixed-Methods Research and Revisiting Triangulation as a Perspective' (2017) 23 *Qualitative Inquiry* 46

Forrest K and Rushton A, 'Children with Relatives Abroad: Assessment for Placement' (1998) 4 *Child and Family Social Work* 153

Galanter M, 'Why the "Haves" Come Out Ahead: Speculations on the Limits of Legal Change' (1974) 9 *Law and Society Review* 95

Gilbert N, Parton N and Skivenes M, 'Changing Patterns of Response and Emerging Orientations' in Neil Gilbert, Nigel Parton and Marit Skivenes (eds), *Child Protection Systems: International Trends and Orientations* (OUP, 2011)

Gilbert N, Parton N and Skivenes M, 'Introduction' in Gilbert N, Parton N and Skivenes M (eds), *Child Protection Systems: International Trends and Orientations* (OUP, 2011)

Goicoechea I and Warren B, 'National Organs and Central Authorities under HCCH Conventions' in Paul Beaumont and Jayne Holliday (eds), *A Guide to Global Private International Law* (Hart, 2022)

Gössl S and Lamont R, 'Connecting Factors' in Paul Beaumont and Jayne Holliday (eds), *A Guide to Global Private International Law* (Hart, 2022)

Gould JB and Barclay S, 'Mind the Gap: The Place of Gap Studies in Sociolegal Scholarship' (2012) 8 *Annual Review of Law and Social Science* 323

Greene M, 'On the Inside Looking In: Methodological Insights and Challenges in Conducting Qualitative Insider Research' (2014) 19 *The Qualitative Report* 1

Habermas J, 'Law as a Medium and Law as an Institution' in Gunther Teubner (ed), *Dilemmas of Law in the Welfare State* (Walter de Gruyter, 1988)

Habermas J, *The Theory of Communicative Action Vol 2* (Nachdr, Beacon, 1987)

Hallett N, Garstang J and Taylor J, 'Kinship Care and Child Protection in High-Income Countries: A Scoping Review' (2021) *Trauma, Violence and Abuse* 1

Halliday S and Morgan B, 'I Fought the Law and the Law Won? Legal Consciousness and the Critical Imagination' (2013) 66 *Current Legal Problems* 1

Harrington K, 'Child A and Child B: A Serious Case Review' (Oxfordshire Safeguarding Children Board 2017)

Harwin J et al, 'A National Study of the Usage of Supervision Orders and Special Guardianship over Time (2007–2016)' (2015) Nuffield Foundation

Harwin J et al, 'Care Demand and Regional Variability in England: 2010/11 to 2016/17' (2018) Centre for Child and Family Justice Research, Lancaster University

Harwin J et al, 'The Contribution of Supervision Orders and Special Guardianship to Children's Lives and Family Justice' (2019) Centre for Child & Family Justice Research, Lancaster University

Harwin J, *Making Care Orders Work: A Study of Care Plans and their Implementation* (Stationary Office 2003)

Henrich D, 'Family Law Across Frontiers: Facts, Conflicts, Trends' in Nigel Lowe and Gillian Douglas (eds), *Families Across Frontiers* (Kluwer Law International, 1996)

Holliday J and Beaumont P, 'Introduction' in Paul Beaumont and Jayne Holliday (eds), *A Guide to Global Private International Law* (Hart, 2022)

Honorati C and Keyes M, 'Parental Responsibility, Custody and Access' in Paul Beaumont and Jayne Holliday (eds), *A Guide to Global Private International Law* (Hart, 2022)

Home Office, Multi Agency Working and Information Sharing Project Final Report (Home Office, 2014)

Howe D, 'Child Abuse and the Bureaucratisation of Social Work' (1992) 40 The Sociological Review 491

Howe KR, 'Against the Quantitative-Qualitative Incompatibility Thesis or Dogmas Die Hard' (1988) 17 Educational Researcher 10

Hunt J, Macleod A and Thomas C, *The Last Resort: Child Protection, the Courts and the 1989 Children Act – Studies in Evaluating the Children Act 1989* (Stationary Office, 1999)

Hunt J, *Two Decades of Research on Kinship Care* (Family Rights Group, 2020)

Hunt J, 'Practising Kinship Care: The Perspectives of Specialist Social Workers' (2021) Cardiff University, Kinship

Jay M et al, 'Who cares for children? Population Data for Family Justice Research' (2017) Lancaster University, Appendix I

Johnson RB and Onwuegbuzie AJ, 'Mixed Methods Research: A Research Paradigm whose time has come' (2004) 23 *Educational Researcher* 14

Jones R, *The Story of Baby P: Setting the Record Straight* (Policy Press, 2014)

Josephs I, 'Forced Adoption: Punishment Without Crime' (Forced Adoption) https://forced-adoption.com accessed 28 April 2022

Keddell E, 'Going home: Managing 'risk' through relationship in returning children from foster care to their families of origin' (2011) 11 *Qualitative Social Work* 604

Kinship Care Alliance, 'Delivering Good Practice Initial Assessments of Family and Friends Carers in the Context of Covid-19' (June 2020) Coram BAAF, Family Rights Group

Kruger T and Samyn L, 'Brussels II bis: Successes and Suggested Improvements' (2016) 12 *Journal of Private International Law* 132

Kruger, T 'Habitual Residence: The Factors that Courts Consider' in Paul Beaumont, Mihail Danov, Katarina Trimmings and Burcu Yüksel (eds), *Cross Border Litigation in Europe* (Hart, 2017)

Lagarde P, Explanatory Report on the 1996 Hague Child Protection Convention, Proceedings of the Eighteenth Session (1996), *Tome II, Protection of Children* (The Hague, SDU, 1998)

Laming WH, *The Victoria Climbié Inquiry: Report of an Inquiry by Lord Laming* (HMSO, 2003)

Lamont R and Fenton-Glynn C, 'Cross-Border Public Care and Adoption Proceedings in the European Union' (2016) 38 *Journal of Social Welfare and Family Law* 94

Lamont R, 'Care Proceedings with a European Dimension under Brussels IIa: Jurisdiction, Mutual Trust and the Best Interests of the Child' (2016) 28 *Child and Family Law Quarterly* 67

Lamont R, 'Central Authorities and the European Judicial Network: Cross-border cooperation as a mechanism for advancing children's rights in Europe' in Helen Stalford and Ingi Iusmen (eds), *The EU as a Children's Rights Actor: Law, Policy and Structural Dimensions* (Verlag Barbara Budrich, 2016)

Lamont R, 'The Development of Child Protection Across International Borders for Children at Risk of Harm' in Gillian Douglas, Mervyn Murch and Victoria Stephens (eds), *International and National Perspectives on Child and Family Law* (Cambridge University Press, 2018)

Larsson B et al, 'Planning and Supporting Permanence in Long-Term Foster Care' (2021) Nuffield Foundation

Lazić V et al, *Regulation Brussels IIbis Guide for Application* (Asser Institute, 2018)

Lenaerts K, 'The Best Interests of the Child Always Come First: The Brussels II bis Regulation and the European Court of Justice' (2013) 20 *Jurisprudence* 1302

Lehouq E and Taylor W, 'Conceptualizing Legal Mobilization: How Should We Understand the Deployment of Legal Strategies?' (2000) 45 *Law & Social Inquiry* 166

Lipstein K, 'The Hague Conventions on Private International Law, Public Law and Public Policy' (1959) 8 *The International and Comparative Law Quarterly* 506

Lipstein K, 'One Hundred Years of Hague Conferences on Private International Law' (1993) 24 *International and Comparative Law Quarterly* 553

Lowe N and Setright H, 'Transferring the Problem – How Art 15 of the Revised Brussels II Regulation Operates in the Public Law Context' (2017) *International Family Law* 13

Lowe N and White R, *Wards of Court* (Butterworths, 1979)

Lowe N, 'The 1996 Hague Convention on the Protection of Children – A Fresh Appraisal' (2002) 14 *Child and Family Law Quarterly* 191

Lowe N, 'The Growing Influence of the European Union on International Family Law: A View from the Boundary' (2003) 56 *Current Legal Problems* 439

Lowe N and Nicholls M, *The 1996 Hague Convention on the Protection of Children* (LexisNexis, 2012).

Macdonald J and Moylan LJ, 'Family Courts Informing Consular Authorities of Proceedings' (18 April 2019) International Family Justice Office

Marshall A, 'Injustice Frames, Legality, and the Everyday Construction of Sexual Harassment' (2003) 28 *Law & Social Inquiry* 659

Martiny D, 'The Impact of the EU Private International Law Instruments on European Family Law' in Jens M. Scherpe (ed), *European Family Law Vol 1* (Elgar, 2016)

Marvel A, 'The U.N. Convention on the Rights of the Child and the Hague Conference on Private International Law: The Dynamics of Children's Rights Through Legal Strata' (1996) 6 *Transnational Law & Contemporary Problems* 271

Masson J, 'Intercountry Adoption: A Global Problem or a Global Solution?' (2001) 55 *Journal of International Affairs* 141

Masson J et al, *Care Profiling Study* (Ministry of Justice, 2008)

Masson J et al, 'Partnership by Law: The Pre-Proceedings Process for Families on the Edge of Care Proceedings' (2013) School of Law, University of Bristol and the Centre for Research on Children and Families, University of East Anglia

Masson J, 'Recognition of Adoption Orders: A Problem for the Courts of England and Wales?' (2016) 46 *Family Law* 1113

Masson J, 'Disruptive Judgments' (2017) 29 *Child and Family Law Quarterly* 401

Masson J et al, *Child Protection in Court: Outcomes for Children* (School of Law, University of Bristol and the Centre for Research on Children and Families, University of East Anglia, 2019)

McEleavy P, 'The Brussels II Regulation: How the European Community has Moved into Family Law' (2002) 51 *International and Comparative Law Quarterly* 883

McEleavy P, 'The European Court of Human Rights and the Hague Child Abduction Convention: Prioritising Return or Reflection?' (2015) 62 *Netherlands International Law Review* 365

McEwan-Strand A and Skivene M, 'A Child-Centered Court of Human Rights? Strand Lobben v Norway (30 Nov. 2017)' (Strasbourg Observers, 3 January 2018) https://strasbourgobservers.com/2018/01/03/a-child-centred-court-of-human-rights-strand-lobben-v-norway-30-nov-2017 accessed 23 February 2022

McGlynn C, 'The Europeanisation of Family Law' (2001) 13 *Child and Family Law Quarterly* 35

Miller E, '"I Ran Away to France to Keep My Baby"' (BBC News, 4 April 2019) https://www.bbc.co.uk/news/stories-47802296 accessed 7 March 2022

Ministry of Justice, 'Children in Family Justice Data Share: The Public Law Applications to Orders (PLATO) Tool' (MOJ, 2015)

Morrison T, 'Working together to safeguard children: challenges and changes for inter-agency co-ordination in child protection' (2000) 14 *Journal of Interprofessional Care* 36

Munby J, 'View from the President's Chambers (3): The process of reform: expert evidence' (2013)

Munby J, 'President's Guidance of 10 November 2014: The International Child Abduction and Contact Unit' (2014)

Munby J, 'View from the President's Chambers: Care Cases – The Looming Crisis' (2016)

Munro E, The Munro Review of Child Protection: Final Report (Department for Education, 2011)

Munro E and Gilligan R, 'The 'dance' of kinship care in England and Ireland: Navigating a course between regulation and relationships' (2013) 22 *Psychosocial Intervention* 185

Nadelmann K, 'Mancini's Nationality Rule and Non-Unified Legal Systems: Nationality versus Domicile' The American Journal of Comparative Law' (1969) 17 *The American Journal of Comparative Law* 418

Nandy S et al, 'Spotlight on Kinship Care Using Census Microdata to Examine the Extent and Nature of Kinship Care in the UK at the turn of the Twentieth century' (2001) University of Bristol
Naughton D and Fay K, 'Of Kin and Culture US Children and International Kinship Care Placements' (2003) 27 *Adoption & Fostering* 30
Nelken D, 'The Gap Problem in the Sociology of Law: A Theoretical Review' (1981) 35 *Windsor Yearbook of Access to Justice* 45
Ní Shúilleabháin M, 'Ten Years of European Family Law: Retrospective Reflections from a Common Law Perspective' (2010) 4 *International & Comparative Law Quarterly* 1021
Ní Shúilleabháin M, 'Surrogacy, System Shopping, and Article 8 of the European Convention on Human Rights' (2019) 33 *International Journal of Law, Policy and The Family* 104
Novick G, 'Is There a Bias Against Telephone Interviews in Qualitative Research' (2008) 31 *Research in Nursing and Health* 391
Nussbaum A, 'The Rise and Decline of the Law-of-Nations Doctrine in the Conflict of Laws' (1942) 42 *Columbia Law Review* 189
Nygh P, 'The Hague Convention on the Protection of Children' (1998) 45 *Netherlands International Law Review* 1
Olwig KF, 'Narratives of the children left behind: Home and identity in globalised Caribbean families' (1999) 25 *Journal of Ethnic and Migration Studies* 267
Palinkas L et al, 'Purposeful sampling for qualitative data collection and analysis in mixed method implementation research' (2015) 42 *Administration and Policy in Mental Health*
Papendorf K, 'Juridification, Marginalised Persons and Competence to Mobilise the Law', in Olaf Halvorsen Rønning and Ole Hammerslev (eds), *Outsourcing Legal Aid in the Nordic Welfare States* (Palgrave Macmillan, 2017)
Parra-Aranguren G, 'Explanatory Report on the Convention on Protection of Children and Co-Operation in Respect of Intercountry Adoption' Proceedings of the Seventeenth Session (1993), tome II, Adoption – co-operation The Hague, SDU, 1994
Parton N, 'Social Work, Child Protection and Politics: Some Critical and Constructive Reflections' (2014) 44 *British Journal of Social Work* 2042
Parton N, 'Addressing the Relatively Autonomous Relationship Between Child Maltreatment and Child Protection Policies and Practices' (2020) 3 *International Journal on Child Maltreatment* 19
Pedriana N, 'From Protective to Equal Treatment: Legal Framing Processes and Transformation of the Women's Movement in the 1960s' (2006) 111 *American Journal of Sociology* 1718
Pfund PH, 'Intercountry Adoption: The 1993 Hague Convention: Its Purpose, Implementation, and Promise' (1994) 28 *Fam LQ* 53
Pertegás M and Beaumont P, 'Hague Conference on Private International Law' in Paul Beaumont and Jayne Holliday (eds), *A Guide to Global Private International Law* (Hart, 2022)
Pfund PH, 'The Developing Jurisprudence of the Rights of the Child – Contributions of the Hague Conference on Private International Law' (1997) 3 *ILSA Journal of International and Comparative Law* 665
Philip G et al, '"I had no hope, I had no help at all": insights from a first study of fathers and recurrent care proceedings' (2020) 10 *Societies* 8
Ponnert L and Johansson S, 'Juridification and Standardisation: Two Legal Dimensions Influencing Contemporary Child Protection' (2018) 48 *The British Journal of Social Work* 2020
Pound R, 'Law in Books and Law in Action' (1910) 44 *American Law Review* 12
Prabhat D, *Britishness Belonging and Citizenship: Experiencing Nationality Law* (Policy Press Bristol, 2018)
Preston R, 'English councils need £2.7bn more for children's social care by 2025, LGA warns government' (Community Care, 25 October 2021) https://www.communitycare.co.uk/2021/10/25/english-councils-need-2-7bn-more-for-childrens-social-care-by-2025-lga-warns-government/ accessed 4 March 2022

Preston R, 'English councils need £2.7bn more for children's social care by 2025, LGA warns government' Community Care (25 October 2021) https://www.communitycare.co.uk/2021/10/25/english-councils-need-2-7bn-more-for-childrens-social-care-by-2025-lga-warns-government/ accessed 4 March 2022

Preston-Shoot M, Roberts G and Vernon S, 'Values in Social Work Law: Strained Relations or Sustaining Relationships?' (2001) 23 *Journal of Social Welfare and Family Law* 1

Richardson G, 'Impact Studies in the United Kingdom' in Marc Hertogh and Simon Halliday (eds), *Judicial Review and Bureaucratic Impact: International and Interdisciplinary Perspectives* (Cambridge University Press, 2004)

Rosén M, Arneback E and Bergh A, 'A Conceptual Framework for Understanding Juridification of and in Education' (2021) 36 *Journal of Education Policy* 822

Sarat A, 'Legal Effectiveness and Social Studies of Law: On the Unfortunate Persistence of a Research Tradition' (1985) 9 *Legal Studies Forum* 23

Schofield G et al, 'The Search for Stability and Permanence: Modelling the Pathways of Long-Stay Looked After Children' (2005) 37 *British Journal of Social Work* 619

Schuz R, 'Policy Considerations in Determining the Habitual Residence of a Child and the Relevance of Context' (2001) 11 *Journal of Transnational Law and Policy* 101

Schuz R, 'Commentary on RCB as Litigation Guardian of EKV, CEV, CIV and LRV v The Honourable Justice Colin James Forrest', in Helen Stalford, Kathryn Hollingsworth, Stephen Gilmore (eds), *Rewriting Children's Rights Judgments: From Academic Vision to New Practice* (Hart Publishing, 2017)

Schuz R, 'Disparity and the Quest for Uniformity in Implementing the Hague Child Abduction Convention' (2014) 9 *Journal of Comparative Law* 7

Selman P, 'Intercountry Adoption in the New Millennium; The "Quiet Migration" Revisited' (2002) 23 *Population Research and Policy Review* 205

Silberman L, 'The 1996 Hague Convention on the Protection of Children: Should the United States Join?' (2000) 34 *Fam. L.Q.* 239

Silberman L, 'The Hague Convention on Child Abduction and Unilateral Relocations by Custodial Parents: A Perspective from the United States and Europe-Abbott, Neulinger, Zarraga' (2018) 63 *Oklahoma Law Review* 733

Silbey SS, 'After Legal Consciousness' (2005) 1 *Annual Review of Law and Social Science* 323

Skivenes M and Thoburn J, 'Pathways to Permanence in England and Norway: A Critical Analysis of Documents and Data' (2016) 67 *Children and Youth Services Review* 152

Smith J, 'Quantitative Versus Qualitative Research: An Attempt to Clarify the Issue' (1983) 12 *Educational Researcher* 6

Snow D et al, 'The Emergence, Development, and Future of the Framing Perspective: 25+ Years Since "Frame Alignment"' (2014) 19 *Mobilization: An International Quarterly* 23

Stalford H, *Children and the European Union: Rights, Welfare and Accountability* (Oxford: Hart Publishing, 2012)

Sumption S and Walsh PW, 'EU Migration to and From the UK' (Migration Observatory, 15 February 2022) https://migrationobservatory.ox.ac.uk/resources/briefings/eu-migration-to-and-from-the-uk/ accessed 28 April 2022

Teubner G, 'Juridification: Concepts, Aspects, Limits, Solutions' in Robert Baldwin, Colin Scott and Christopher Hood (eds), *A Reader on Regulation* (OUP, 1998)

Thoburn J, 'Reunification of children in out-of-home care to birth parents or relatives: A synthesis of the evidence on processes, practice and outcomes' (2009) Deutsches Jugendinstitut

Thue H, 'Connecting Factors in International Family Law' in Nigel Lowe and Gillian Douglas (eds), *Families Across Frontiers* (Kluwer Law International, 1996)

Torremans P (ed), *Cheshire, North & Fawcett, Private International Law* (15th edn, OUP, 2017)

Trimmings K, *Child Abduction within the European Union* (Hart Publishing, 2013)

Trimmings K, 'Transfer of Jurisdiction and the Best Interests of the Child' (2016) 3 *CLJ* 471

W de Steiger M, 'Rapport Explcatif: Convention du 5 octobre 1961 concernant la compétence des autorités et la loi applicable en matière de protection des mineurs' (1960) HCCH

Wade J et al, Investigating Special Guardianship: Experiences, Challenges and Outcomes' (Department for Education, 2014)

Walker L, 'The Impact of the Hague Abduction Convention on the Rights of the Family in the Case-Law of the European Court of Human Rights and the UN Human Rights Committee: The Danger of Neulinger' (2010) 6 *Journal of Private International Law* 649

Wastell D et al, 'Children's Services in the Iron Cage of Performance Management: Street-Level Bureaucracy and the Spectre of Švejkism: Iron Cage of Performance Management' (2010) 19 *International Journal of Social Welfare* 310

Wate R, 'Serious Case Review Shi-Anne Downer (Birth Name) AKA Keegan Downer' (Birmingham Safeguarding Children Board, 2017)

Weller M, 'Mutual Trust: In Search of the Future of European Union Private International Law' (2015) 11 *Journal of Private International Law* 64

Wessels M et al, 'The Disconnect Between Community-Based Child Protection Mechanisms and the Formal Child Protection System in Rural Sierra Leone: Challenges to Building an Effective National Child Protection System' (2012) 7 *Vulnerable Children and Youth Studies* 211

Williams J, 'Social Work, Liberty and Law' (2004) 34 *British Journal of Social Work* 37

Wright M, '"Working the International Child Protection Case"' (2019) 41 *Journal of Social Welfare and Family Law* 15

Yekini A and Beaumont P, 'Pragmatism and Private International Law' in Paul Beaumont and Jayne Holliday (eds), *A Guide to Global Private International Law* (Hart, 2022)

Yüksel B and Trimmings K, 'Choice of Law Aspects of Non-Consensual Adoption of Eastern European Children in England and Wales' (2017) 3 *International Family Law* 202

Zermatten J, 'The Best Interests of the Child Principle: Literal Analysis and Function' (2010) 18 *International Journal of Children's Rights* 483

INDEX

www.ingramcontent.com/pod-product-compliance
Ingram Content Group UK Ltd.
Pitfield, Milton Keynes, MK11 3LW, UK
UKHW021907150926
475560UK00003B/238

9 781509 977307